Reader's Guide
to
HENRY JAMES, JR.

Reader's Guide
to
HENRY JAMES, JR.

Rudolf Eisler

CENTRUM PRESS
NEW DELHI-110002 (INDIA)

CENTRUM PRESS
H.O.: 4360/4, Ansari Road, Daryaganj,
New Delhi-110 002 (India)
Ph.: 23278000, 23261597

B.O.: No. 1015, Ist Main Road, BSK IIIrd Stage
IIIrd Phase, IIIrd Block,
Bangalore - 560 085 (India)
Tel.: 080-41723429
Visit us at: www.centrumpress.com

Reader's Guide to Henry James, Jr.

First Edition, 2009

ISBN 978-93-80106-90-8

PRINTED IN INDIA

Printed at Balaji Offset, Delhi.

Contents

Contents

Preface

The events of Mr. James's life—as we agree to understand events—may be told in a very few words. His race is Irish on his father's side and Scotch on his mother's, to which mingled strains the generalizer may attribute, if he likes, that union of vivid expression and dispassionate analysis which has characterized his work from the first. There are none of those early struggles with poverty, which render the lives of so many distinguished Americans monotonous reading, to record in his case: the cabin hearth-fire did not light him to the youthful pursuit of literature; he had from the start all those advantages which, when they go too far, become limitations.

He was born in New York city in the year 1843, and his first lessons in life and letters were the best which the metropolis—so small in the perspective diminishing to that date—could afford. In his twelfth year his family went abroad, and after some stay in England made a long sojourn in France and Switzerland. They returned to America in 1860, placing themselves at Newport, and for a year or two Mr. James was at the Harvard Law School, where, perhaps, he did not study a great deal of law. His father removed from Newport to Cambridge in 1866, and there Mr. James remained till he went abroad, three years later, for the residence in England and Italy which, with infrequent visits home, has continued ever since.

He had already printed a tale—"The Story of a Year"—in the "Atlantic Monthly," when I was asked to be Mr. Fields's assistant in the management, and it was my fortune to read Mr. James's second contribution in manuscript. "Would you take it?" asked my chief. "Yes, and all the stories you can get from the writer." One is much securer of one's judgment at twenty-nine than, say, at forty-five; but if this was a mistake of mine I am not yet old enough to regret it. The story was called "Poor Richard," and it dealt with the conscience of a man very much in love with a woman who loved his rival. He told this rival a lie, which sent him away to his death on the field,—in that day nearly every fictitious personage had something to do with the war,—but Poor Richard's lie did not win him his love. It still seems to me that the situation was strongly and finely felt.

One's pity went, as it should, with the liar; but the whole story had a pathos which lingers in my mind equally with a sense of the new literary qualities which gave me such delight in it. I admired, as we must in all that Mr. James has written, the finished workmanship in which there is no loss of vigor; the luminous and uncommon use of words, the originality of phrase, the whole clear and beautiful style, which I confess I weakly liked the better for the occasional gallicisms remaining from an inveterate habit of French.

Author

Chapter 1

Introduction

Henry James, O.M. (April 15, 1843(1843-04-15) – February 28, 1916), son of theologian Henry James Sr., brother of the philosopher and psychologist William James and diarist Alice James, was an American author. He is one of the key figures of 19th century literary realism; the fine art of his writing has led many academics to consider him the greatest master of the novel and novella form.

He spent much of his life in England and became a British subject shortly before his death. He is primarily known for a series of major novels in which he portrayed the encounter of America with Europe. His plots centered on personal relationships, the proper exercise of power in such relationships, and other moral questions. His method of writing from the point of view of a character within a tale allowed him to explore the phenomena of consciousness and perception, and his style in later works has been compared to impressionist painting.

James insisted that writers in Great Britain and America should be allowed the greatest freedom possible in presenting their view of the world, as French authors were.

His imaginative use of point of view, interior monologue and unreliable narrators in his own novels and tales brought a new depth and interest to realistic fiction, and foreshadowed the modernist work of the twentieth century. An extraordinarily productive writer, in addition to his voluminous works of fiction he published articles and books of travel writing, biography, autobiography, and criticism, and wrote plays, some of which were performed during his lifetime with moderate success. His theatrical work is thought to have profoundly influenced his later novels and tales. Henry James was born on April 15, 1843 in New York City into a wealthy family. His father, Henry James Sr. was one of the best-known intellectuals in mid-nineteenth-century America. In his youth James traveled back and forth between Europe and America. He studied with tutors in Geneva, London, Paris, Bologna and Bonn. At the age of 19 he briefly attended Harvard Law School, but preferred reading literature to studying law. James published his first short story, "A Tragedy of Errors" two years later, and devoted himself to literature. In 1866-69 and 1871-72 he was a contributor to *The Nation* and *Atlantic Monthly*.

From an early age James had read the classics of English, American, French and German literature and Russian classics in translation. His first novel, *Watch and Ward* (1871), was written while he was traveling through Venice and Paris. After living in Paris, where he was contributor to the *New York Tribune*, James moved to England, living first in London and then in Rye, Sussex. During his first years in Europe James wrote novels that portrayed Americans living abroad. In 1905 James visited America for the first time in twenty-five years, and wrote "Jolly Corner". Among James' masterpieces are *Daisy Miller* (1879), where the young and innocent American, Daisy finds her values in conflict with European sophistication and *The Portrait of a Lady* (1881) where again a young American woman becomes a victim of her provincialism during her travels in Europe. *The Bostonians* (1886) was set in the era of the rising feminist movement.

What Maisie Knew (1897) depicted a preadolescent young girl, who must choose between her parents and a motherly old governess. In *The Wings of the Dove* (1902) an inheritance destroys the love of a young couple. James considered *The Ambassadors* (1903) his most "perfect" work of art. James's most famous short story must be "The Turn of the Screw", a ghost story in which the question of childhood corruption obsesses a governess. Although James is best known for his novels, his essays are now attracting a more general audience. Between 1906 and 1910 James revised many of his tales and novels for the New York edition of his complete works. His autobiography, *A Small Boy And Others*, appeared in 1913 and was continued in *Notes Of A Son And Brother* (1914). The third volume, *The Middle Years*, appeared posthumously in 1917. The outbreak of World War I was a shock for James and in 1915 he became a British citizen as a declaration of loyalty to his adopted country and in protest against the US's refusal to enter the war. James suffered a stroke on December 2, 1915. He died three months later in London on February 28, 1916. He was cremated at Golders Green Crematorium and his ashes are interred at Cambridge, Massachusetts.

James early formed the ambition of pursuing a career as a man of letters. His first published work was a review of a stage performance, "Miss Maggie Mitchell in *Fanchon the Cricket*," published in 1863, that reflected a life-long interest in the actor's art. From an early age James read, criticized, and learned from the classics of English, American, French, Italian, German and (in translation) Russian literature. In 1863, he anonymously published his first short story, *A Tragedy of Error*. Until his fiftieth year he supported himself by writing, principally by contributing extensively to illustrated monthly magazines in the United States and Great Britain, but after his sister's death in 1892 his royalties were supplemented by a modest income from the family's properties in Syracuse, New York. Until late in life his novels were serialized in magazines before book publication, and he wrote the monthly installments as they were due, allowing him little opportunity to revise the final work. To supplement his income he also wrote frequently for newspapers, and from 1863 to his death he maintained a strenuous schedule of publication in a variety of genres and media.

In his criticism of fiction, the theater, and painting he developed ideas concerning the unity of the arts; he wrote two full-length biographies, two volumes of memoirs of his childhood and a long fragment of autobiography; 22 novels, including two left unfinished at his death, 112 tales of varying lengths, fifteen plays, and dozens of travel and topical essays. Biographers and critics have identified Henrik Ibsen, Nathaniel

Hawthorne, Honoré de Balzac, and Ivan Turgenev as important influences. He heavily revised his major novels and many of his stories for a selected edition of his fiction, whose twenty-three volumes formed an artistic autobiography which he called "The New York Edition" to emphasize his continuing ties to the city of his birth. In his essay *The Art of Fiction,* and in prefaces to each volume of *The New York Edition,* James explained his views of the art of fiction, emphasizing the importance to him of realist portrayals of character as seen through the eyes and thoughts of an embodied narrator.

At several points in his career James wrote plays, beginning with one-act plays written for periodicals in 1869 and 1871 and a dramatization of his popular novella *Daisy Miller* in 1882.

From 1890 to 1892, he made a concerted effort to succeed commercially on the London stage, writing a half-dozen plays of which only one, a dramatization of his novel *The American,* was produced. This play was performed for several years by a touring repertory company, and had a respectable run in London, but did not earn very much money for James.

His other plays written at this time were not produced. The effort was made avowedly to improve his finances, and after his sister Alice's death in 1892, as he had a modest independent income, he halted his theatrical efforts. In 1893, however, he responded to a request from actor-manager George Alexander for a serious play for the opening of his renovated St. James's Theatre, and James wrote a long drama, *Guy Domville,* which Alexander produced.

There was a noisy uproar on the opening night, January 5, 1895, with hissing from the gallery when James took his bow after the final curtain, and the author was considerably upset. The incident was not repeated, the play received good reviews, and had a modest run of five weeks and was then taken off to make way for Oscar Wilde's *The Importance of Being Earnest,* which Alexander thought would have better prospects for the coming Season. After the stresses and disappointment of this effort James insisted that he would write no more for the theater, but within weeks had agreed to write a curtain-raiser for Ellen Terry. This became the one-act "Summersoft", which he later rewrote into a short story, "Covering End", and then expanded into a full-length play, *The High Bid,* which had a brief run in London in 1907, when James made another concerted effort to write for the stage. He wrote three new plays, two of which were in production when the death of Edward VII May 6, 1910 plunged London into mourning and the theaters were closed.

Discouraged by failing health and the stresses of theatrical work, James did not renew his efforts in the theater, but recycled his plays as successful novels. *The Outcry* was a best-seller in the United States when it was published in 1911. During the years 1890-1893 when he was most engaged with the theater, James wrote a good deal of theatrical criticism and assisted Elizabeth Robins and others in translating and producing Henrik Ibsen for the first time on the London stage. Biographer Leon Edel was the first to call attention to the importance of the "theatrical years" 1890-1895 for James's later work.

Following the commercial failure of his novel *The Tragic Muse,* in 1890, James renounced novel writing and dedicated himself to short fiction and plays, which he described as related forms. Between 1890 and 1895, he sketched in his notebooks plots and themes of nearly all his later novels, which he first conceived as short stories or plays.

The structure of his late novels was "scenic" in James's special sense, in that they followed the scene-by-scene structure of a French play in the classical mode, and he freely translated short stories into plays and vice versa. The use of an observer's consciousness and the sense of the action as a performance became most marked in James's fiction in and after the 1890s. Failing to make a commercial success on the stage, however, and finding that the stresses of theatrical work were difficult for him to sustain, he returned to the writing of long, serialized novels, which again became the mainstay of his income. With his new private income as well, he was able to maintain a country house and rooms in London. Leon Edel argued in his psychoanalytic biography that James was deeply traumatized by the opening night uproar that greeted *Guy Domville,* and that it plunged him into a prolonged depression. The successful later novels, in Edel's view, were the result of a kind of self-analysis, expressed in James's fiction, which partly freed him from his fears.

Other biographers and scholars have not accepted this account, however; the more common view being that of F.O. Matthiessen, who wrote: "Instead of being crushed by the collapse of his hopes [for the theater]. . . he felt a resurgence of new energy." James returned to the United States in 1904-1905 for a lecture tour to recoup his finances and to visit his family. His essays describing that visit, published as *The American Scene,* were perhaps his most important work of social commentary. In them he described the rise of commerce and democracy, the impact of free immigration on American culture, and his agonized sense that his deeply felt American nationality was threatened by these upheavals.

PSYCHOLOGICAL CHARACTERIZATIONS

James never married, he was also a virgin, and after settling in London proclaimed himself "a bachelor" and regularly rejected suggestions that he marry. After his death, critics speculated on the cause of his bachelorhood. F. W. Dupee, in several well-regarded volumes on the James family, originated the theory that James had been in love with his cousin Mary ("Minnie") Temple, but that a neurotic fear of sex kept him from admitting such affections: "James's invalidism . . . was itself the symptom of some fear of or scruple against sexual love on his part."

Dupee used an episode from James's memoir *A Small Boy and Others,* recounting a dream of a Napoleonic images in the Louvre, to exemplify James's romanticism about Europe, a Napoleonic fantasy into which he fled.This analysis seemed to support literary critics like Van Wyck Brooks and Vernon Parrington who had condemned James's expatriation, and who criticized his work as effeminate and deracinated. Leon Edel used it as the premise of his own masterly biography, which held the field for many years.

Dupee had not been given access to the James family papers, however, and had worked principally from James's published memoir of his older brother, and the limited collection of letters edited by Percy Lubbock, which was heavily weighted toward James's last years. Dupee's account, perhaps as a result, portrayed James as a man moving directly from childhood, when he trailed after his older brother, to an elderly invalidism.

As more material became available to scholars, including the diaries of contemporaries and hundreds of affectionate and sometimes erotic letters written by James to younger men, the picture of neurotic celibacy gave way to a portrait of a closeted homosexual. As author Terry Eagleton has stated, "...gay critics debate exactly how repressed his (probable) homosexuality was..."James's letters to expatriate American sculptor Hendrik Christian Andersen have attracted particular attention.

James met the 27-year-old Andersen in Rome in 1899, when James was 56, and wrote letters to Andersen that are intensely emotional: "I hold you, dearest boy, in my innermost love, & count on your feeling me—in every throb of your soul". In a letter of May 6, 1904 to his brother William, James referred to himself as "always your hopelessly celibate even though sexagenarian Henry".

How accurate that description might have been is the subject of contention among James's biographers, but the letters to Andersen were occasionally quasi-erotic: "I put, my dear boy, my arm around you, & feel the pulsation, thereby, as it were, of our excellent future & your admirable endowment." To his homosexual friend Howard Sturgis, James could write: "I repeat, almost to indiscretion, that I could live with you. Meanwhile I can only try to live without you," and it is only in letters to young gay men that James refers to himself as their "lover". James wrote to young men who are now thought to have been homosexual or bisexual, who made up a large fraction of his close male friends. In a letter to Howard Sturgis, following a long visit, James refers jocularly to their "happy little congress of two". In letters to Hugh Walpole, James pursues involved jokes and puns about their relationship, referring to himself as an elephant who "paws you oh so benevolently" and winds about Walpole his "well meaning old trunk". The privately printed letters to Walter Berry have long been celebrated for their lightly veiled eroticism.

However, James wrote to fellow-novelist Lucy Clifford: "Dearest Lucy! What shall I say? when I love you so very, very much, and see you nine times for once that I see Others! Therefore I think that—if you want it made clear to the meanest intelligence—I love you more than I love Others." In another example he wrote to his New York friend Mary Cadwalader Jones:

Dearest Mary Cadwalader. I yearn over you, but I yearn in vain; & your long silence really breaks my heart, mystifies, depresses, almost alarms me, to the point even of making me wonder if poor unconscious & doting old Célimare [Jones' pet name for James] has "done" anything, in some dark somnambulism of the spirit, which has...given you a bad moment, or a wrong impression, or a "colourable pretext"...However these things may be, he loves you as tenderly as ever; nothing, to the end of time, will ever detach him from you, & he remembers those Eleventh St. matutional *intimes* hours, those telephonic matinées, as the most romantic of his life...

His long friendship with American novelist Constance Fenimore Woolson, in whose house he lived for a number of weeks in Italy in 1887, and his shock and grief over her suicide in 1894, are discussed in detail in Leon Edel's biography and play a central role in a study by Lyndall Gordon.

Edel conjectured that Woolson was in love with James and killed herself in part because of his coldness. Gordon builds on Edel's account and adds her own speculation that James felt guilt at having sabotaged Woolson's work. Woolson's biographers have strongly objected to Edel's account, however,, and have generally portrayed James as a friend who advanced Woolson's career. Novick in his more recent account argues that the available evidence shows that James suffered strong emotions prompted by the apparent suicide of a friend and colleague, but that there is no evidence Woolson was in love with him or that he was the cause of her death.

James is one of the major figures of trans-Atlantic literature. His works frequently juxtapose characters from the Old World (Europe), embodying a feudal civilization that is beautiful, often corrupt, and alluring, and from the New World (United States), where people are often brash, open, and assertive and embody the virtues — freedom and a more highly evolved moral character — of the new American society.

James explores this clash of personalities and cultures, in stories of personal relationships in which power is exercised well or badly. His protagonists were often young American women facing oppression or abuse, and as his secretary Theodora Bosanquet remarked in her monograph *Henry James at Work*:

When he walked out of the refuge of his study and into the world and looked around him, he saw a place of torment, where creatures of prey perpetually thrust their claws into the quivering flesh of doomed, defenseless children of light... His novels are a repeated exposure of this wickedness, a reiterated and passionate plea for the fullest freedom of development, unimperiled by reckless and barbarous stupidity.

Critics have jokingly described three phases in the development of James's prose: "James the First, James the Second, and The Old Pretender" and observers do often group his works of fiction into three periods. In his apprentice years, culminating with the masterwork *The Portrait of a Lady,* his style was simple and direct (by the standards of Victorian magazine writing) and he experimented widely with forms and methods, generally narrating from a conventionally omniscient point of view. Plots generally concern romance, except for the three big novels of social commentary that conclude this period. In the second period, as noted above, he abandoned the serialized novel and from 1890 to about 1897, he wrote short stories and plays. Finally, in his third and last period he returned to the long, serialized novel. Beginning in the second period, but most noticeably in the third, he increasingly abandoned direct statement in favor of frequent double negatives, and complex descriptive imagery.

Single paragraphs began to run for page after page, in which an initial noun would be succeeded by pronouns surrounded by clouds of adjectives and prepositional clauses, far from their original referents, and verbs would be deferred and then preceded by a series of adverbs. The overall effect could be a vivid evocation of a scene as perceived by a sensitive observer.

In its intense focus on the consciousness of his major characters, James's later work foreshadows extensive developments in 20th century fiction. Then and later many readers find the late style difficult and unnecessary; his friend Edith Wharton, who admired him greatly, said that there were passages in his work that were all but incomprehensible. H.G. Wells harshly portrayed James as a hippopotamus laboriously attempting to pick up a pea that has got into a corner of its cage. Some critics have claimed that the more elaborate manner was a result of James taking up the practice of dictating to a secretary. He was afflicted with a stutter and compensated by speaking slowly and deliberately.

The late style does become more difficult in the years when he dictates, but James also was able to revise typewritten drafts more extensively, and his few surviving drafts show that the later works are more heavily revised and redrafted. In some cases this leads critics to prefer the earlier, unrevised versions of some works because the older style is thought to be closer to the original conception and spirit of the work, *Daisy Miller* being a case in point: most of the current reprints of this novel contain the unrevised text.

On the other hand, the late revision of the early novel *The Portrait of a Lady* is generally much preferred to the first edition, even by those who dislike the late style, because of the power of the imagery and the depth of characterization, while his shorter late fiction, such as *The Turn of the Screw*, is considered highly accessible and remains popular with readers. More important for his work overall may have been his position as an expatriate, and in other ways an outsider, living in Europe.

While he came from middle-class and provincial belongings (seen from the perspective of European polite society) he worked very hard to gain access to all levels of society, and the settings of his fiction range from working class to aristocratic, and often describe the efforts of middle-class Americans to make their way in European capitals.

He confessed he got some of his best story ideas from gossip at the dinner table or at country house weekends. He worked for a living, however, and lacked the experiences of select schools, university, and army service, the common bonds of masculine society. He was furthermore a man whose tastes and interests were, according to the prevailing standards of Victorian era Anglo-American culture, rather feminine, and who was shadowed by the cloud of prejudice that then and later accompanied suspicions of his homosexuality. Edmund Wilson famously compared James's objectivity to Shakespeare's:

One would be in a position to appreciate James better if one compared him with the dramatists of the seventeenth century—Racine and Molière, whom he resembles in form as well as in point of view, and even Shakespeare, when allowances are made for the most extreme differences in subject and form. These poets are not, like Dickens and Hardy, writers of melodrama — either humorous or pessimistic, nor secretaries of society like Balzac, nor prophets like Tolstoy: they are occupied simply with the presentation of conflicts of moral character, which they do not concern themselves about softening or averting. They do not indict society for these situations: they regard them as universal and inevitable. They do not even blame God for allowing them: they accept them as the conditions of life.

It is also possible to see many of James's stories as psychological thought-experiments. *The Portrait of a Lady* may be an experiment to see what happens when an idealistic young woman suddenly becomes very rich. In many of his tales, characters seem to exemplify alternate futures and possibilities, as most markedly in "The Jolly Corner", in which the protagonist and a ghost-doppelganger live alternate

American and European lives; and in others, like *The Ambassadors,* an older James seems fondly to regard his own younger self facing a crucial moment.

Although any selection of James's novels as "major" must inevitably depend to some extent on personal preference, the following books have achieved prominence among his works in the views of many critics. The first period of James's fiction, usually considered to have culminated in *The Portrait of a Lady,* concentrated on the contrast between Europe and America. The style of these novels is generally straightforward and, though personally characteristic, well within the norms of 19th century fiction.

Roderick Hudson (1875) is a Künstlerroman that traces the development of the title character, an extremely talented sculptor. Although the book shows some signs of immaturity—this was James's first serious attempt at a full-length novel — it has attracted favorable comment due to the vivid realization of the three major characters: Roderick Hudson, superbly gifted but unstable and unreliable; Rowland Mallet, Roderick's limited but much more mature friend and patron; and Christina Light, one of James's most enchanting and maddening femmes fatale. The pair of Hudson and Mallet has been seen as representing the two sides of James's own nature: the wildly imaginative artist and the brooding conscientious mentor.

Although *Roderick Hudson* featured mostly American characters in a European setting, James made the Europe–America contrast even more explicit in his next novel. In fact, the contrast could be considered the leading theme of *The American* (1877). This book is a combination of social comedy and melodrama concerning the adventures and misadventures of Christopher Newman, an essentially good-hearted but rather gauche American businessman on his first tour of Europe. Newman is looking for a world different from the simple, harsh realities of 19th century American business. He encounters both the beauty and the ugliness of Europe, and learns not to take either for granted.

James wrote *Washington Square* (1880), a deceptively

simple tragicomedy that recounts the conflict between a dull but sweet daughter and her brilliant, domineering father. The book is often compared to Jane Austen's work for the clarity and grace of its prose and its intense focus on family relationships.

James was not particularly enthusiastic about Jane Austen, so he might not have regarded the comparison as flattering. In fact, James was not enthusiastic about *Washington Square* itself. He tried to read it over for inclusion in the *New York Edition* of his fiction (1907–09) but found that he could not. So he excluded the novel from the edition. But other readers have enjoyed the book enough to make it one of the more popular works in the entire Jamesian canon.

In *The Portrait of a Lady* (1881) James concluded the first phase of his career with a novel that remains his most popular long fiction. The story is of a spirited young American woman, Isabel Archer, who "affronts her destiny" and finds it overwhelming.

She inherits a large amount of money and subsequently becomes the victim of Machiavellian scheming by two American expatriates. The narrative is set mainly in Europe, especially in England and Italy. Generally regarded as the masterpiece of his early phase, *The Portrait of a Lady* is not just a reflection of James's absorbing interest in the differences between the New World and the Old, but covers themes of personal freedom, moral responsibility, betrayal, and sexuality.

In the 1880s James wrote *The Bostonians* (1886), a bittersweet tragicomedy that centers on: Basil Ransom, an unbending political conservative from Mississippi; Olive Chancellor, Ransom's cousin and a zealous Boston feminist; and Verena Tarrant, a pretty protege of Olive's in the feminist movement. The story line concerns the contest between Ransom and Olive for Verena's allegiance and affection, though the novel also includes a wide panorama of political activists, newspaper people, and quirky eccentrics. James followed with *The Princess Casamassima* (1886), the story of an intelligent but confused young London bookbinder, Hyacinth

Robinson, who becomes involved in far left politics and a terrorist assassination plot. The book is something of a lone sport in the Jamesian canon for dealing with such a violent political subject. But it is often paired with *The Bostonians*, which is concerned with political issues.

Just as James was beginning his ultimately disastrous attempt to conquer the stage, he wrote *The Tragic Muse* (1890). This novel offers a wide, cheerful panorama of English life and follows the fortunes of two would-be artists: Nick Dormer, who vacillates between a political career and his efforts to become a painter, and Miriam Rooth, an actress striving for artistic and commercial success. Huge casts of supporting characters helps and hinder their pursuits. The book reflects James's consuming interest in the theater and is often considered to mark the close of the second or middle phase of his career in the novel. After the failure of his "dramatic experiment" James returned to his fiction and began to probe his characters' consciousness. His style started to grow in complexity to reflect the greater depth of his analysis. *The Spoils of Poynton* (1897), considered the first example of this final phase, is a half-length novel that describes the struggle between Mrs. Gereth, a widow of impeccable taste and iron will, and her son Owen over a houseful of precious antique furniture.

The story is largely told from the viewpoint of Fleda Vetch, a young woman in love with Owen but sympathetic to Mrs Gereth's anguish over losing the antiques she patiently collected. James continued the more involved, psychological approach to his fiction with *What Maisie Knew* (1897), the story of the sensitive daughter of divorced and irresponsible parents. The novel has great contemporary relevance as an unflinching account of a wildly dysfunctional family. The book is also a notable technical achievement by James, as it follows the title character from earliest childhood to precocious maturity.

The third period of James's career reached its most significant achievement in three novels published just after the turn of the century. Critic F. O. Matthiessen called this "trilogy" James's major phase, and these novels have certainly received intense critical study. It was the second-written of the books, *The Wings of the Dove* (1902) that was the first published. This novel tells the story of Milly Theale, an American heiress stricken with a serious disease, and her impact on the people around her. Some of these people befriend Milly with honorable motives, while others are more self-interested. James stated in his autobiographical books that Milly was based on Minny Temple, his beloved cousin who died at an early age of tuberculosis. He said that he attempted in the novel to wrap her memory in the "beauty and dignity of art".

The next published of the three novels, *The Ambassadors* (1903), is a dark comedy that follows the trip of protagonist Lewis Lambert Strether to Europe in pursuit of his widowed fiancée's supposedly wayward son. Strether is to bring the young man back to the family business, but he encounters unexpected complications. The third-person narrative is told exclusively from Strether's point of view. In his preface to the *New York Edition* text of the novel, James placed this book at the top of his achievements, which has occasioned some critical disagreement. *The Golden Bowl* (1904) is a complex, intense study of marriage and adultery that completes the "major phase" and, essentially, James's career in the novel. The book explores the tangle of interrelationships between a father and daughter and their respective spouses. The novel focuses deeply and almost exclusively on the consciousness of the central characters, with sometimes obsessive detail and powerful insight.

James was particularly interested in what he called the "beautiful and blest *nouvelle*", or the longer form of short narrative. Still, he produced a number of very short stories in which he achieved notable compression of sometimes complex subjects. The following narratives are representative of James's achievement in the shorter forms of fiction. Just as the contrast between Europe and America was a predominant theme in James's early novels, many of his first tales also explored the clash between the Old World and the New. In "A Passionate Pilgrim" (1871), the earliest fiction that James included in the *New York Edition*, the difference between America and Europe erupts into open conflict, which leads to a sadly ironic ending. The story's technique still seems somewhat inexpert, with passages of local colour description occasionally interrupting the flow of the narrative. But James manages to craft an interesting and believable example of what he would call the "Americano-European legend".

James published many stories before what would prove to be his greatest success with the readers of his time, "Daisy Miller" (1878). This story portrays the confused courtship of the title character, a free-spirited American girl, by Winterbourne, a compatriot of hers with much more sophistication. His pursuit of Daisy is hampered by her own flirtatiousness, which is frowned upon by the other expatriates they meet in Switzerland and Italy. Her lack of understanding of the social mores of the society she so desperately wishes to enter ultimately leads to tragedy. As James moved on from studies of the Europe-America clash and the American girl in his novels, his shorter works also explored new subjects in the 1880s. "The Aspern Papers" (1888) is one of James's best-known and most acclaimed longer tales. The storyline is based on an anecdote that James heard about a Shelley devotee who tried to obtain some valuable letters written by the poet. Set in a brilliantly described Venice, the story demonstrates James's ability to generate almost unbearable suspense while never neglecting the development of his characters.

Another fine example of the middle phase of James's career in short narrative is "The Pupil" (1891), the story of a precocious young boy growing up in a mendacious and dishonorable family. He befriends his tutor, who is the only adult in his life that he can trust. James presents their relationship with sympathy and insight, and the story reaches what some have considered the status of classical tragedy. "The Altar of the Dead", first published in James's collection *Terminations* in 1895 after the story failed of magazine publication, is a fable of literally life and death significance. The story explores how the protagonist tries to keep the remembrance of his dead friends, to save them from being forgotten entirely in the rush of everyday events. He meets a woman who shares his ideals, only to find that the past places what seems to be an impassable barrier between them. Although James was not religious in any conventional sense, the story shows a deep spirituality in its treatment of mortality and the transcendent power of unselfish love.

The final phase of James's short narratives shows the same characteristics as the final phase of his novels: a more involved style, a deeper psychological approach, and a sharper focus on his central characters. Probably his most popular short narrative among today's readers, "The Turn of the Screw" (1898) is a ghost story that has lent itself well to operatic and film adaptation. With its possibly ambiguous content and powerful narrative technique, the story challenges the reader to determine if the protagonist, an unnamed governess, is correctly reporting events or is instead an unreliable neurotic with an overheated imagination. To further muddy the waters, her written account of the experience—a frame tale—is being read many years later at a Christmas house party by someone who claims to have known her.

"The Beast in the Jungle" (1903) is almost universally considered to be one of James's finest short narratives, and has often been compared with *The Ambassadors* in its meditation on experience or the lack of it. The story also treats other universal themes: loneliness, fate, love and death. The parable of John Marcher and his peculiar destiny speaks to anyone who has speculated on the worth and meaning of human life. Among his last efforts in short narrative, "The Jolly Corner" (1908) is usually held to be one of James's best ghost stories. The tale describes the adventures of Spencer Brydon as he prowls the now-empty New York house where he grew up. Brydon encounters a "sensation more complex than had ever before found itself consistent with sanity".

Beyond his fiction, James was one of the more important literary critics in the history of the novel. In his classic essay *The Art of Fiction* (1884), he argued against rigid proscriptions on the novelist's choice of subject and method of treatment. He maintained that the widest possible freedom in content and approach would help ensure narrative fiction's continued vitality. James wrote many valuable critical articles on other novelists; typical is his insightful book-length study of his American predecessor Nathaniel Hawthorne. When he assembled the *New York Edition* of his fiction in his final years, James wrote a series of prefaces that subjected his own work to the same searching, occasionally harsh criticism. For most of his life James harbored ambitions for success as a playwright. He converted his novel *The American* into a play that enjoyed modest returns in the early 1890s. In all he wrote about a dozen plays, most of which went unproduced.

His costume drama *Guy Domville* failed disastrously on its opening night in 1895. James then largely abandoned his efforts to conquer the stage and returned to his fiction. In his *Notebooks* he maintained that his theatrical experiment benefited his novels and tales by helping him dramatize his characters' thoughts and emotions. James produced a small but valuable amount of theatrical criticism, including perceptive appreciations of Henrik Ibsen. With his wide-ranging artistic interests, James occasionally wrote on the visual arts. Perhaps his most valuable contribution was his favorable assessment of fellow expatriate John Singer Sargent, a painter whose critical status has improved markedly in recent decades. James also wrote sometimes charming, sometimes brooding articles about various places he visited and lived in. His most famous books of travel writing include *Italian Hours* (an example of the charming approach) and *The American Scene* (most definitely on the brooding side).

James was one of the great letter-writers of any era. More than ten thousand of his personal letters are extant, and over three thousand have been published in a large number of collections. A complete edition of James's letters began publication in 2006 with two volumes covering the 1855–1872 period, edited by Pierre Walker and Greg Zacharias. James's correspondents included celebrated contemporaries like Robert Louis Stevenson, Edith Wharton and Joseph Conrad, along with many others in his wide circle of friends and acquaintances. The letters range from the "mere twaddle of graciousness" to serious discussions of artistic, social and personal issues. Very late in life James began a series of autobiographical works: *A Small Boy and Others, Notes of a Son and Brother*, and the unfinished *The Middle Years*. These books portray the development of a classic observer who was passionately interested in artistic creation but was somewhat reticent about participating fully in the life around him. Henry James was only twenty-two when he wrote *The Noble School of Fiction* for *The Nation*'s first issue in 1865. He wrote, in all, over two hundred essays and book, art and theater reviews for the magazine.

James's work has remained steadily popular with the limited audience of educated readers to whom he spoke during his lifetime, and remained firmly in the British canon, but after his death American critics, such as Van Wyck Brooks, expressed hostility towards James's long expatriation and eventual naturalization as a British citizen. Other critics like E.M. Forster complained about what they saw as James's squeamishness in the treatment of sex and other possibly controversial material, or dismissed his style as difficult and obscure, relying heavily on extremely long sentences and excessively latinate language. Vernon Parrington, composing a canon of American literature, condemned James for having cut himself off from America. Although these criticisms have by no means abated completely, James is now widely valued for his psychological and moral realism, his masterful creation of character, his low-key but playful humour, and his assured command of the language. In his 1983 book, *The Novels of Henry James*, Edward Wagenknecht offers an assessment that echoes Theodora Bosanquet's:

> "To be completely great," Henry James wrote in an early review, "a work of art must lift up the heart," and his own novels do this to an outstanding degree... More than sixty years after his death, the great novelist who sometimes professed to have no opinions stands foursquare in the great Christian humanistic and democratic tradition. The men and women who, at the height of World War II, raided the secondhand shops for his out-of-print books knew what they were about. For no writer ever raised a braver banner to which

all who love freedom might adhere. Early biographies of James echoed the unflattering picture of him drawn in early criticism. F.W. Dupee, as noted above, characterized James as neurotically withdrawn and fearful, and although Dupee lacked access to primary materials his view has remained persuasive in academic circles, partly because Leon Edel's massive five-volume work, published from 1953 to 1972, seemed to butress it with extensive documentation.

Michael Anesko, Fred Kaplan, and Sheldon Novick, working from primary materials have disputed the factual basis of Dupee's and Edel's accounts.

Other critics and biographers have disputed Edel's interpretations and conclusions. James has also figured in at least a half-dozen novels. Colm Tóibín used an extensive list of biographies of Henry James and his family for his widely admired 2004 novel, *The Master*, which is a third person narrative with James as the central character, and deals with specific episodes from his life during the period between 1895 and 1899.

Author, Author, a novel by David Lodge published in the same year, was based on James's efforts to conquer the stage in the 1890s.

In 2002 Emma Tennant published *Felony: The Private History of The Aspern Papers*, a novel that fictionalized the relationship between James and American novelist Constance Fenimore Woolson and the possible effects of that relationship on *The Aspern Papers*.

The published criticism of James's work has reached enormous proportions. The volume of criticism of *The Turn of the Screw* alone has become extremely large for such a brief work.

The Henry James Review, published three times a year, offers criticism of James's entire range of writings, and many other articles and book-length studies appear regularly. Some guides to this extensive literature can be found on the external sites listed below.

Perhaps the most prominent examples of James's legacy in recent years have been the film versions of several of his novels and stories. Three of James's novels were filmed by the team of Ismail Merchant and James Ivory: *The Europeans* (1978), *The Bostonians* (1984) and *The Golden Bowl* (2000). The Iain Softley-directed version of *The Wings of the Dove* (1997) was successful with both critics and audiences.

Helena Bonham Carter received an Academy Award nomination as Best Actress for her memorable portrayal of Kate Croy. Agnieszka Holland's *Washington Square* (1997) was well received by critics, and Jane Campion tried her hand with *The Portrait of a Lady* (1996) but with much less success. In earlier times Jack Clayton's *The Innocents* (1961) brought *The Turn of the Screw* to vivid life on film, and William Wyler's *The Heiress* (1949), adapted from *Washington Square,* won four Academy Awards, including a Best Actress award for Olivia de Havilland as Catherine Sloper.

Most of James's work has remained continuously in print since its first publication, and he continues to be a major figure in realist fiction, influencing generations of novelists. Testifying to his importance, a character named "Henry James" appears in at least a half-dozen novels, as noted above, the best-known of which is *The Master* by Colm Toibin.

Such disparate writers as Joyce Carol Oates with *Accursed Inhabitants of the House of Bly* (1994), Louis Auchincloss with *The Ambassadress* (1950), Tom Stoppard with *The Real Thing* (1982), and Alan Hollinghurst with *The Line of Beauty* (2004) were explicitly influenced by James's works.

James was definitely out of his element when it came to music, but Benjamin Britten's operatic version of "The Turn of the Screw" (1954) has become one of the composer's most popular works. William Tuckett converted the story into a ballet in 1999.

Even when the influence is not so obvious, James can cast a powerful spell. In 1954, when the shades of depression were thickening fast, Ernest Hemingway wrote an emotional letter where he tried to steady himself as he thought James would: "Pretty soon I will have to throw this away so I better try to be calm like Henry James.

Did you ever read Henry James? He was a great writer

who came to Venice and looked out the window and smoked his cigar and thought."

The odd, perhaps subconscious or accidental allusion to "The Aspern Papers" is striking. And there are the real oddities, like the Rolls-Royce ad which used Strether's famous words: "Live all you can; it's a mistake not to." That's more than a little ironic, considering *The Ambassadors'* sardonic treatment of the "great new force" of advertising.

Chapter 2

Sexual Orientation Imbued in his Fiction

James belonged to a prominent American family, whose cultural milieu consisted of the intelligentsia of New England, and whose scholarly and social connections extended throughout Europe. His father, Henry James, Sr., was a noted Swedenborgian philosopher and man of letters, a friend of Ralph Waldo Emerson and Thomas Carlyle. Because Henry Sr. favored frequent changes of scenery, the James children spent their childhood divided between the United States and Europe, and were educated on both continents. The family returned to New England before war broke out between the states, and while helping to extinguish a fire in Newport, Henry Jr. sustained what he later called "an obscure hurt." This injury became the source of much biographical and critical speculation about the cause of the author's lack of sexual interest in women.

Henry's eldest brother, William, who went on to become an acclaimed philosopher and psychologist, showed early artistic and academic promise. Henry Jr. attempted to define a space for himself distinct from both his brother and his father. In the early 1860s, Henry began to write short stories and reviews for the *Atlantic Monthly, The Nation,* and the *North American Review*. Attracted by the European cultural environment, Henry traveled throughout Europe for fifteen months but was forced to return to the United States in April 1870, because of financial difficulties. James then managed to secure a position as the *New York Tribune* correspondent in

Paris and sailed again for Europe in 1875. He decided to make England his permanent home and resided in London until 1897, when he retired to Lamb House, in Rye.

In 1914, on the outbreak of World War I, the author became involved in the war effort, and devoted much time and energy to the support of British troops. Disturbed by the U.S. government's reluctance to enter the war, James became a British citizen in 1915. He received one of England's highest honors in 1916, an Order of Merit; shortly thereafter, his health deteriorating, James died of a stroke in Lamb House on February 28, 1916. James's writing career was long and productive. He published nearly thirty novels and novellas, in addition to a myriad of short stories, travel sketches, and critical essays. With the advent of *Daisy Miller,* in 1878, he claimed a place in London's distinguished writing circle, boasting, at one point, that he had accepted more than 107 dinner invitations in one social season.

James won literary acclaim for his artistic devotion to the form of the novel, innovating the dramatic presentation of character and perfecting the technique of narrative "point of view."

By the 1890s, however, his writings had begun to lose their popular appeal. As one commentator noted, James was the most famous novelist in Europe who was never read. In an effort to reestablish his popularity (and to bolster his finances), James turned to drama. His efforts met with minimal success, and when he was booed off the stage at the London opening of *Guy Domville* in January 1895, he decided to restrict his literary endeavors to writing short stories and novels.

Although James's later fiction was never to meet with the popularity of his earlier writings, it always elicited favorable critical reviews. Indeed, at the turn of the century, the author produced the three novels of the "Major Phase"—*The Ambassadors* (1903), *The Wings of the Dove* (1902), and *The Golden Bowl* (1904)—which are generally regarded as his literary masterpieces.

James's many close friendships with women have received a great deal of critical and biographical attention. Following the author's lead in his autobiographical *Notes of a Son and Brother* (1914), critics concentrated on James's early involvement with his cousin Minny Temple, whose death in 1870 was thought to be one of the reasons behind his decision to remain single. James maintained a warm friendship with Constance Fenimore Woolson, and some biographers have speculated that her suicide in 1894 was due to her inability to establish a reciprocal romantic relationship with James.

RECLAIMING JAMES'S HOMOSEXUALITY

Yet, despite (or perhaps, because of) the scholarly scrutiny focused on James's friendships with women, his sexuality and sexual preferences remained shrouded until the 1980s and 1990s. Richard Hall has claimed that heterosexual critics of James have been unable to decipher the signs of his homosexuality, and although some pioneering critics, like Robert K. Martin, argued in the 1970s that James's sexual orientation imbued his fiction, the bulk of Jamesian scholarship remained under the influence of the "official" biographical data. Since the 1980s, however, interest in James's sexuality has led to a reappraisal of his life and writings. A number of insightful analyses of his novels have been produced, leading to a reassessment of James as a gay literary figure, and lending his novels' famous "ambiguity" a different hue.

Whether James's homosexuality was active remains an open question (Hugh Walpole told a story of how he propositioned James, only to meet with a horrified, "I can't! I can't!"), but, as Fred Kaplan demonstrates in his 1992 biography, *The Imagination of Genius,* the author had a number of intimate relationships with young men. In 1876, James met and fell in love with Paul Joukowsky, a young Russian painter and intellectual. Although his association with Joukowsky was short-lived, the friendships he established with men like Jonathan Sturges and Morton Fullerton were to endure for many years. These friendships appear to have been primarily spiritual and asexual, but his attachment to Hendrik Andersen, a young sculptor, generated an intensely erotic correspondence. James treasured his relationship with

Andersen, and this relationship was to provide him with a source of joy throughout his later life.

JAMES ON OSCAR WILDE

James was ambivalent about his own sexuality, and his ambivalence is perhaps most apparent in his response to Oscar Wilde. James was by no means an advocate of gay rights, and was, in fact, horrified by Wilde's flamboyant sexuality (as well as jealous of Wilde's popularity).

In letters to intimate friends, he spoke of the Wilde trial in no uncertain terms, drawing attention to his view that Wilde's fate was hideously, atrociously dramatic & really interesting. ... It is the squalid gratuitousness of it all ... of the mere exposure—that blurs the spectacle. But the *fall* ... to that sordid prison-cell & this gulf of obscenity over which the ghoulish public hangs & gloats—it is beyond any utterance of irony or any pang of compassion!

He was never in the smallest degree interesting to me—but this hideous human history has made him so—in a manner. James also refused to sign the petition circulated in 1896 requesting a pardon for Wilde. Of course, one can speculate that Wilde's fate made no small impression on James, and strengthened his desire to keep his own relationships private and hidden from public view.

RELATIONSHIPS BETWEEN MEN (AND WOMEN) IN JAMES'S FICTION

Although James was praised for his innovative portrayals of women (particularly of the "American girl," whom he made famous), many of his novels also focus on relationships between men. As Leland S. Person, Jr. has demonstrated, James's writings often construct, deconstruct, and reconstruct masculinity in a number of intriguing ways. The author's first acknowledged novel, *Roderick Hudson* (1876), traces the development of a friendship between an older and wealthy art connoisseur, Rowland Mallett, and his protégé, the brilliant sculptor, Roderick Hudson. The passages devoted to the budding friendship between the two men are among the most powerful in the novel; and though the friendship is doomed and, indeed, the novel concludes with Hudson's suicide, the young sculptor's impact on Mallett's life provides the focal point of the text.

In *The Bostonians*, published in 1885, James shifts his literary focus and dramatizes a relationship between two Boston women. The latent lesbianism in the novel has received a great deal of critical attention, and in 1978, Judith Fetterley contested conventional views of the relationship between Olive Chancellor and Verena Tarrant as "deranged" and "abnormal." Fetterley points out that the novel was inspired by Henry's sister, Alice, and her longtime companion, Katherine Loring, and argues that "James's understanding of their relationship, though at times critical, is imbued by a genuine sympathy. Thus, if one looks to the external context surrounding the conception of *The Bostonians*, one can find only support for the love between Olive and Verena."

Fetterley's analysis engenders a different reading of Olive and Verena's association, but this association, much like the male homoerotic relationships in James's literary oeuvre, is doomed within the text. *The Bostonians* details how a Southern macho hero, Basil Ransom, intrudes into the women's friendship, ultimately "winning" Verena, and leaving Olive bereft. The portrayal of Ransom's virility, and the problems exposed therein, however, also work to undercut and subvert traditional representations of masculinity. The critique of normative role-playing, which is an important aspect of *The Bostonians* and of a number of James's later fictions, often underpins the construction of the famous Jamesian observer. The observer—a man outside the social circle represented in the texts, who records the foibles of those whom he is watching—is frequently in a position to analyse and comment on the structure of normative heterosexual relations.

In *The Sacred Fount* (1901), for example, the observer-figure narrates the story, and hypothesizes that, in the heterosexual relationships he is evaluating, the elder partner draws energy from the younger, who weakens as a result. In *The Ambassadors*, traditionally hailed as James's masterpiece, Lambert Strether, an aging male character, performs the role of the observer. Strether travels to Paris, on behalf of his fiancée, to watch over and return to her her errant son, Chad Newsome. Through Chad and his paramour, Marie de Vionnet, Strether learns to embrace life and to "live all you can." Repudiating his fiancée and his female confidante in Paris, Newsome embarks on a new life, alone, but rejuvenated. The seemingly disinterested position of the observer, therefore, often gives way to a friendship with a younger man, which empowers the observer to repudiate conventional restrictions.

MALE FRIENDSHIP IN JAMES'S SHORT STORIES

James's short stories frequently focus on the theme of male friendship. Texts like "The Pupil" (1890) portray homoerotichomoerotic relationships between older men and their protégés, and trace enriching, if short-lived, associations. In "The Author of Beltraffio" (1884), a young critic attempts to resolve the domestic difficulties of his literary hero, Mark Ambient, only to find that his intervention into Ambient's marriage indirectly causes the death of Ambient's son. In "The Middle Years" (1893), a relationship develops between a dying author and a young doctor at a resort. This relationship enriches the doctor's cultural existence, but also results in his poverty, since his attention to the author enrages his female patron, who cuts the doctor out of her will.

As Eve Kosofsky Sedgwick has argued, *The Beast in the Jungle* (1903) comprises a case study of "homosexual panic." Moreover, stories like "The Jolly Corner" (1908), which involves a protagonist who confronts himself as he might have been had he not left America for a solitary existence in Europe, dramatize the ways in which the protagonist comes to embrace heterosexual love. Even though the above might suggest that James's portrayals of women suffer as a result of the privileged male relationships in his short stories, and to a certain extent this is so, at the same time, James's treatment of women is also deft and skillful, and has led many feminist critics to applaud his representations of femininity. James, a man of his time, did not support women's rights (and was frequently quite dismissive of female writers), but his female characters are among the most positively represented in British and American literature.

In turn, although James's ambivalence toward gay love and lifestyles propels his fiction, his portrayals of male friendships are provocative and powerful. Indeed, the fated nature of these relationships testifies not only to James's inability to conceive of a space wherein homosexual love might be dramatized in fruition, it also points to the pall cast by the Wilde trials, wherein the specter of Oscar shadowed the comportment of many gay men of his age. James, caught within a myriad of conflicting cultural positions—an American living in Europe, a gay man living in a normative heterosexual world—was able to channel his own marginality into literary texts that document the anxieties of his age, be they social, sexual, or cultural. In so doing, this closeted gay man was able to transform his personal difficulties into novels that represent and document a crucial stage in the development of homotextual traditions.

Chapter 3

The Question of James's Americanism

Henry James was born an American and died an Englishman. He might never have formally transferred his allegiance had it not been for the War and our long delay in espousing the Allied cause. He became a British subject in July, 1915. The transfer had, however, been virtually made many decades earlier. Of the two ruling passions of James, one was surely his passion for "Europe." Of this infatuation the reader will find the most explicit record in his fragmentary book of reminiscences, *The Middle Years* (1917), record and whimsical apology which may well serve the needs of other Americans pleading indulgence for the same offence. James loved Europe, as do all "passionate pilgrims," for the thick-crowding literary and historical associations which made it seem more alive than the more bustling scene this side the water. Going to breakfast in London was an adventure,—being not, as at Harvard, merely one of the incidents of boarding, but a social function, calling up "the ghosts of Byron and Sheridan and Scott and Moore and Lockhart and Rogers and *tutti quanti.*"

In America, James had never so taken breakfast except once with a Boston lady frankly reminiscent of London, and once with Howells fresh from his Venetian post, and so "all in the Venetian manner." Everybody in Victorian London had, as he calls it, references—that is, associations, appeal to the historic imagination; and, as he humorously confesses, "a reference was then, to my mind, whether in a person or an object, the most becoming ornament possible." It was "with bated breath" that he approached the paintings of Titian in the old National Gallery; and when, in the presence of the Bacchus and Ariadne, he became aware, at the same moment, of the auburn head and eager talk of Swinburne, his cup for that day ran over. With the best of introductions to the Rome of Story, the London of Lord Houghton, the highest ambition of James was to establish "connections" of his own with a world in which everything so bristled with connections; and it is he who lets us know with what joy he found himself, on the occasion of his first visit to George Eliot, running for the doctor in her service, since thereby "a relation had been dramatically determined."

American patriotism, little less since the Civil War than before, has steadily contended that America does as well as Europe as a background for fiction, pointing to the epic dimensions and the epic hopes of existence on this continent. Less expansive critical dispositions have continued to feel that the human past of the country has not been large enough to match the landscape; that the present at any given moment has lacked the stability, the solidarity, which alone might afford the novelist a firm texture of reality in his representations; that the simplicity of American manners, being merely provincial rather than fittingly republican, renders impossible the subtleties and nuances of European fiction. Of the principal later novelists Howells held, on the whole, the broadest views. He built, with some limitations, on what he saw before him, not unconscious of Europe but aware that the way to a body of American fiction was action as well as argument and that in the production of a national literature imagination begets imagination. Mark Twain, without much reflection but with powerful instincts in the matter, wrought in the fashion of all great autochthons—as if his native land were the centre of the world. Henry James, at the other extreme, never ceased to regard America as essentially an outlying region of European, more specifically of Anglo-Saxon, civilization.

The differing governments of England and the United States were simply nothing to him, who knew and cared so little for man as a political animal. For this craftsman in language it was language which outlined the empire of the English and bound its various parts together in spite of such surface matters as ocean and revolution. He was a loyalist to the tongue of England. And of course speech was for him but a symbol of all the customs which he thought of as centering in or about London and to which he drew near and nearer with a passion of return which implies an atavistic hankering in the blood. In other words, Henry James was a patriot to his race, and his final transfer of citizenship, though immediately called forth by his sense of America's procrastination in the World War, was but the outward sign of a temperamental repatriation already complete. The process began early under the deliberate guidance of a father, Henry James, Sr., a remarkable metaphysician and theologian, who sought to make his sons citizens of the world by never allowing them to take root in any particular religion, political system, ethical code, or set of personal habits.

Born in New York, Henry James had the most desultory schooling, under the most diverse teachers, in New York, Albany, Geneva, London, Paris, Newport, Geneva again, Bonn, and again Newport, studying now mathematics, now languages, reading a good deal of Latin and a little Greek, dabbling in Fourier and Ruskin, drawing a little, immersing himself in the British magazines and the *Revue des deux Mondes*, and from a very early period writing stories after the model of Balzac. A circle which contained at once the elder Henry James and his son William was out of contact with few of the important ideas then stirring; and the father was accustomed to bring into the household many of the eminent Europeans who visited the United States from time to time. The Civil War would possibly have enlisted Henry, as it did his two younger brothers, but for his uncertain health; and it did without doubt mark him deeply. "It introduced into the national consciousness," Henry James wrote in 1879, by the "national consciousness" undoubtedly meaning his own as well, "a certain sense of proportion and relation, of the world being a more complicated place than it had hitherto seemed, the future more treacherous, success more difficult ... [a perception] that this is a world in which everything happens."

His non-participation in the war at first hand appears also to have developed—hardly aroused—in him a sense that his' essential rôle was to be that of a spectator of life. At any rate, instead of going to war he went to Harvard in 1862, for some vague reason to the Law School, which touched him hardly at all in comparison with the men of letters whom he encountered in Boston or Cambridge, in particular Charles Eliot Norton and William Dean Howells. Through them he became a contributor of critical articles to the *Nation* and the *North American* and of stories to the *Atlantic* and the *Galaxy*. The "open editorial hand" which Howells held out to him from the *Atlantic* during the summer of 1868, Henry James said, "was really the making of me, the making of the confidence that required help and sympathy and that I should otherwise, I think, have strayed and stumbled about a long time without acquiring. You showed me the way and opened me the door." New England, however, could not satisfy him.

Early in 1869 he made the passionate pilgrimage to Europe which, in various forms, provides the theme for so immense a portion of his work: England, Switzerland, Italy, France in turn met his "relish for the element of accumulation in the human picture and for the infinite superpositions of history." Singular contrast between the behaviour of the Innocent Abroad and the Passionate Pilgrim! Without anything like so deep a sense for history as Mark Twain, Henry James had not Mark Twain's ignorance to sustain him against the magnetic pull of Europe; nor had the younger man a touch of that indigenousness which restored Mark Twain to his original continent. Lacking any strong roots into the American soil, Henry James, though he returned to Cambridge in 1870 for two years, and after a further European sojourn during 1872–1874, for one year more, now succumbed to the centripetal pull which all along had been acting upon him, and in 1875 finally decided that his future belonged to Europe.

For a year he tried Paris, where he met Turgenev and the Flaubert group—Edmond de Goncourt, Daudet, Maupassant,

Zola; but he there felt too much a foreigner for comfort, and late in 1876 he settled for good in London, the natural home of his imagination. With *Roderick Hudson* (1876) James concluded the long years of experimentation through which, as had Hawthorne before him, he seriously ascended to his art. His first novel, *Watch and Ward,* issued as a serial in the *Atlantic* during 1871, was a trivial performance. Of the more than a score of short stories he published before his homesick hegira, he later cared to preserve but three. The discarded trifles betray a strong influence of Hawthorne, particularly *The Romance of Certain Old Clothes,* with its dusky scene laid in eighteenth-century America and its ghostly, inconclusive conclusion; *De Grey: a Romance,* the study of an ancestral curse dubiously inherited by a New York family from its European forebears; and *The Last of the Valerii,* wherein a young Roman nobleman digs up a statue of Venus from his garden and fatally reverts to the worship of her pagan loveliness.

No such dominant magic as Hawthorne's, however, quite invests these tales; Henry James belonged to a different universe, with a different heaven and hell. Nor could be even as well as the Hawthorne of *The Seven Vagabonds,* for instance, succeed with little adventures into the picaresque like *Professor Fargo,* with its tawdry traveling showmen. James came nearer to achieving the considered sobriety of George Eliot, whom he admired; and he tucked himself as far as he could under the edge of the mantle of Balzac. In *Travelling Companions* is foreshadowed James's later skill in the description of ancient landscape and architecture; in *At Isella,* his habit of rounding out a story from the most flying hint; and in *The Sweetheart of Mr. Briseux,* at least in patches, his smoothly ironical, dexterously enwinding style. The stiffness and scrawniness of youth appears more obviously in his purely American stories than in those narrated against a European background, as were all the three he salvaged from these days of experiment—*A Passionate Pilgrim* (1871), *The Madonna of the Future* (1873), *Madame de Mauves* (1874).

Madame de Mauves is a sort of American Una among European lions, the snowy wife of a sinful Frenchman who first hates her because she will neither "submit basely nor rebel crookedly" and then melodramatically blows his brains out because, when he has fallen in love with her, she cannot forgive him. Theobald, in the affecting *Madonna of the Future,* has for twenty years nursed in Florence the vision of a flawless Madonna which he means to paint, only to find out at last that he has dawdled away his powers and chances: his adored model has grown coarse, his hand cannot execute his beautiful plan. *A Passionate Pilgrim* carries an overwrought American to England to claim a fortune, as Hawthorne's *Ancestral Footstep* had done. The plot is nearly as romantic as Hawthorne would have made it; the chief concern is the sensations of the ardent traveller in the presence of that charm which maddens, in Henry James, the "famished race." This concern, too, makes up a large bulk of *Roderick Hudson,* the account of a young sculptor who, thanks to a friendly patron, is suddenly lifted from the naked, rectangular society of Northampton, Massachusetts, and set down in Rome in the hope that something great will come of his genius under circumstances luxuriantly propitious.

His vein proves thin and he goes, with unconvincing promptitude, to pieces, and then on to fall to death over a Swiss precipice. James subsequently admitted that the element of time in this novel should have been better handled; that he had borrowed more from the intensity of the dramatist than, as novelist, he could offer security for. But he still felt willing to acknowledge as his own the skill with which he had represented the entire action—Roderick's aspiration and descent, his unfaithfulness to Mary Garland and his passion for Christina Light—through the consciousness of Rowland Mallet, who, though he does not speak in the first person, renders the narrative something the same service that Miles Coverdale renders in *The Blithedale Romance.* Without at the moment quite understanding it, James was working toward that admirable technique, in which he is practically supreme among novelists—the technique of concentration which makes his novels as compact as tales and which allows his tales to run without dilution of emphasis almost to the dimensions of novels. Now established in London, James sedulously worked at making himself a purer Anglo-Saxon than he believed he could be anywhere along the periphery of the race, forgetful, it seems, that Anglo-Saxons are explorers and colonizers no less truly than huggers of the insular hearth.

As an American with proper introductions he went into penetralia of English society which novelists in the Islands do not easily reach unless they are born to them. He learned, after a struggle and occasional relapses, to like both the weather and the manners of Britain, exposing himself to both those cooling experiences, except for a few brief visits to France and Italy, during five remarkably busy years. The critical doctrines which sustained him he collected and put forth in *French Poets and Novelists* (1888), much of it written during his earlier years on the Continent. "Realism," he said, "seems to us with 'Madame Bovary' to have said its last word"; but he felt that for the most part Flaubert's knowledge was greater than his imagination. James admired GeorgeSand's magnificent flow and colour, which he oddly compared to that of Spenser in *The Faerie Queene,* but he thought she had too little form and too much optimism: "We suspect that something even better [than optimism] in a novelist is that tender appreciation of actuality which makes even the application of a simple coat of rose-colour seem an act of violence." Balzac, of course, James greatly preferred to either Flaubert or George Sand, for his great range and close texture: "He has against him," James however added, "that he lacks that slight but needful thing—charm."

The informing imagination absent from Flaubert, the substantial texture absent from George Sand, the charm absent from Balzac—all these James found in his great master and favourite Turgenev, whom in 1874, so little had he been translated further west than Paris, it was still possible to include among French novelists. Turgenev had, it seemed to James, "a deeply intellectual impulse toward universal appreciation"; he had form and grace and tenderness and irony. When James says that "the blooming fields of fiction" can hardly show "a group of young girls more radiant with maidenly charm" than Turgenev's, or when he says that these girls "have to our sense a touch of the faintly acrid perfume of the New England temperament—a hint of Puritan angularity," the remark throws a long light ahead on James's own deep concern with the characters of women. And he must have had in mind a parallel between Turgenev and himself when he wrote that "Russian society, like our own, is in process of formation, the Russian character is in solution, in a sea of change, and the modified, modernized Russian, with his old limitations and his new pretensions, is not, to an imagination fond of caressing the old, fixed contours, an especially grateful phenomenon."

James still drew considerably, and was long to draw, upon the "sprawling continent" at his back; but he was "fond of caressing the old, fixed contours" of Europe. He sustained his position as an expatriate in his subtle study of *Hawthorne* (1879), which he had been asked by John Morley to contribute to the English Men of Letters series and in which the recent disciple of Hawthorne, while delicately appreciating the master, wrote into almost every page his accusation of provincialism against the entire American nation.

"Certain national types," he answered to Howells's comment that it is no more provincial for an American to be very American than for an Englishman to be very English, "are essentially and intrinsically provincial." If James during these acclimatizing years reflected almost constantly upon the "international situation" it was because he stood in that situation himself. A good deal of what it meant for him may be found ripely remembered in his posthumous autobiographical fragment *The Middle Years.* But he had thousands of companions under the same spell in varying degrees: those of his nationality who, the Civil War being now over and methods of travel in Europe easier than in the home-keeping days of the republic, annually swarmed to Europe for vacations of culture.

Whether Henry James sympathized with their aspirations or satirized their numerous awkwardnesses in the midst of manners less casual than those of the United States, he could not overlook them or that simplicity which he identified with provinciality. The ground they traversed furnished him a sort of literary terrain which excited his imagination precisely as the frontier, on which another set of Americans had faced the new as these Americans faced the old, had excited the imagination of Fenimore Cooper.

Highly ironical as it may seem, it is still not highly fanciful to say that *The American* (1877), begun in Paris in 1875 at a time when James, though delighting in the art and companionship of Turgenev, was yet feeling somewhat excluded from French society, sprang from James's conception of a romantic American gesture quaintly like that of Daniel Boone renouncing the settlements, the gesture on which Cooper founded the character of Leather-Stocking. It was, as James subsequently explained, "the situation, in another country and an aristocratic society, of some robust but insidiously beguiled, some cruelly wronged, compatriot: the point being in especial that he should suffer at the hands of persons pretending to represent the highest possible civilisation and to be of an order in every way superior to his own."

But when the opportunity for vindication came, the American, as James conceived him, "in the very act of forcing it home would sacrifice it in disgust," not out of forgiveness but out of so great contempt for those who had wronged him that he was unwilling to touch them even in a rich revenge. Nor does the plot at large fall, in its romantic qualities, below this instigating gesture. Christopher Newman, intensely self-made and American, is in love with the widowed daughter of the intensely ancient and French house of Bellegarde, which, though the daughter loves him in return, snubs him, snatches the lady from him, and drives her into a convent. Then, though Newman has found out that her mother and brother murdered her father, the American, making his large gesture, refuses to let the ax descend. Claire de Cintré, lovely as she is made out, belongs with the heroines who are too limp for life though not for romantic tragedy; the mother and brother, James himself admitted, in real life would have been remarkably careful to get hold of Newman's money—through marrying Mme. de Cintré to him if need be—before showing him too much scorn.

Nor is Newman excessively convincing; "before the American business-man, as I have been prompt to declare, I was absolutely and irredeemably helpless, with no fibre of my intelligence responding to his mystery." Yet these imperfect elements are tangled in a fine net of charm. Though the style is sparer, sharper than James's style was to become, its texture is here firm with adroit allusions and observant wit, while the background of Paris abundantly though unobtrusively fills the picture. Vain as it must be to strive for all the perfections of Balzac, Flaubert, George Sand, and Turgenev at once, here still was something that looked toward a synthesis of their excellences—with a singular alloy from the older type of American romance which rejoiced to set the American hero patriotically up above the European crowd. As if to redress the balance or to atone for this patriotic zeal, *The Europeans* (1878) subjects two charming persons from Europe, though with some of America in their blood, to the deadly seriousness which Henry James remembered as prevailing in the suburbs of Boston.

There is caricature in his Wentworths, with their large square house and large square consciences; there is perhaps less of it in the European cousins who find here so little use for the virtues of joy or flexibility; but the conflict of manners is nevertheless presented with nearly as much detachment as brilliance. Following it came two shorter novels—*nouvelles*—also equipoised between the hemispheres. *An International Episode* (1879), which shows an American girl insulted by an English duchess and her daughter and then taking such revenge as she can by refusing to marry the duchess's son, vexed the British, who in such matters were accustomed to look for satire entirely on their own side. *Daisy Miller* (1879) enraged the United States, where it was thought an aspersion upon American girlhood to represent an entirely virtuous but innocently daring young woman from Schenectady as conducting herself in Switzerland and Italy in a manner which confuses, and worse than confuses, a half-Europeanized young American who loves her. Fault was naturally found with Winterbourne, the man in the case, who as an American might have been expected to understand Daisy's behaviour as any average American would. But of course to have found fault reveals the naïve temper of criticism in the late seventies.

Henry James had done nothing more reprehensible than to make international comedy out of the situation chosen by Milton for his *Comus.* Daisy wears her rustic innocence to the revels, and, though traduced, would have emerged safely had Winterbourne been true to the simple faith of his nation. *Washington Square* (1881) James called "a tale purely American, the writing of which made me feel acutely the want of the 'paraphernalia'" of an established civilization.

This want, however, did not prevent his making a dainty masterpiece, lucid and quiet and cool, ironical yet tender, out of his story of how poor dull Catherine Sloper dreamed she had a true lover and then found he was only a fortune-hunter after all. The fashion in which James here constantly explains America to his readers, as if they were of course to be Europeans, hints that he had traveled a long way from his native shores in a half-dozen years, as indeed he had. His concern in the international situation had begun to wear thin. It was, nevertheless, at this point in his career that he produced the first of his books which may be characterized as magnificent, *The Portrait of a Lady* (1881).

Although Isabel Archer belongs in the charming line of those American girls whom James subtly traces through their European adventures, she is more important than any who had gone before her. She is but incidentally American, made so for the convenience of a creator who chose to display her as moving across a scene already lighted by his imagination and familiarized by his art. James saw in her the type of youth advancing toward knowledge of life; of youth at first shy and slight in its innocence but flowering under the sun of experience to the fullest hues and dimensions of a complexity which might under different circumstances have lain dormant; of youth growing irresistibly to meet the destiny which growth compels. Had James belonged to another school he might have preferred a young man for protagonist; as it was he preferred to watch the more subterranean alchemies which, with the fewest possible external incidents, gradually enrich this sort of woman to maturity. The methods of his narrative were suggested by his theme.

He would scrupulously keep the centre of his subject within Isabel's consciousness, careful not to make her an egoist but equally careful to reveal her qualities by his notation of the delicate refraction which the scenes and personages of her career undergo in passing through her. Working thus, he could not skimp her story. "I would build large," he determined, "in fine embossed vaults and painted arches, as who should say, and yet never let it appear that the chequered pavement, the ground under the reader's feet, fails to stretch at every point to the base of the walls." His scene shifts spaciously from Albany to the Thames, among English country houses more ripe and ample than anything James had yet described, on to Paris, Florence, Rome—"the inimitable France and the incomparable Italy." Nothing hurries the stream of the narrative, which has time for eddies and shallows, broad stretches of noon and deep ominous pools. Isabel, being young and desirable, and like most of James's heroines allowed no career beside that incident to her sex, gets much of her education from being loved—by the too aggressive Bostonian Caspar Goodwood, by the healthy, manly Lord Warburton, by her cousin Ralph Touchett, most whimsical and wistful and charming of all Henry James's men, and by the dilettante Gilbert Osmond.

She marries Osmond only to find out finally that she had been coldly tricked into the marriage by Madame Merle, whom Isabel has thought her best friend when the woman is in reality Osmond's mistress anxious to get money for their illegitimate child. Something in the intricate, never quite penetrable fibre of the heroine sends her in the end back to her husband for the sake of her stepdaughter, thinking, it seems, that she thereby encounters her destiny more nobly than in any previous chapter of it. The conclusion, on various grounds, does not satisfy, but it consistently enough rounds out Isabel's chronicle. Praise can hardly exaggerate the skill with which James at first warily investigates as from without the spirit of the fresh young girl, gradually transfers the action to her consciousness, and thenceforth with almost no appearance of art reduces his story to the terms of her realization of her fate. In something of this delaying fashion life dawns upon its victims. "'Tis surely a graceful, ingenious, elaborate work," James wrote of the *Portrait* to Stevenson, who disapproved of it, "with too many pages, but with (I think) an interesting subject and a good deal of life and style." He might justly have said that as to life it was unfailing and as to style all gold and ivory.

In his next two novels, *The Bostonians* (1886) and *The Princess Casamassima* (1886) he relinquished the advantage of international contrast. The first deals with a group of American oddities somewhat stridently set on improving the status of women. Henry James himself belonged with the school of those who hold, in a phrase which must almost have driven him to a different position, that woman's place is the home. He brought to his narrative the tory disposition to satire, and filled the book with sharp caustic portraits and an unprecedented amount of caricature. His Bostonians recall that angular army of transcendentalists whom Lowell's essay on Thoreau hung up once for all in its laughable alcove of New England history. James regards them only too obviously from without, choosing as the consciousness through which they are to be represented an engaging young reactionary from Mississippi, Basil Ransom, who invades this fussy henyard and carries away its prized heroine, Verena Tarrant, on the very eve of her great popular success as a lecturer in behalf of her oppressed but rising sex.

By such a scheme James was naturally committed to making his elder feminists all out as unpleasant persons, preying on Verena's youth and charm and enthusiasm, and bound to keep her for their campaign no matter what that it might cost her in the way of love and marriage. But more than James's own prejudices and his technical device contribute to a certain insufficiency in *The Bostonians.* It is too largely skeleton, without the blood which might have come from heartier sympathies, without the flesh with which James might have been able to round out a "purely American" tale had he not forgotten so much about American life. He had forgotten, or at least ceased to care greatly about it. Two visits to his native country during 1881–1883 had left him still hungry for Europe, from which after 1883 he was not to return for over twenty years. *The Princess Casamassima* is wholly European as to setting and characters.

In it the bewildering Christina Light of *Roderick Hudson,* now a discontented princess dabbling in revolution, appears again with a maturer mystery of temperament and an achieved diversity of whim. The romantic strain which James had lately been repressing here rose unashamed to the surface and invented a cock-and-bull yarn about a vast, malignant, ramifyingsecret society which—not unlike that in Brockden Brown's *Ormond* so long before—was supposed to underlie the whole of modern Europe, ready at almost any moment to break out and set thrones and governments toppling. With the Princess is involved the pathetic Hyacinth Robinson, unacknowledged son of a lord and yet a book-binder by trade, who falls first into the vicious coils of the militant socialists, then into the kindly, though as it turns out no less fatal, coils of the Princess Casamassima, learns to admire the aristocracy, and comes to a tragic end.

The story, James said, proceeded directly from his habit of walking the streets of London and reflecting upon the possible lot of some person who should have been produced by this civilization and yet should be condemned, as James decidedly had not been, to witness it from outside—that is, from outside the world of fashion and intelligence. Would not such a humble hero, if sensitive enough, long for all the privileges of such a civilization, plot against them when denied them, fall in love with them when invited to share them even transiently? *The Princess Casamassima* is James's answer to his question; it is, moreover, a superb *tour de force.* Although written as from some timid boudoir or club or milder hearth which trembles fantastically at devouring socialists, the book pleases by its variety and swiftness. It has, in the vulgar sense, a plot.

And it is evidence, too, how thorough was the process of saturation going on in its author, that the background, splendid or sordid, of this novel is crowded with aspects of reality in the still life and racy yet believable characters to an extent that makes *The Bostonians* seem by comparison flat and empty. If the international novels had shown the "dense categories of dark arcana" of European life threatened by Americans, and *The Princess Casamassima* by revolution, *The Tragic Muse* (1890) showed them threatened by art. Nicholas Dormer resigns his seat in Parliament to become a mere portrait painter, to the ineffable horror of his very political mother and fiancée and patron. Parallel to his career is that of Miriam Rooth, who without at first being a lady contrives to become, with the help of genius, a great actress, incidentally refusing, for the sake of her art, a rising diplomat who proposes to make her the most brilliant lady in Europe. The conflict between art and "the world" had early struck James as "one of the half-dozen great primary motives."

That conflict had governed and shaped his own career. So far as he had been a partizan at all in his pictures of life he had sided with "the world" in its compacter, urbaner phases as against uncivilized crudity and cruelty. But now, standing at the centre of the compact, urbane "world," he studied the phenomenon of genius which deflects Nick Dormer from all that his caste regards as desirable or even respectable; and which makes Miriam seem "important" as a human being in spite of her shortcomings as an ornament of society. That singular personage Gabriel Nash, who has no art but the art of living and who has no rôle in the novel but that of chorus, sums up the general problem. "It's the simplest thing in the world; just take for granted our right to be happy and brave. What's essentially kinder and more helpful than that, what's more beneficent? But the tradition of dreariness, of stodginess, of dull dense literal prose, has so sealed people's eyes that they've ended by thinking the most natural of all things the most perverse." Such notes the æsthetic movement in England had been striking for a decade, but only Pater had struck them with the sustained power or linked sweetness of *The Tragic Muse,* and Pater had written about the long past instead of producing, as James here does, a marvelous document on the artistic life of his own immediate days.

Peter Sherringham from watching Miriam arrives at a perception "of the perfect presence of mind, unconfused, unhurried by emotion, that any artistic performance requires and that all, whatever the instrument, require in exactly the same degree: the application, in other words, clear and calculated, crystal-firm as it were, of the idea conceived in the glow of experience, of suffering, of joy." Such a statement implies that James had found a new aristocracy to imagine about—an aristocracy essentially more cosmopolitan than the shining barbarians of his "perpetual Piccadilly" and his innumerable country houses. This shift in the objects of his imagination was connected with certain external facts. The popular success which James had hardly tasted except in the case of *Daisy Miller* but which he had confidently expected would be won by *The Bostonians* and *The Princess Casamassima,* had failed him. He felt hurt and mystified, for, contrary to the general notion, he desired more numerous plaudits than he got.

He wanted money, though he had a competency; he wanted the power that comes from recognition. For these reasons more than any other he gave the five years of 1889–1894 very largely to the writing of plays, working enormously without any substantial reward, and finally concluding early in 1895 that "you can't make a sow's ear out of a silk purse." The same period, and partly the same motive, turned him from full-length novels. "I want," he had written to Stevenson in 1888, "to leave a multitude of pictures of my time, projecting my small circular frame upon as many different spots as possible,... so that the number may constitute a total having a certain value as observation and testimony." Of these briefer stories a notably large number deal with problems of the artistic life in its clashes with "the world." *The Author of*

Beltraffio (1885) had exhibited the wife of that pagan-spirited author as so afraid of her husband's influence upon their son that she actually—if not quite deliberately—lets the boy die to save him from the fearful contamination. *The Aspern Papers* (1888) recounts the strife between the former mistress of the famous Jeffrey Aspern and the critic who wants to publish the poet's letters.

In *The Lesson of the Master* (1892) Henry St. George's lesson to his disciple is that perfection in art may not normally be hoped for by a man whose powers are drawn away by wife and children. To *The Yellow Book* James contributed three studies richly suited to the purposes of a periodical aiming to erect a temple of art in the midst of British Philistia: *The Death of the Lion* (1894), in which the genius Neil Paraday dies neglected in a country house while his hostess gets credit for being his patron; *The Coxon Fund* (1894), laughably modernizing Coleridge into the parasite Frank Saltram who sponges on the rich and devoted and foolish; *The Next Time* (1895), about poor Ralph Limbert who fails in his struggles to boil the pot because he is incapable of anything less than masterpieces, no matter how hard he tries. This group of stories may be said to end with *The Figure in the Carpet* (1896), with Hugh Vereker explaining to his critics how it is they must look in the whole of a writer's work for the "primal plan," the string his pearls are strung on, the complex figure in the Persian carpet of his art. "If my great affair's a secret," said Vereker, "that's only because it's a secret in spite of itself.... I not only never took the smallest precaution to make it so, but never dreamed of any such accident." So Henry James might have reasoned in his own behalf.

Obscurity was his destiny not his design. He had set out to record certain subtle relationships that he perceived binding men and women together in the human picture, and he would not call it his fault if his perceptions had proved more delicate than those of the reading public. He had tried to make national contrasts interesting; he had tried to diversify his matter in the great novels of the eighties; he had tried a new literary form in his plays and had, restricting himself for a time as to dimensions, written about the artistic life as no one had ever done in English. Nothing had availed him with the wider audience. He now gave up the battle, reconciled himself to his limited fate, discovered the house at Rye which was to be his permanent residence till the end of his life, and settled down to the untrammeled practice of his art. Nothing could be more autobiographical, in a sense, than this later work of Henry James, exquisitely reproducing as it so often does the adventures of exquisite souls among thorns and pitfalls.

To robuster dispositions he appears, of course, to be making an incredible fuss over nothing to speak of, and he did cease to interest any but that small group capable of caring about passions so delicate as these. But art may be great without being popular, just as now and then some magnificent radiance of personality may light up a narrow corner. A flawless story published in 1895, *The Altar of the Dead,* somewhat forecasts James's final type. It is the tale—almost an apologue—of a George Stransom who at an altar privately maintained in a dim church sets up, one after another, candles for his dead, himself gradually perfected by his worship until at last he can complete the symmetry of his ritual by setting up a final candle to the memory of his bitter enemy, now forgiven. This narrow corner of existence glows with the whitest, purest light of a noble imagination. James's themes, however, rarely rose quite so high. He chose to walk closer to the ground of usual events, expanding and elevating not the deeds of his characters but their sentiments.

In *The Spoils of Poynton* (1897) the action is only a sordid squabble between a widow and her son over the possession of a house made beautiful with objects of art which she has collected there for a lifetime but which by the hard English law now belong not to her but to him and the stupid bride he means to take. Round this central strife the story grew from a tale to a novel, from a vivid episode to a drama richly conceived and decorated. Another novelist might have abused the law; some other might have sided with son or mother. Henry James reveals his drama through a third person, the gentle, unselfish Fleda Vetch, who shares the mother's passion for beautiful things but who loves the son. James lacked the moral arithmeticwhich taught Howells in *The Rise of Silas Lapham* that wisdom demands the strictest economy in sacrifice: Fleda Vetch, though Owen Gereth loves her and not Mona Brigstock, renounces him without lifting a hand, and condemns, along with herself, son and mother and doubtless wife to pain—and all seemingly with James's approbation.

But though in this regard sentimental and immoral, *The Spoils of Poynton* as regards structure, proportion, texture, style, is accomplished perfection, the result of methods now matured and working upon their materials with absolute competence, without sign of effort or haste. It was natural that in imagining the world in its impact upon tender intelligences, Henry James should have made use of children as his focuses of sensation. *What Maisie Knew* (1897) records the disgusting annals of a "fast" set in London through the mystified innocence of Maisie Farange, whose father and mother, divorced and both married again, toss her back and forth from one to the other in the intervals of incessant infidelity. She sees the outer facts of these obscene menages—joined together, by the way, through the liaison of the step-parents—without comprehending their inner horror. She is like a flower blooming in a filthy pool, by her shy beauty making the contrast a dreadful thing. That contrast is the plot. Charming though Maisie appears in her own right, and ugly as her companions are in theirs, the interest lies essentially in the relations between them and her.

The spectator, aware that in time her innocence will sink down and the dirty flood overwhelm her, constantly winces. Still worse horrors, however, threaten in *The Turn of the Screw* (1898), an almost incomparable short story which, as a sort of moral sequel to *What Maisie Knew*, exhibits two children so corrupted by wicked servants that words will not utter the evil in them. Although a certain symbolism hints at the nature of this particular evil, James was careful not to identify it exactly. Horror multiplies with the vagueness. Maisie is menaced by a bad example which is understood however hated; Miles and Flora appear to have been exposed to dim cosmic forces of evil which surround mankind as in the old

Puritan cosmos, now and then expressed in actual sin but always huger than anything which can come of them. *The Awkward Age* (1899), also concerned with the young, brought James back from his far explorations to polite comedy again, to the problem of the young girl in a society full of innuendo and intrigue. But Nanda Brookenham's experiences are swathed in such countless folds of reference and gossip that, artfully as the drama is expounded, it comes to the ear with a muffled sound, like agreeable voices heard speaking at a distance which lets the actual words die away on the wind.

Five hundred pages of such matter strain the most loyal attention to irritation if not to disgust. And much the same thing must be said of *The Sacred Fount* (1901), which has a soul the size of a short story and a body enlarged to the size of a novel by the solicitude with which James walks round and round his theme, hinting, hinting, hinting. A consequence of the exuberant insinuation with which he worked in the first five years of his freedom from hope in the public was that the public found itself, by the reports of those who had read these later books, confirmed in its disposition to neglect him. From these years dates the legend that he had consciously, almost spitefully, evolved a style which no one could read but which it was a jolly game to laugh at. The laughter grew into a cloud which obscured, and still in most quarters continues to obscure, the three superb novels with which, in prolific succession, he brought his art to its peak: *The Wings of the Dove* (1902), *The Ambassadors* (1903), *The Golden Bowl* (1904). As if with some recurrence of his younger interests, he deals in each of the three with the old situation of Americans in Europe, but in a spirit no longer so reproachful toward them as being merely provincial or dowdy.

James had ceased to be worried over the petty blunders of his travelling countrymen, now that he felt himself securely European and no longer felt the responsibility which once had brought compatriotic blushes to his cheek. Like Mr. Longdon in *The Awkward Age*, an elderly Englishman who has retired to the country but is now drawn back to London again, James's Americans in his maturest masterpieces bring into a fast and loose society certain old-fashioned virtues and graces, such as simplicity, truthfulness, monogamy, solvency. Even Lambert Strether in *The Ambassadors,* who, having friend from the naughtinesses of Paris, himself surrenders to the beautifully beguiling universe he has entered—even Strether holds fast to the integrity which has all along given strength to his natural sympathy and which will not allow him to profit by his amiable betrayal of his mission. Strether's being an American who can be contrasted with Europeans, however, does not exhaust his function. He stands also for a common enough human type, the individual brought up in a limited community who discovers too late, or almost too late, what richness, what content, what joy might have awaited him in some fuller existence.

"Live all you can; it's a mistake not to," Strether says in a speech which Henry James himself pointed out to be the essence of *The Ambassadors.* "It doesn't so much matter what you do in particular so long as you have your life. If you haven't had that what *have* you had?" With some such precepts Pater had talked of the counted number of pulse-beats and had counseled a life lived at the flame. And in that transcendentalist New England which James partially inherited, Emerson and Thoreau had constantly urged the need of fullness and intensity of life. Strether's situation flawlessly fits James's idea. To get the largest value from them James had of course to make Strether another of his exquisite intelligences—rather too exquisite for his upbringing; he had, too, to make this abundant life into which Strether is initiated a life of lovely line and colour, of gorgeous vesture and sweet, subtle, intoxicating atmosphere.

All James's old powers came in upon him, with his new freedom. The execution of *The Ambassadors,* which he thought his most perfectly constructed novel, is as richly imaginative as it is deliberate. James had annually increased the distance between his art and improvisation. He built novels now as architects do cathedrals, planning every stone in advance, testing every material, calculating every stress, visualizing every "elevation." Without any impetuous drive of narrative to carry him on, or the clashes of melodrama, he peculiarly needed anxious prevision and conscientious workmanship. *The Golden Bowl* excellently illustrates this. Maggie Verver, an American girl, marries an Italian prince living in London, and her widowed father marries her friend Charlotte Stant. But there had been between Charlotte and the Prince before their marriages a secret intimacy which afterwards is resumed. With the fictive paraphernalia customary to such cases—jealousy, peeping, revelations, revenges—James of course has nothing to do.

He would no more have brought the matter into the courts than would Maggie Verver and her quiet father. For James, as for Maggie, the evil of the situation consisted less in the sin of adultery than in the ugliness of stealth and deceit. The problem is to bring the hidden offense into light, and the plot is merely the process by which the various characters, one after another, first only gradually, accidentally, then with suspicions hurrying dreadfully into convictions, discover and are discovered. When the truth has come up into the light, the story ends, with Verver and his wife departing for America. Tenuous as the substance may seem to any first glance, *The Golden Bowl* is still solidly constructed beneath its sumptuous garment of phrases and clauses; careless of moral considerations as it may seem to any moralistic eye, it still glows with condemnation of the ugly and the sordid facts which here disrupt a charming microcosm. The story suggests the coming of a great summer sun after a midnight of slinking ghosts.

In *The Wings of the Dove* the beauty and power of truth and goodness receive a tribute which has rarely been paid them in sophisticated novels. As Isabel Archer in *The Portrait of a Lady* has risen magnificently to meet life, so here Milly Theale magnificently rises to meet death. The book is the drama of her "inspired resistance." Without gross or overt agonies, she struggles to experience "as many of the finer vibrations as possible, and so achieve, however briefly and brokenly, the sense of having lived." James made her a New Yorker, the last of her family, rich and free, as the best way he could imagine to endow her with all the ages, and he took her of course to Europe to inherit her domain. There her battle and collapse, since she moves through her fate like a reigning princess, draw a whole circle with and after her; and in the end her tragedy shakes them all. The particular blackness against which she is exhibited is the scheme of Kate Croy and her lover Merton Densher to make Milly believe he is in love with her in order that before her death she may leave him her fortune.

Yet so radiant is the whiteness of Milly's character that, though the plot superficially succeeds, the plotters are separated by disgust at their own shame. Every dexterity was required in such a story to keep Milly from seeming a prig or at best a tedious saint. James avoids this fatal defect by revealing her not so much in her words and deeds as in the effect she has on those who devotedly or selfishly surround her. She stands, as it were, in the beauty from every angle and which themselves report her quest of a crowded existence during her numbered days. As she slowly fades under her malady the mirrors have an increasing task, until at last she is no longer visible except in them, where eventually her image lingers even after her death. Such puissance as hers does not lapse with bodily extinction, but lasts on as a remembered effluence of loveliness. If *The Ambassadors* is the best constructed of these three novels, and *The Golden Bowl* the most subtly suggestive, *The Wings of the Dove* is most elevated, most tender, most noble.

They issued from what might be called the Indian summer of James's career as an American. "Europe," he wrote in 1902, "has ceased to be romantic to me, and my own country, in the evening of my days, has become so." But his longing did not survive the visit which he lustrously chronicled in *The American Scene* (1907). From New Hampshire to Florida, from New York to California, the sensations awakened by the roaring continent overwhelmed him. Like an astronomer come down from his tower into the town, James fled back with his hands to his ears. The remainder of his life was more fragmentary than the rounded period 1896–1904. He resumed for a little while his theatrical ambitions; he wrote more short stories; he worked at the two novels, *The Sense of the Past* (originally begun in 1900) and *The Ivory Tower*, which, though incomplete when posthumously published in 1917, have the special interest that the second of them employs the American scene and both are accompanied by the dictated notes which he latterly made to assist him in his composition; and he carried avowed autobiography through *A Small Boy and Others* (1913), *Notes of a Son and Brother* (1914), and the unfinished *The Middle Years* (1917).

The war shattered his peace beyond repair. This lover of art who had not taken the trouble to form an opinion concerning the Dreyfus case, who had little more to say of the Boer War than that it doubled his income tax, who had vaguely hoped that the war with Spain might educate Americans as imperialism had educated the English, who had looked with candid contempt upon the Irish aspirations for freedom, now woke to the crisis of the world with a passion which ceased only with his death in 1916. There was nothing complicated in his loyalty, nothing critical in his attitude toward the drama being enacted. His "Europe"—France, England, Italy—had been assailed in utter wantonness; the barbarians were pounding at the gates and might at any moment break in to befoul the pavements and violate the shrines of his sacred city. His own distant country looked on without lifting a helping hand, and he saw no better way to signify his protest and his allegiance than by becoming a British citizen in 1915, declaring "civis Britannicus sum" with a Roman boast, and ending his career, as he had begun it, on the note of romance.

Criticism must take account of the vast gulf across which those who like Henry James view with contempt those who do not, and in return those who do not like him view with incredulity those who do. Casual gossip says that his style by its obscurity has fixed the gulf there. While this indubitably operates with regard to certain of his later works, it can have nothing to do with *The American*, or *The Europeans*, or *Daisy Miller*, or *Washington Square*, or *The Portrait of a Lady*, which are all as pellucid as a clean spring. And even in the elaborate, maturer books the style is obscure only in the sense that it speaks of matters less blunt and tangible than those which most fiction deals with. Nor will the cosmopolitan aspect of his themes entirely explain the hindering gulf, as has been argued by patriots who wish to punish him for his expatriation. The three metropolises—New York, London, Paris—which mark the triangle of his chosen territory are objects of curiosity for an enormous audience. Indeed, nationalism hurts James worse than internationalism: he suffers from the sensitiveness to national differences which kept him concerned too much with them and too little with the universal human likenesses which transcend nationality.

He was actually less able to forget his American origin than such an unhesitant son of America as Whitman, for instance, who, taking his native land for granted, could send his imaginations out to all the corners of the world without worrying at the national boundaries thus crossed. Neither may James's failure to touch the wider world he really aimed at be accounted for by his unceasing labors to perfect his technique of representation. These concerned himself alone, or such fellow craftsman or connoisseurs as find in his prefaces to the New York Edition (1907–09) the most remarkable commentaries ever made upon the art of fiction. James's essential limitation may rather accurately be expressed by saying that he attempted, in a democratic age, to write courtly romances. He did not, naturally, go back for his models to the *Roman de la Rose* or *Morte d'Arthur* or Sidney's *Arcadia* or the *Grand Cyrus*. But he did devote himself to those classes in modern society which descend from the classes represented by the romancers of the Middle Ages and the Renaissance.

His characters, for the most part, neither toil nor spin, trade nor make war, bear children in pain nor bring them up with sacrifices. The characters who do such things in his novels are likely to be the servants or dependents of others more comfortably established. His books consequently lack the interest of that fiction which shows men and women making some kind of way in the world—except the interest which can be taken in the arts by which the penniless creep into the golden favor of the rich or the socially unarrived wriggle into an envied caste. James is the laureate of leisure. Moreover the leisure he cared to write about concerns itself in not the slightest degree with any action whatsoever, even games or sports. Love of course concerns it, as with all novelists. Yet even love in this chosen universe must constantly run the gauntlet of a decorum incomprehensible to all but the initiate. Decorum is what damns James with the public.

In one of Chrétien de Troyes's romances Lancelot, on his way to rescue Guinevere from a most precarious situation, commits the blunder of riding part of the way in a cart and thereby brings upon himself a disgrace which his most gallant deeds can scarcely wipe out. Sensible citizens who may have happened upon this narrative in the twelfth century probably felt mystified at the pother much as do their congeners in the twentieth who stare at the wounds which James's heroes and heroines suffer from blunders intrinsically no more serious than Lancelot's. How much leisure these persons must enjoy, the sensible citizen thinks, to have evolved and to keep up this mandarin formality; and how little use they make of it! Only readers accustomed to such decorums can walk entirely at ease in the universe James constructed. But they have the privileges of a domain unprecedented and unmatched in modern literature. It is not merely that he is the most fascinating historian of the most elegant society of the century.

He is the creator of a world immensely beautiful in its own right: a world of international proportions, peopled by charming human beings who live graceful lives in settings lovely almost beyond description; a world which vibrates with the finest instincts and sentiments and trembles at vulgarity and ugliness; a world full of works of art and learning and intelligence, a world infinitely refined, a world perfectly civilized. In real life the danger to such a world is that it may be overwhelmed by some burly rush of actuality from without. In literature the danger is that such a world will gradually fade out as dreams fade, and as the old romances of feudalism have already faded. Elaborate systems of decorum pass away; it is only the simpler manners of men which live forever.

Chapter 4

The Eighties and Their Kin

VARIED TYPES

The decade 1880–1890 produced more good novels than any other American decade. Howells was then at his height in *A Modern Instance, The Rise of Silas Lapham, Indian Summer, A Hazard of New Fortunes;* Mark Twain in *The Adventures of Huckleberry Finn, A Connecticut Yankee in King Arthur's Court;* Henry James in *Washington Square, The Portrait of a Lady, The Princess Casamassima, The Tragic Muse.* It was the decade which saw the beginnings and the most brilliant successes of Francis Marion Crawford, the story-teller par excellence among American novelists, and Frank R. Stockton, delightful inventor of joyous extravaganza.

It was the decade of Wallace's *Ben-Hur,* of Cable's *The Grandissimes,* of E. W. Howe's *The Story of a Country Town,* of Blanche Willis Howard's *Guenn,* of Helen Hunt Jackson's *Ramona,* of Henry Adams's *Democracy* and John Hay's *The Bread-Winners,* of Constance Fenimore Woolson's *East Angels,* of Margaret Deland's *John Ward, Preacher,* of Edward Bellamy's *Looking Backward.* In spite of the popularity of the short story, the novel prospered. The publication of novels serially in magazines had not yet begun to decline. Criticism of the art attained a high dignity inthe hands of Howells and Henry James; Bayard Tuckerman wrote *A History of English Prose Fiction* (1882) which included American authors; and Sidney Lanier used his lectures on *The English Novel* (1883) as the vehicle for a load of passionate opinions concerning literature. By the eighties practically all the types of fiction known to the

United States had been invented and all of them were in use.

Domestic sentimentalism of course still walked its everlasting way of tears with an abundant audience. The romance of adventure, though degraded to the dime novel for the most part, asked no quarter from the critical. The historical tale kept up its ancient habits with the past, sweetening and decorating it. The international novel, sometimes rather the exotic romance, was having its day, not only in Howells and James but in various followers. Local colour, tending toward the romantic, divided the principal field with realism, tending away from it. The novel with some sort of purpose continued to be a tool ready to almost every hand. And there were also certain gaily whimsical stories of a sort new to the country if not to the language. The novels of the eighties cannot be reduced to any such simple formulas as suffice with the romance of Cooper's school or with the tearful tales of the fifties. They show diversities of style and structure, of artistic and moral attitude, as well as topographical variety. In general they represent a decisive advance in simplicity and reality.

Characters were now no longer required to speak the stilted language or to feel the quivering sentiments that had once seemed symptoms of nobility of soul. At the same time, but little advance had been made in the direction of studied raciness or strenuous naturalism. Howells's honest decency set the tone for the period. As the master was often saved from seeming thin and tame only by his unfailing grace and mellow wisdom, the disciples, inferior in these respects, did not always escape thinness or tameness. The preoccupation with local colour encouraged love of surfaces, if not a satisfaction with surfaces alone; so that, though the local colour novel was likely to be a more serious performance than the short story of the type, it nevertheless suffered from the contagion of triviality. The fiction of the eighties suffered, too, from the delicate contagion of gentility.

At the best it imparted daintiness and charm; at the worst, timidity and bloodlessness. The violent currents of political life during the decade, which brought a new party into power for the first time in a quarter of a century; the rising warfare upon established economic privilege; the rapid growth in luxury and sophistication—these but faintly appear in the novels which the decade brought forth, except for those specifically designed to redress grievances or to expose wrongs. Ordinarily, ideas played but a small part. Nor was this absence of ideas compensated for, again except in special cases, by large ranges of personality or depths of passion or impressive beauty or truth. The lives which these novels represent have little to do with the clash of the times in religious or moral, any more than in political, matters. Even in the love affairs which make up the great bulk of all such narratives the complications are of the simplest and the psychology simpler still. The very young do most of the loving, innocently, pathetically, hardly ever realistically or tragically. If love is simple, so is livelihood.

While many of the novels do indeed concern themselves with the poor, it is the more or less contented poor of the older American villages where no serious poverty existed. In but few cases do the heroes and heroines of the eighties contend with the society in which they live, and then rarely indeed with the approval of their authors. Fiction, in short, had not assumed the heavier burdens laid on it by a subsequent generation, but existed largely for entertainment. If it was thus limited in certain directions, so was it freed in others. It recognized no obligation to be polemic, though it could be so on occasion.

It did not look relentlessly for victims of the social order who might be elevated into champions of a higher truth. It did not feel obliged to take many exceptions to the broad average current of human existence. It chose the simpler emotions for the reason that American character was simple. It preferred to make as much of the cheerful aspects of life as possible, because that was the general American preference, even when there was much unpleasantness to be blinked at.

With such a temper prevalent, the style of fiction naturally became lighter and gayer. It discarded the blocks of description which the older romances had admitted and the showers of tears which had immediately preceded the Civil War. Having taken stock of technical methods, it varied its structures with its themes, gave an increased attention to dialect and dialogue, studied the problems of proportion and emphasis. The decade made a highly eclectic use of foreign models. Lanier devoted nearly a half of his study of the English novel to George Eliot, who was influential in many quarters. The writers of local colour novels in not a few instances showed traces of Thomas Hardy. *Ben-Hur* recalls both Bulwer-Lytton and Victor Hugo.

Aldrich and Cable and Bunner had obviously read such Frenchmen as Merimée, About, Daudet, Maupassant, though with reservations. Toward the end of the decade Zola began to be heard, particularly railed at, however, by the orthodox. Henry James and Howells investigated and expounded Turgenev; James added most of the French novelists of the time; Howells added Dostoevsky and his master passion Tolstoy, as well as the Spanish Galdós, Valdés, Valera, and the Italian Verga; while both Howells and James had something to say of almost every eminent European who practised fiction. Though eclectic, the American novel was not unwarrantably imitative. It had certain traditions of its own and followed them.

It was faithful to American life, at least to those phases which it chose to record. Its points of view were clearly national. Without achieving methods as distinctive as those of the short story, the American novel was still a distinctively, unmistakably native product. In the department of domestic sentimentalism the most widely read rivals of E. P. Roe and his kind who appeared in the eighties happened both to be Lancashire women resident in America: Frances Hodgson Burnett, whose *Little Lord Fauntleroy* (1886) moistened millions of uncritical eyes with its account of the American child instructing the British aristocracy in democratic manners: and Amelia Edith Barr, whose swift, kindly pen played over all the fields of fiction except the distinguished. In the romance of adventure Anna Katharine Green Rohlfs made something of a new departure with her very successful detective stories, and Captain (later General) Charles King became the first novelist of the American army, with his brisk stories of field and camp and military post. The historical novel, for which Howells and James cared so little, suffered some neglect, though *Ben-Hur* belonged to that form and *A Connecticut Yankee* burlesqued it; John Esten Cooke worked in it till his death in 1886; Marion Crawford handled past and present with almost equal ease; and at the end of the decade several writers began to point forward to the historical-romantic "best sellers" which crowded the nineties.

The older fashion of sea tales and foreign adventure, now fallen into abeyance, had been succeeded by the milder comedy of international manners, as handled by Howells and James. Mark Twain, of course, handled it humorously, and Crawford, when he liked, with vigorous knowledge. A tragic note infrequent in these international comedies was struck by Blanche Willis Howard's *Guenn* (1884), the story of an American painter in a Breton village and the hopeless, fatal love which he awakens in a young girl there. Most such novels represented their Americans as a little bewildered by the superior complexity of European manners; to Guenn, wild and simple, Hamor seems rich and strange and great. The story, founded, it is said, on the actual experience of a painter who is still living, charmingly preserves the spirit of a day when American artists were mad with the love of France and swarmed over it in pursuit of the beauty and quaintness which at the moment seemed to reside there as nowhere else.

Novels of foreign life might have flourished more numerously had it not been for the zest with which the rarer materials of existence were pursued at home. Better though the local colour writers were in short stories than in novels, their longer novels cannot be overlooked. Bret Harte, in such attempts as *The Story of a Mine* (1878), *Maruja* (1885), *Cressy* (1889), *A Waif of the Plains* (1890), as in other brief novels like them, did no more than to expand short stories with a loss of effectiveness in proportion as he expanded them. And *Gabriel Conroy* (1876), a long novel, for all the novelty and even riches of its contrasts of California civilizations, is lamentably deficient as regards conception, structure, and suspense. With certain touches here and there of Harte's romantic charm or insinuating irony, it is for the most part mere melodrama, without even the distinction of being swift or thrilling as melodrama should be.

The contrast of Californian civilizations led Helen Hunt Jackson to write one of the most moving of American romances. In *A Century of Dishonor* (1881) she had begun her indictment of the United States government for its treatment of the Indians. In *Ramona* (1884) she carried the indictment further, bringing her passion to bear in a new guise. What *Uncle Tom's Cabin* had done to make known the wrongs of the black slaves, *Ramona* attempted to do for the red wards of the nation. It was no longer possible to take Fenimore Cooper's attitude toward the Indian as a lofty child of nature; since Cooper's day there had been the wars with the Sioux and the massacre of Custer. Mrs. Jackson eluded the difficulty by making Ramona, the heroine, and her Temecula husband Alessandro so near to high caste Mexicans in colour and nurture that their wrongs as Indians seem hardly typical of the real grievances of their unfortunate race. They suffer little more from the invading Yankees than do the proudest Mexicans.

Indeed, the true conflict and injustice occur between the old Californians, Indian or Spanish, and the predacious vanguard of the Anglo-Saxon conquest. For Mrs. Jackson California had been a splendid paradise of patriarchal estates, in vast fertile valleys, steeped in a drowsy antiquity, and cherished by fine, unworldly priests. Against this rich background she set a story which begins in peace, blackens to hard and ugly tragedy, and then grows at the end to peace again. The pomp of the setting, the strength of the contrasts, the eloquence, the intensity, the passionate colour—these dominate, almost submerge, the problem with which the narrative is concerned; but they also tend to lift it above controversy, into those higher regions of the imagination in which particular acts of injustice take on a universal significance, in which blunders become tragedies not temporary accidents. *Ramona* was a local colour novel which had a passionate aim and a large historical background as well as quaint surfaces. Two novels of the Mississippi Valley, G. W. Cable's *The Grandissimes* (1880) and E. W. Howe's *The Story of a Country Town* (1883), illustrate the range which the type permitted. *The Grandissimes* is to New Orleans what Irving's Knickerbocker *History* might have been to New York had Irving given himself less to comic history and more to witty romance.

For his period Cable chose the year of the purchase of Louisiana by the United States, but the entire history of the old province lies behind his narrative, constantly showing through; for his scene he chose New Orleans, but action shifts, at least by report, to plantation and bayou, forest and swamp. No other American novel represents such a mingling of races: French and Spanish and German and Yankee, Creole and quadroon, Indian aborigines, and negro slaves who speak a strange jargon of French and English but who have the instincts of Africa in their blood.

This New Orleans is a city of austere castes and almost incomprehensible customs, never too obviously explained, though hinted at with laughing dexterity. The central plot, which shows the houses of Grandissime and De Grapion at war and then reconciles and unites them by marriage, loses itself, unfortunately, in a maze of episodes. But the episodes glitter under a treatment and a style to the last degree allusive, sparkling, felicitous. By comparison, *The Story of a Country Town* moves with the cold tread and hard diction of a saga. It has, indeed, various romantic elements: there is a mill in a dark wood; the church bell tolls fitfully in high winds; certain of the characters prowl about ominously midnight after midnight. The author, whose first book this was, apparently did not know how to give it the sense of locality. It is as if the bare, sunburned Kansas plain, on which the action passes, had no real depth, no mystery in itself, no native motif but the smoldering discontent of an inarticulate frontier.

If it lacks locality, so does it lack relief, comedy, poetical touches, and above all that flowing optimism which too often weakened the books of the period. *The Story of a Country Town* is the sternest, the grimmest of American novels—and it was published the same year as Mark Twain's joyous *Life on the Mississippi*. If happiness or gaiety ever lighted up Fairview and Twin Mounds Howe's story does not tell it. There is something symbolic about the figure of the narrator's father, the Rev. John Westlock, who outwardly practises the most ferocious Calvinism and yet is daily haunted by gorgeous processions of sin sweeping before his eyes, until he runs off with a vulgar woman to an existence more miserable than the first.

Symbolic, too, is Lytle Biggs, who serves as impudent chorus with a cynicism that plays over the face of the story, cheapening and corroding all it touches. Howe wrote about Twin Mounds as Crabbe wrote about the English village—determined, it seems, to paint it "As Truth will paint it, and as Bards will not": a neighborhood as barren of beauty and elevation as of lakes and mountains; dogmatic without being religious, ambitious enough without having any intelligent aims, industrious but futile. A Parisian never wrote more contemptuously of provincial life. And yet beneath this cold exterior, which will not let the narrative or the dialogue be flexible for one moment, lurks authentic power.

No shallow mind could have conceived the blind, black, impossible passion of Joe Erring, who loves like a backwoods Othello; no tepid mind could have conducted such a passion through its catastrophe to the purgation and tranquillity which succeed. That Howe, though he wrote another novel or two, ended his career as a novelist almost where he began it, meant a grave loss to American fiction. He made himself a successful country journalist, a wise and ineffably disillusioned country sage; but the energy of his imagination sought other channels than the novel.

Howe had taken a step beyond Edward Eggleston on the way to that stiffening of the conscience which brought the naturalism of the next decade, but in the eighties he had no fellow except Joseph Kirkland of Illinois, who wrote the crude, truthful *Zury* (1887). Elsewhere local colour produced few novels that need to be called by name. Cable wrote others for Louisiana: Charles Egbert Craddock now and then turned away from the short story with her Tennessee material; as did

Sarah Orne Jewett in New England, H. C. Bunner in New York, and Richard Malcolm Johnston in Georgia.

An unusual control over a diversity of sections appears in the work of Constance Fenimore Woolson, a grandniece of Fenimore Cooper, who during the eighties had a promise that seemed to rank her little below Howells and James and Crawford. She lived in turn in the Great Lakes region, particularly Mackinac, in the devastated, reviving South of Reconstruction times, and in Italy, applying her art to all of her neighborhoods. Henry James found her deserving of a fairly extended critique from a pen which did not often condescend to the underwoods of literature. Her stories are perhaps as good as her novels, but she has not quite survived by virtue of either.

And yet *East Angels* (1886), that glowing, rich-hued picture of the Florida of the tourist, just misses being a classic. To be mistress of all the local colors will not make a writer even a minor classic unless something else is added—some superior grace as in Cable or superior veracity as in E. W. Howe. Little as most of the novels of the period touched upon its public affairs, some of them were not silent. Albion Winegar Tourgée's *A Fool's Errand* (1879) called attention to the problem of the freedman. Henry Adams in *Democracy* (1880) drew a caustic picture of society and politics in Washington—a city strangely neglected in American literature, which can hardly point to a dozen political novels of any merit whatever.

John Hay's *The Bread-Winners* (1884) made a sensation by its defence of the old economic order against the increasing claims of labour. Margaret Deland's *John Ward, Preacher* (1888), like the exactly contemporary *Robert Elsmere* of Mrs. Humphry Ward, aroused wide controversy by its account of a husband and wife so divided on doctrinal grounds that their lives are shattered. In the American novel it is the husband who is orthodox and the wife who is latitudinarian, but here as in the English book stress falls upon the consequences to love of such a difference. Though no civilized human being can now do more than stare at the zeal which impels John Ward in his efforts to save his wife's soul by teaching her to believe in the fires of hell, by no means all the passion of the book has faded out. In the same year with *John Ward* appeared a work of fiction which caught the immediate public as hardly any book of its theme had ever done before.

The book was Edward Bellamy's *Looking Backward 2000–1887,* and the theme was communism. Hundreds of thousands of copies were sold with a tumult of acclamation; the book went round the world; a political party—the Nationalist party—was founded on Bellamy's doctrines. Howells's *A Hazard of New Fortunes* and his Altrurian writings bear witness to the influence Bellamy exerted in literary circles. Reversing the scheme of *The Connecticut Yankee* Bellamy allows his narrator to sleep until the year 2000 and then to wake upon a Utopian Boston which, like the rest of the world, has moved forward, without revolution, to a rational adjustment of production and distribution, and has perfected the conditions of human life. In his glad millennium all capital belongs to the community and all labour contributes to it; the inequality of reward has disappeared, for men and women all share alike, however different may be the tasks to which they are assigned by the most careful selection; intelligent planning has increased the wealth of the community, wealth has increased leisure, and leisure has increased joy and goodness.

Bellamy's specific solutions of the ancient problem matter less to the history of American fiction than the fact that he found an enormous public ready to snatch from his romance some sort of consolation in a vast discontent. At the opposite pole from Bellamy was Frank R. Stockton (1834–1902), in whom whimsy reached something like its apogee. Stockton, a Philadelphian, first worked at wood-engraving but deserted it for literature, which he reached by the unusual avenue of fairy tales and juvenile journalism. As in his fairy tales he had made his fanciful creatures behave, as far as possible, after the manner of the real world, so into his maturer stories of the real world he constantly infused a fairy irresponsibility. His earliest important book, *Rudder Grange* (1879), illustrates all his qualities. The suggestion came from an actual maid in Stockton's household, whom he called Pomona both in fact and in fiction, and around whose preposterous deeds and words and tastes he built up a little cycle of improbabilities.

Pomona, after a youth largely devoted to the kind of literature that entranced Tom Sawyer, marries a farmer who has ague at the altar; spends her honeymoon partly in a lunatic asylum as guest not inmate; and later has a child which so much occupies her mistress that the master of the house hires another child to amuse himself with. The household which Pomona adorns is joyfully mad. Part of the time it inhabits a canal boat. Later it lets its house so that master and mistress can have the fun of tenting on the estate, though after a little they become bored and take refuge in their own house, which is that same day deserted by the pair which has leased it but now prefers to live in the tent, which they have discovered without knowing to whom it belongs. Still later the Rudder Grangers find a deserted tavern in which they take immense delight, disturbed only by travelers who insist on being entertained there. To the outward eye the novel resembles realism.

The characters look real, they speak like beings who are real enough. But their adventures are the adventures of a Gilbert and Sullivan opera—one rollicking confusion which, so popular did it prove, had later to be continued in *The Rudder Grangers Abroad* (1891) and *Pomona's Travels* (1894). Stockton's fancy found the short story peculiarly congenial, and the dilemma he invented for his brief tale *The Lady or the Tiger?* (1882) won him his largest single applause. On the whole, however, his masterpiece was *The Casting Away of Mrs. Lecks and Mrs. Aleshine* (1886), which also had a sequel, *The Dusantes* (1888). The dauntless Mrs. Lecks and Mrs. Aleshine come, like Pomona, from reality, from two middle-aged women who knew too little of the world outside of their village ever to be surprised at anything which could possibly happen to them elsewhere. To them in the story it happens that they are wrecked in the Pacific Ocean, paddle themselves in life-preservers, using oars as brooms, to an island which might have been deserted but which instead has a comfortable house on it, and there begin housekeeping as cheerfully as if they were in Meadowville, scrupulously depositing each week in a ginger jar on the mantelpiece a sum for board, minus a fair charge for their services in doing the housework.

After a train of incidents which joyfully, though not too obviously, parody all the literature of shipwreck, they are restored to the United States; but they have left behind them a letter which so piques the curiosity of the real owners, the Dusantes, that those migratory personages follow Mrs. Leeks and Mrs. Aleshine and their companions to the United States, especially to return the money which Mr. Dusante is far too hospitable to be willing to keep.

Mr. Dusante, who has an adopted mother with him, encounters in Mrs. Leeks a moral principle equal to his own and finds she will not take back the money; the sequel is largely devoted to the fate of the ginger jar. If Stockton's fantastic invention is here at its most luxuriant, so is his manner at its gravest. His tongue is only stealthily in his check, and his voice is as calm and level as if he were reciting the multiplication table. Thus inspired liars lie—sailors back from distant voyages and yarning to landlubbers, cowboys "stringing" tenderfeet with tales of local dangers, Sindbads and Munchausens. Stockton dictated his stories lying comfortably in a hammock in summer and in an easy chair in colder weather.

His delight in circumstantial mendacity was so unfailing that he often spun his matter out too thin, and he never concerned himself with the problem of structure beyond what he needed to give point to an episode. His variety came largely from within. At the same time, he was observant of costume and dialect. He amused himself particularly with the negroes and certain odd whites whom he encountered in the South (Virginia was latterly his home) and who make *The Late Mrs. Null* (1886) a continual delight. In New Jersey, where he spent much of his life within surburban distance of New York, he constantly studied the village types, and above all the sailors along the coast, whose habits with regard to the sobre truth fell in admirably with his own. Stockton's mariners are among his happiest devices. They furnish a natural excuse for fibbing, and they themselves, rakish and tarry, give comic opera touches which nothing else in Stockton quite equals. The three seamen who in *The Dusantes* tattoo the barn and set out onions according to nautical designs may be said to head the humorous crew, but they have many rivals for preëminence. Stockton's invention rarely flagged. *The Adventures of Captain Horn* (1895) plays with the search for hidden treasure in South America: its sequel, *Mrs. Cliff's Yacht* (1896), goes larking among pirates, who interested Stockton in other books as well. He cheerfully perlustrated the strangest climes and ages, with a blithe inconsequence heaping all his visions together, as if he were some jovial Spenser taking a vacation in Fairyland.

He delighted, too, in imaginary science, like that which in *The Great Stone of Sardis* (1898) proves that the centre of the earth is one immense crystal, and in imaginary machines such as those for making war prohibitive in *The Great War Syndicate* (1889). In such directions he carried his fooling to an extravagance and a tenuity which have punished him with inpermanence, the fate, indeed, of lighter comedy. But in his three or four genuine successes he achieved more with merry farce than any other American novelist. Stockton should have credit, too, for his services in rendering popular the briefer type of novel called in America the novelette, the vogue of which was established during the eighties and early nineties.

With Stockton may be mentioned Eugene Field, much better known for his verse and his comic skits than for his fiction, and yet the author of at least one novel—if it may be called a novel—which has achieved among book-lovers a little immortality. *The Love Affairs of a Bibliomaniac* (1896) chronicles no passions more violent than the desire for books, but it chronicles that desire in forms as diversified as Field's own career as a collector, and in a tone as piquant and whimsical as that of his own personality.

The tale is packed with charming episodes and vagaries recognizable by all the book-hunting tribe; indeed, it exhibits, in an unpretentious way, an unusual erudition playing over the amiable regions of literature which Field himself had explored. But the bibliomaniac of the narrative, though largely studied from Field's own tastes, is also an actual creation, extended, if not enlarged, from the life by the addition of adventures which every book-collector has imagined himself as having, and portrayed with the sprightly humour and wistful grace which Field generally reserved for his verse.

Something like the same quaint or homely touches may be found in two other novels of the period which both exploit elderly, eccentric, charming heroes: F. Hopkinson Smith's *Colonel Carter of Cartersville* (1891), displaying the type of old school Virginia gentleman now firmly fixed in the popular imagination; and Edward Noyes Westcott's *David Harum* (1898), a novel dominated by a shrewd, racy-tongued upstate New Yorker who holds a comfortable place in the long American tradition of the unlettered philosopher and humorist.

Chapter 5

Remembering Henry James Jr

HIS PASSION FOR "EUROPE"

But it is only in the light of his other ruling passion that we can rightly understand the force of his passion for Europe. Even more rooted was his love for art, the art of representation. All his pilgriming in London and elsewhere was by way of collecting a fund of material to draw upon "as soon as ever one should seriously get to work." And is it surprising that he should have been impressed with the greater eligibility of the foreign material; that his impressions of New York and Boston seemed to him "negative" or "thin" or "flat" beside the corresponding impressions of London?

The old world was one which had been lived in and had taken on the expressive character of places long associated with human use. It was not simply the individual object of observation, but the "cross-references"; or, again, the association of one object with another and with the past, making up altogether a "composition." Whatever person or setting caught his attention, it was always because it "would fall into a picture or a scene." Of the heroine of *The American,* a young French woman of rank, the hero observed that she was "a kind of historical formation."

And along with his material, James found abroad a favourable air in which to do his work. There he found those stimulating contacts, there he could observe from within those movements in the world of art, which were of such prime importance for his own development. Lambert Strether, in *The Ambassadors,* represents the deprivations of a man of letters, strikingly suggestive in many ways of James himself, condemned to labour in the provincial darkness of "Woollett, Massachusetts." In all this our American author seems identified with anything but the American scene; and the case is not altered when we consider his stories on the side of form.

His form is not American, nor his preoccupation with form. It is as strictly international as that of Poe. James was a profound admirer of Hawthorne; but so was he an admirer of Balzac and of George Sand, and it is probably to later models than any of these that he owes whatever is most characteristic in his technique.

There is at any rate nothing here drawn from American sources rather than from European; nothing which we can claim as our production. Yet we have reasons for our claim upon him. This very passion for Europe, as he has exhibited it in himself and in so many of his creatures, this European "adventure" of Lambert Strether and Isabel Archer (of *The Portrait of a Lady*)—what more purely American product can be conceived? Even to the conscientiousness with which young James did his London sightseeing, mindful of his own feeble health, which threatened to cut it short, and above all mindful "that what he was doing, could he but put it through, would be intimately good for him!"

AMERICANS IN HIS STORIES

Altogether his theme turned out to be quite as much American character as European setting. We must not forget how predominantly his novels, and how frequently his short stories, have for their subject Americans,—Americans abroad, or even Americans at home seen in the light of foreign observation. In this connection the novels in particular may be divided into three groups, falling chronologically into three periods. In the first period, extending from *Roderick Hudson* to *The Bostonians,* 1875 to 1885, the leading characters are invariably Americans, though the scene is half the time abroad. In the second period, from *The Princess Casamassima* to *The Sacred Fount,* 1885 to 1901, the novels confine themselves rather strictly to English society. In the third period, from *The Wings of the Dove* to the novels left unfinished at the author's death, 1902 to 1917, James returned to his engrossing, and by far his most interesting, theme of Americans in Paris or Venice or London.

Not a very original contribution to literature is the American scene itself—the New York of *Washington Square* (1881), the Boston of *The Europeans* (1878) and *The Bostonians;* and none of these novels was included by James in the New York Edition. His American settings are but palely conceived; and his figures do not find here the proper background to bring them out and set off their special character. But the crusading Americans—variegated types, comic and romantic—with the foreign settings in which they so perfectly find themselves, these make up a local province as distinct in colour and feature as those of Cable and Bret Harte, —a province quite as American, in its way, and for the artist quite as much of a *trouvaille,* or lucky strike. These Americans abroad fall naturally into two classes. The first are treated in the mildly comic vein, as examples of American crudeness or simplicity. Such are the unhappy Ruck family of *The Pension Beaurepas,*—poor Mr. Ruck who had come abroad in hopes of regaining health and escaping financial worries, and his ladies whose interest in the old world is confined to the shops where money can be spent.

Perhaps we might refer to this class Christopher Newman, the self-possessed and efficient American business man, hero of *The American* (1877); though in his case the comedy of character is by no means broad, and is strictly subordinate to the larger comedy of social contrast. In general, these people are treated not unkindly; and there is the one famous instance of *Daisy Miller,* in which the fresh little American girl is so tenderly handled as to set tears flowing—a most unusual proceeding with James. Generally the Americans emerge from the international comedy with the reader's esteem for sterling virtues not always exhibited by the more sophisticated Europeans. In the later group of stories in particular, the American character, presented with no hint of comic bias, actually shines with the lustre of a superior spiritual fineness.

This is what Rebecca West has in mind in her somewhat impatient reference to James's characters as American old maids, or words to that effect.

TRANSCENDENTALISM

And here we have the very heart of his Americanism, if we may make bold to call it that. There is something in James's estimate of spiritual values so fine, so immaterial, so indifferent to success or happiness or whatever merely practical issues, as to suggest nothing so much as the transcendentalism of Emerson, the otherworldliness of Hawthorne. There is here a psychology not of Scott or Thackeray, not even of George Eliot, still less of any conceivable Continental novelist; and one can hardly refer it to any but a New England origin.

PARENTAGE AND EDUCATION

William James, the novelist's grandfather, was an Irishman settled in Albany. He was described in a New York newspaper of 1832 as "the Albany business man"; and he laboured so well at business that he left several millions to be divided among twelve heirs. Otherwise the relatives of the novelist were quite innocent of practical affairs. His father, Henry James, was a philosopher-clergyman, a friend of Emerson's, who carried with him everywhere the entire works of Swedenborg. Henry James, Jr., was born 15 April, 1843, in New York; but he went to Europe as a babe in arms. Two years later, still in long clothes and waggling his feet, he noted from the carriage window "a stately square surrounded with highroofed houses and having in the centre a tall and glorious column"—the reader will recognize the Place Vendôme. From the earliest times, in New York and Albany, all his conceptions of culture had a transatlantic origin. The caricatures of Gavarni, Nash's lithographs of *The Mansions of England,* the novels of Dickens read aloud in the family circle,—these fed his imagination.

He and his brothers went regularly to a New York bookseller for a boys' magazine published in London. Even their sense of a "political order" was derived from Leech's drawings in *Punch.* Their education was amazingly various and spasmodic,—better adapted, one might suppose, to the formation of novelists than of philosophers. Dozens of private schools and tutors succeeded one another in bewildering rapidity in New York, not to speak of later instruction in Bonn and Geneva, in Paris and London. All this while the main occupation of the future novelist was the contemplative observation of character. The world of Albany and New York was a world not of vulgar persons but of artistic "values." Everyone was interesting as a "type": type of "personal France" or of French "adventuress" (referring to early governesses), type of orphan cousins, type of wild young man. Cousin Henry was a kind of Mr. Dick, cousin Helen a kind of Miss Trotwood. James's account in *A Small Boy and Others* shows him in those early days a mere vessel of impressions suitable to the uses of art.

All this was fostered by the kind of discipline, or no discipline, maintained by their metaphysical father. For religion, the boys went to all the churches, and, we gather, in much the spirit in which they approached any other æsthetic experience. As for livelihood, or occupation, the father was always inclined to discourage any immediate decision upon that point, lest a young man might prematurely limit the development of his inner life. We are reminded how small a place is taken in the stories of James by what men do to earn a living. In America, it seemed, there were—apart from the unique case of Daniel Webster—but two possible destinies for a young man. Either he went into business or he went to the dogs. But the immediate family and connections of James were always aspiring to that more liberal foreign order in which was offered the third alternative of a person neither busy nor tipsy,—a cultivated person of leisure.

NEWPORT, BOSTON, CAMBRIDGE

In 1860 the family went to live in Newport, so that the older brother might work in the studio of William Morris Hunt; and Henry, who had earlier haunted the galleries of Paris with his brother, welcomed this occasion to frequent a place devoted to the making of pictures. In 1862, William being at Lawrence Scientific School, Henry entered the Harvard Law School; still noting, in boarding-house or lecture-room, personalities, chiaroscuro, *mise en scène,* more than the precedents of law. The Civil War was the one distinctly American fact which seems to have penetrated the consciousness of Henry James.

While he was prevented by lameness from going to war himself, it was brought home to him, for one thing, by the participation of two of his brothers. But the war, like everything else, was followed by him, however breathlessly, as a spectacle rich in artistic values. In 1864 the family were living in Boston, and from 1866 they were definitely settled in Cambridge, William entering the Harvard Medical School in that year; and in these days the young author was forming excitingly important literary connections. One friendship dating from this time was that with E. L. Godkin, editor of the newly founded *Nation.* But most important no doubt was that with the Nortons of Shady Hill, who later introduced him to London society.

RESIDENCE ABROAD

In 1870 died the person to whom James refers with the greatest personal affection, his cousin Mary Temple, the model for Milly Theale in *The Wings of the Dove,* as he tells us, and also—as we guess—for Isabel Archer of *The Portrait of a Lady* and more than one other of his loveliest American women. Of her death he says "we felt it together as the end of our youth." So far he brings the family record in his *Notes of a Son and Brother* (1914). Meanwhile in 1869 occurred the visit to London recorded in *The Middle Years.* To 1872 belongs a perhaps equally memorable visit to Italy. And from that time forward until his death, 28 February, 1916, he lived abroad; during the first years largely in Italy and France ("inimitable France" and "incomparable Italy"), and then, from about the year 1880, in the England of his adoption—making his bachelor home in London or in the old Cinque Port of Rye. But he continued almost to the end to publish his novels and tales in the great

American magazines, so that his first appeal was generally to the public here.

Evidences of the honour in which he was held in England were the Order of Merit conferred upon him at New Year's, 1916; and his portrait by Sargent, undertaken on the occasion of his seventieth birthday, at the invitation of some two hundred and fifty English friends. At the outbreak of the War, none was more enthusiastic for the cause of the Allies, which was associated with everything he held most precious. His feeling for England at this time, on looking out across the channel from his Sussex home, is described in what is perhaps his latest piece of writing, *Within the Rim,* published in the *Fortnightly Review* in August, 1917. It has been said that his mortal illness was provoked by the vigour with which he took up the work of relief for suffering Belgium and France.

MISCELLANEOUS WRITINGS; COLLECTED STORIES

James began his literary career as an anonymous contributor of reviews to *The North American Review* and *The Nation;* and such reviews and literary news-letters he continued to write for many years. Only a small part of his critical writing has appeared in book form; and it still remains for the curious to trace the development of his literary theory from the beginning. His books of fiction were frequently supplemented, too, with books of impressions, in which he might commune at length with the spirit of places,—English, French, American, Italian. He also wrote many plays, a few of which made brief appearances on the London stage. But they were "talky" and untheatrical; and he succeeded neither in purging the theatre of the commercialism he deprecated nor even in taking the public fancy himself. His first attempts at fiction were printed in *The Atlantic Monthly* and *The Galaxy;* but he hardly emerges as an author of account before the appearance of *The Passionate Pilgrim* in 1871.

His first important novel was *Roderick Hudson,* published in *The Atlantic* in 1875. His first and only approach to popularity, whether in long or short story, was made by *Daisy Miller* in 1878. The New York Edition of his novels and tales, published during the years 1907 to 1909, is of the greatest interest because of the extended discussion of his own work and the account of his imaginative processes found in the Prefaces. It is, however, very far from being a complete collection even of his works of fiction. It is simply the choice made by James at that late date, and according to his taste as it had then developed, of such of his stories as he wished to be known by. It remains to be seen how far posterity will submit to his judgment in the matter.

EARLIER NOVELS

The threefold grouping of his novels already suggested was in connection with the treatment of American themes. In reference to form and method a more illuminating division would be one of two periods: first, *Roderick Hudson* to *The Tragic Muse,* 1875–1890; and second, *The Spoils of Poynton* to *The Sense of the Past,* 1896–1917. In the novels of the first group, he includes, in general, more material than in the later ones, more incident, a greater number of characters, a more extended period of time; and he treats his material in the larger, more open, more lively manner of the main English tradition. He also chooses, in the earlier period, what may be considered more ambitious themes in the matter of psychology. In *Roderick Hudson,* for example, he undertakes to trace the degeneration of a man of genius, a young American sculptor, when given the freedom of the artistic life in Rome.

This evolutionary—or revolutionary—process of character, suggestive of George Eliot, is a "larger order' than he would ever have taken on in the later period. In *The Tragic Muse* he reverts to the theme of the artistic temperament—this time in disagreement with the world of affairs; and he develops it by means of two great interrelated stories, one dealing with an actress, one with a painter. In the later years he would not have undertaken thus to tell two stories at the same time; and perhaps the artistic temperament itself would have seemed to him too ambitious a theme. In the earlier period, again, we find him sometimes treating subjects touching on political or the more practical social problems, though indeed his interest was never primarily in the problems. *The Bostonians* is a somewhat satirical study, at one and the same time, of the Boston character and of feminism; while in *The Princess Casamassima* the leading persons are revolutionary socialists, and political murder lurks in the background.

Probably the best, as well as the best liked, of the earlier novels is *The Portrait of a Lady* (1881), which records at length the European initiation of a generous-souled American girl.

SHORT STORIES

In the course of six years between the first and second periods no novel of James was published; but during that interim came the culmination of his long activity as a short-story writer.

It was his tendency always to subordinate incident to character, to subordinate character as such to situation—o the relations among the characters; and in situation or character, to prefer something rather out of the ordinary, some aspect or type not too obviously interesting but calling for insight and subtlety in the interpretation.

Good examples, in the short story, of this predilection are *The Pupil, The Real Thing,* and *The Altar of the Dead,* all appearing in the early nineties; and a little later, *The Beldonald Holbein* and *The Turn of the Screw,* most haunting of ghost stories. In *The Beldonald Holbein* the beautiful great lady has chosen for her companion a supposedly unattractive middle-aged American woman, who will admirably serve as a foil to her beauty.

But certain painters of her acquaintance having discovered that the foil is herself remarkably "beautiful"—that is, distinguished, significant of feature, a subject worthy of Holbein—it becomes necessary to send her back home and get another companion with less character engraved upon her countenance.

How one of the artists gets his revenge by painting Lady Beldonald in all the splendour of her mediocrity is not the point of interest; the point of interest is the fine discrimination shown by artist—and author, and reader—in evidence of their superior good taste. Each tale of James is thus an "initiation" into some social or artistic or spiritual value not obvious to the vulgar. And each tale is a quiet picture, a social study, rather than the smart anecdote prescribed by our doctors of the "short-story."

James is not rigorous in his limitation of the short story to the magazine length; so that his tales are as likely to take the form of the more leisurely *nouvelle* as of the brief and sketchy *conte.* And so it was not surprising to find a tale intended originally for a magazine short story enlarging itself by insensible degrees into what is practically a novel.

Such was the case with *The Spoils of Poynton,* one of his finest stories, which has the length of a novel, together with the restricted subject-matter, the continuity, and economy of the short story. But these traits, it is clear, had already grown to be James's ideals for a narrative of whatever length.

They were the ideals of many of the foreign novelists whose personal influence had swayed him in Paris; and to a considerable extent those of George Eliot, whose influence upon him must have been mediate, working through her French imitators, as well as emanating directly from her own work.

More and more, serious novelists were denying themselves the breezy and picturesque variety of materials, the broad free stroke, of the old masters, in favour of a dramatic limitation, a dramatic closeness of weave, a scientific minuteness of detail, an intimate psychological notation, and a pictorial (as distinguished from picturesque) consistency of tone—all of which we find in their extremest development in the later novels of James.

This is what makes the international character of his art. Note should be taken, of course, of a certain fussiness and long-windedness, as well as a certain tendency to the abstract, which are partly to be set down to the score of personal idiosyncrasy. But in general he is clearly following the ideals of George Eliot, of Flaubert, of Turgenev.

Perhaps too we should admit the suggestion of F. M. Hueffer, who would trace back the lineage of James, through

Stendhal and other French writers, ultimately to Richardson, the early master of the technique of manifold fine strokes,. of the close and sentimental study of souls.

LATER NOVELS

Along with *The Spoils of Poynton* may be mentioned, among the later novels, *The Sacred Fount* (1901) and *What Maisie Knew* (1897) as partaking somewhat of the nature of long short stories. *What Maisie Knew is,* by the way, in a class by itself, not merely for reasons of technique too special to be considered here, but also by reason of the great charm of the little girl—so naïve, so earnest, so much a lady and so much a girl, whose experience of evil is the subject of the story.

For the full-fledged novels of the later period, it will suffice to state briefly the themes of *The Awkward Age* (1899) and *The Golden Bowl* (1904)—without prejudice, however, to the special claims of *The Ambassadors,* the novel considered by James himself to be his most perfect work of art. *The Awkward Age* is concerned with the adjustment called for in a certain London circle by the emergence of the *jeune fille* and the consideration due her innocence of the world.

The adjustments prove to be very extensive, but almost wholly subjective, and leaving things very much where they were before so far as any outward signs go. The book is almost literally all talk,—the talk of people the most "civilized" and "modern," people the most shy of "vulgarity," who have ever been put in a book. It is a fascinating performance—for those who have the patience to read it. *The Golden Bowl* is a study of a theme not unlike that of *The Portrait of a Lady.* It is the story of an American girl who marries an Italian prince, and the strategy by which she wins his loyal affection. The time covered is much shorter than that in the *Portrait,* the important characters only about half as many, the amount of action much smaller: and there is little change of scene as compared with the earlier novel.

The length of the book is about the same; and the space saved by these various economies is devoted to the leisurely development of a single situation as it shaped itself gradually in the minds of those participating, the steady deepening of a sense of mystery and misgiving, the tightening of emotional tension, to a degree that means great drama for all readers for whom it does not mean a very dull book.

For many readers it certainly means a very dull book. In this recipe for a story almost everything has been discarded which was the staple of the earlier English novel, even of George Eliot,—exciting incident, dramatic situation, highly coloured character and dialogue, humour, philosophy, social comment.

Indeed, we may almost say the story itself has been thrown out with the rest. For in the later novels and tales of James there is not so much a story told as a *situation revealed;* revealed to the characters and so to us; and the process of gradual revelation, the calculated "release" of one item after another—that is the plot.

It is as if we were present at the painting of a picture by a distinguished artist, as if we were invited to follow the successive strokes by which this or that detail of his conception was made to bloom upon the canvas; and when the last bit of oil had been applied, he should turn to us and say "Now you have heard Sordello's story told."

Some of us would be satisfied with the excitement of having assisted at such a function, considering also the picture which had thus come into being. Others,—and it is human nature, no doubt,—would exclaim in vexed bewilderment "But *I* have heard no *story* told!"

PECULIARITY OF THE JAMES METHOD

The stories of James tend to be records of seeing rather than of doing. The characters are more like patients than agents; their business seems to be to register impressions; to receive illumination rather than to make up their minds and set about deeds.

But this is a way of conceiving our human business by no means confined to these novels; is it not more or less characteristic of the whole period in which James wrote? One passes by insensible degrees from the world of Renan to that of Pater and Swinburne, and thence to that of Oscar Wilde and of writers yet living, in whom the cult of impressions has been carried to lengths yet more extreme.

JAMES AND PATER

Among all these names the most significant here seems to be that of Walter Pater, whose style and tone of writing—corresponding to his intellectual quality and bias—more nearly anticipate the style of James than do those of any other writer, English or French. It does not matter that Pater's subject is the art of the past and James's the life of the present.

No two writers were ever more concerned with mere "impressions," and impressions mean for them discriminations, intimate impressions, subtle and finely sympathetic interpretations. None ever found it necessary, in order to render the special quality of their impressions, to try them in so many different lights, to accompany their statements with so many qualifications and reservations: impulses giving rise to sentences more curiously complex and of longer breath than were ever penned by writers of like pith and moment. They were both of them averse to that raising of the voice, that vehement or emphatic manner, characteristic of the earlier Victorians and supposed to be associated with strong feelings and firm principles.

These reasonable and well-bred writers, if they ever had strong feelings or firm principles, could be trusted to dissimulate them under a tone of quiet urbanity. They abhorred abrupt transitions and violent attitudes. They proceed ever in their discourse smoothly and without marked inflection, softly, as among tea-tables, or like persons with weak hearts who must guard themselves against excitement. There is a kind of hieratic gentleness and fastidiousness,—and yet withal a hint of breathless awe, of restrained enthusiasm,—in the manner in which they celebrate the mysteries of their religion of culture, their religion of art.

AMERICAN FAITH AND EUROPEAN CULTURE

This, we say of James, is anything but American,

indigenous; this is the *Zeitgeist;* this is the spirit of England in the "æsthetic nineties" reacting against the spirit of England in the time of Carlyle.

But then we think of the "passionate pilgrimage" of Isabel Archer and the others; we think of James's *Middle Years;* we think, it may be, of ourselves and eastward prostrations of our own. And we realize that what the romancer has conjured up is a world not strange to our experience.

His genius is not the less American for presenting us, before all things, this vision of a bride rushing into the arms of her bridegroom: vision of the mystic marriage (shall we say?) of new-world faith and old-world culture.

Chapter 6

A Biographic Mystery

In April 1894, a middle-aged gentleman, bearing a load of dresses, was rowed to the deepest part of the Venetian lagoon. A strange scene followed: he began to drown the dresses, one by one. There were a good many, well-made, tasteful, and all dark, suggesting a lady of quiet habits and some reserve.

The gondolier's pole would have been useful for pushing them under the still water. But the dresses refused to drown. One by one they rose to the surface, their busts and sleeves swelling like black balloons. Purposefully, the gentleman pushed them under, but silent, reproachful, they rose before his eyes. The dresses belonged to a writer, widely read at that time, called Constance Fenimore Woolson. She was a great-niece of James Fenimore Cooper, author of *The Last of the Mohicans* (1826) and other frontier tales, and the first American writer to achieve worldwide fame. 'Fenimore', as she was known to choice friends, had combined Western vigour with the quiet manner of a patrician family strongly rooted in the New World.

In 1879 she had settled in Eurcpe, and a few months later met a fellow-expatriate, the distinguished but less popular novelist Henry James. The course of their long friendship was rudely broken when, on the night of 24 January 1894, Fenimore, aged fifty-three, had fallen to her death from her bedroom window in Venice. A mystery has always surrounded this death, but James believed it was no accident. It was suicide. He, alone, was certain. What exactly it was that James knew of Fenimore which convinced him, remains obscure, blurred by his claims that Fenimore, contrary to appearance, had been mad – beyond help. The very urgency of his repeated denials of responsibility calls attention to their tie. So does his attempt to drown her clothes. Henry James was a bachelor of fifty-one at this time, with a high forehead, accentuated by receding hair and a high nose with the faintest bend to it. He had a mobile, sensitive mouth, with a fuller lower lip, firm, not petulant. It was exceptionally wide; parallel to the edge of his eyes.

In repose, it would have shown a long line, slicing through the lower half of his face, had it not been hidden by a brown beard – a natural-looking growth, neither unruly nor too clipped. He dressed in English clothes with too much care to be an Englishman. Some thought he looked like a Russian count; others, a bishop. What friends noticed first were the eyes: light grey and extraordinarily keen (when they were not veiled by his lids), looking at them with complicit amusement or with scorching intensity as though he could see into their secret selves.

He was known for explorations of the inward life: the unvoiced exchange and the drama of hidden motives. These were his skills, as well as a power, beyond that of any other man, to plumb the unknown potentialities of women. Two women, in particular, provoked his attention – a creative attention which claimed them through their untimely deaths. Fenimore was the second of these two women. The first was his cousin Mary Temple, known as Minny, who had died in 1870 at the early age of twenty-four. Where Fenimore was part of his middle years in Europe, Minny had been the real-life 'heroine' of his youth in Newport, Rhode Island.

James saw her as a free spirit, 'a plant of pure American growth', amongst the polished ladies of their time. The very air of Newport was 'vocal with her accents, alive with her movements'. Fenimore was free in a different way: a solitary, mature woman who pursued her ambitions with an intentness that matched his own. In her, James encountered the kind of writer with whom he might share, now and then, the privacy of the artist. The freedoms of these two women went masked, as most nineteenth-century women were masked (whether they knew it or not) by the demands of social consensus: publicly, they fitted themselves to approved models of womanhood. Fenimore appeared to everyone as the needy gentlewoman she in fact was, and this helped to establish her in her career. Her need did her no harm with editors, who found they could combine profit with gallantry towards a lady with a widowed mother and broken-down brother.

She disarmed editors and fellow-writers with modest, self-deprecating letters which go out of their way to stress how inferior was the fortune of a single woman who must write for her living to that of a cherished wife. It is uncertain to what extent she actually believed this in the loneliness she certainly endured, but her best stories subvert contemporary pieties about wifehood and womanly dependence. For herself, Fenimore was strong, serious, and determined to put her work first. She published fifty-eight stories (amongst them her best work), five novels, poems, and travel-writing. Where the freedoms of Fenimore passed scrutiny in the guise of retiring gentlewoman, the freedoms of Mary Temple were acceptable in the guise of vivacious young girl. Intelligent men, all destined for public distinction, surround her in the woods of New Hampshire or on Newport verandahs. Their eyes follow her advance in her buttoned, high-necked dress. She holds her slight form erect as she hugs her arms.

Her eagerness for ideas, her directness, and wide laugh showing all her teeth, seemed to Henry James the embodiment of innocence and untried youth. Yet, with others — his brother, the future psychologist William James, and a law graduate, John Chipman Gray — she was different: less playful, more troubled. Overwhelming questions about human possibility in the face of fate disturb her letters to these men. Why was she less serious towards Henry James? Why did she make fewer demands on her favourite, her 'dearest Harry', who was the fittest to gauge her depth? Mary Temple left behind the mystery of those with promise who die young. An unfinished life cries out for form: this challenge took hold of James with Isabel Archer in *The Portrait of a Lady* (1881), Milly Theale in

The Wings of the Dove (1902), and in a memoir he published in 1914. There was something uncategorisable in Minny. Like his brother William and other gifted men, he saw an uncommon spirit behind the girlish vivacity; but the uncommon was, of course, unwelcome to guardians of gender. Henry's mother — small-minded Mrs James, the ruling angel in the James house — deplored the expanse of Minny's laugh, while Henry's sister, Alice, seething with correct repression, scorned her eager response to every idea.

Given the obscurity and brevity of her existence, it is hard to find the woman behind the fictions. Barring access is the safe label of girlish charm or the unsafe label of 'aggressive': one implies that Mary Temple knew her place as a woman; the other, that she did not. Yet her questions — a dying plea to James or query about the purpose of living — open up an order of existence not to be defined in reductive ways. Fenimore began to publish in 1870, the year of Minny's death. Though she differed in many ways from Minny, she provided a second model of independence. Her looks displeased her, or so she said, but photographs reveal delicate features, curly hair, and a classic profile, set off by a narrow velvet band about her throat. As a 'local colorist' of the latter half of the nineteenth century, Constance Fenimore Woolson did participate in a genre going out of fashion at the time of her death, yet as a watcher of women's lives — the single woman, the exile, the artist — she now invites renewed attention.

Her innovative fables of artists precede those of Henry James. This biography will draw out these two women in their own terms, marking the points at which they intersect with the shaping consciousness of Henry James. It is easy to see how he put his stamp on them, and made them 'Jamesian'. The mystery is why he kept them under wraps: his reasons for doing so, and for the weird behaviour which the circumstances of Fenimore's death provoked, remain to be uncovered. He did not forget them; on the contrary, they return obsessively in his works. James is the most elusive and unwilling of subjects. He rejected the prospect of biography, not only to protect his privacy, but also, we might guess, because he was so much a biographer himself — he well knew the excitements and dangers of biographic power. He drew out others with intent curiosity. In his attaching way, he 'preyed ... upon living beings', as T. S. Eliot recognised.

His experiments in human chemistry, 'those curious precipitates and explosive gases which are suddenly formed by the contact of mind with mind', have in them 'something terrible, as disconcerting as quicksand', which make the character he comes to know, 'uneasily the victim of a merciless clairvoyance'. His awareness of buried possibilities, the gifts of the obscure, and gaps between the facts, invites the infinite challenge of his own life. To approach James at precisely the points he screened raises the issue of the biographer's right to know. Questionable as this is, it does grant access to a more compelling and dangerous character, as well as a new reading of the major novels and a host of puzzling tales. James was a man of secrets, sunk from sight a hundred years ago. Why did he lock away his photograph of Minny Temple? Why, when ten and a half thousand letters of Henry James were allowed to survive, did he make a pact with Fenimore to destroy their correspondence? No other such pact is known.

And why, when Fenimore died, did he travel all the way to Venice to ensure secrecy in April 1894? Sinking her dresses at that time was not, I believe, a casual act, but sign of a strange bond which James guarded with discretion, and which suicide almost exposed. At the height of their relationship, in 1887, they shared a house on the hill of Bellosguardo near Florence. Few knew of this arrangement, and it didn't last — one reason being the scope for scandal. Two other stays abroad were kept wholly secret, as were many short visits. And we might wonder, too, why James, as an old man, forty-four years after Mary Temple's death, destroyed a batch of her letters — philosophic letters, written with undimmed spirit in the face of death — after he had used what he wanted for his memoir. Researchers are increasingly aware 'that interpretation has *already been built into* the documents allowed to survive'. Yet some residue of an alternative story does remain: amongst the leavings, four letters from Mary Temple to Henry James, and a large batch of her letters to John Chipman Gray, the ones James destroyed but Mrs William James had the forethought to copy before handing them over.

Her copy is amongst the James papers at Harvard together with an unnoticed batch of letters from James to Minny's niece Bay Emmet, which bear on the closest fictional re-creation of Minny in *The Wings of the Dove*. In Ohio, there are two records of Fenimore's last days where facts fit with revealing clarity. Four letters from Fenimore to James in the early 1880s fell through the net, while many letters from Fenimore to others lie buried amongst the papers of various men of some importance in their day. James's own letters are, for the most part, too public, too busy, too fulsome to give much away. Now and then, he cast off this social being with raging impatience. The crowded engagements, the comedies of manners in his letters and their effusions of fondness, were a façade for the private action of this most private of lives. His fables of a writer's life instruct us to start with the work. 'My dear sir, the best interviewer's the best reader' is the message of a literary lion for a pleading journalist. 'This last book ... is full of revelations.'

'Revelations?' pants the journalist.

'The only kind that count. It tells you with a perfection that seems to me quite final all the author thinks ...'

James tells us that he understood women almost better than we understood ourselves. 'You see what I am,' says the Jamesian woman to the Jamesian man who befriends her in one of the novels. Minny and Fenimore, and in a sicker way his brilliant sister, Alice, allowed James to 'see' their frustration, their fund of unused 'life', their alertness to the unspoken, and unanswered, passions — as though they had agreed to participate in the form he gave to the potent shadow in which women of the past lived; as though he understood, with them, that what is distinctive in women's lives is precisely what is hidden, not only from the glare of publicity, but from the daylight aspect which women present for their protection — or, it may be, for the protection of those who can't face what they are. James was irresistible to women because he met authenticity without fear, possessed himself of it, and put it out to play on the stage of his imagination.

His knowing, supremely intelligent, ageless, and — yes — irresistible, is what makes James increasingly pertinent. It was necessary to his purpose to engage certain women in ways which remain to be defined. The man who did so is not the socialite James who is exhaustively documented, nor the aesthete, nor the detached observer, nor the Anglicised expatriate — all faces of the legendary Master. Instead, we shall follow an inchoate, troubled man who remained in the making to the end of his life. As such he had two rules: art must have passion, and it must be hard as nails, 'hard as the heart of the writer'. This James is not passive; he is wilful, even ruthless, and stranger than he appeared respectably clothed under an umbrella of benevolence. The real James remained an American: a visionary moralist, he did not indulge in the European vogue for decadence. He was not a cynic. With him, virtue is seen to hold in a period when art-for-art's sake debunks Victorian morality, and Modernism with its array of ineffectual men — Prufrock, Petroushka, Chaplin's little tramp — takes the stage.

The vision of James has outlived the disillusion of the twentieth century; as the Moderns move farther into the past, he is with us, more than ever our contemporary. Only now do we approach the kinds of manhood and womanhood he proposed, not viable in his own age, but possible — essential — in ours. A reinvention of manhood began with Civil War tales where wounded, dying men discover a higher form of manhood than may be found on the battlefield or in the drawing-room. He marked the capacity of men and women to transcend themselves in the face of mortality. The otherness of women made them a focus for an alternative to the pressure of wartime ideals of masculinity: this alternative manhood could take on qualities traditionally assigned to women. James looked beyond the Woman Question, as it was framed in his time, the question of the vote and education in the nineteenth century, the question of professional advance in the twentieth century. When Isabel Archer 'affronts her destiny', she approaches the evolutionary frontier with the question of woman's nature, yet to be addressed. The depths of her nature are 'a very out-of-the-way place, between which and the surface, communication was interrupted'. James wished to promote the power of innocence, a conscious innocence without ignorance or naivety.

The twentieth century favoured *The Turn of the Screw* which toys with perversions of innocence, but his extraordinary women, Isabel Archer and Milly Theale, await a farther future — Milly's wings bear her beyond her lifetime. The women who adored James and whom he came to know in his special way were not submissive, not the helpless muse. Minny and Fenimore had the strength not to relinquish their sense of being. Minny was freer, more familiar with James than anyone would be again. And Fenimore undertook a dialogue with him in stories that re-create him as a beguiling authority who proves a destroyer. Their friction fed on gender reinforced by the antagonisms of popular and high art. Alone, it seems, Mary Temple and Constance Fenimore Woolson were bold enough to cross the uncrossable boundary of that private life. Somewhere lies the clue to what they gave him. Henry James was not shielding some form of love; he was fading out the ghostly companions of his art. And this may have been necessary because he did *not* acknowledge them, openly and visibly, as they perhaps wished and certainly deserved.

If there was love, it was not the usual love of men and women but an intuitive closeness that remained unspoken. We approach, here, ties more intimate than sex, closer than those of family and friends. Genius appears to soar above such ties, a lone phenomenon, but this is romantic myth, perpetuated by James himself in the rarefied solitude of a writer in 'The Private Life'. Genius, though, cannot emerge in a void. Here is a starting point: to challenge the myth of the artist with a truer story of what we might call, for want of a better word, collaboration. To some extent, of course, James invented himself, but he could not have written as he did without partners — female partners, posthumous partners — in that unseen space in which life is transformed into art.

Chapter 7

Criticisms and Interpretations

IF we take him at all we must take him on his own ground, for clearly he will not come to ours. We must make concessions to him, not in this respect only, but in several others, chief among which is the motive for reading fiction. By example, at least, he teaches that it is the pursuit and not the end which should give us pleasure; for he often prefers to leave us to our own conjectures in regard to the fate of the people in whom he has interested us. There is no question, of course, but he could tell the story of Isabel in "The Portrait of a Lady" to the end, yet he does not tell it. We must agree, then, to take what seems a fragment instead of a whole, and to find, when we can, a name for this new kind in fiction. Evidently it is the character, not the fate, of his people which occupies him; when he has fully developed their character he leaves them to what destiny the reader pleases.

The analytic tendency seems to have increased with him as his work has gone on. Some of the earlier tales were very dramatic: "A Passionate Pilgrim," which I should rank above all his other short stories, and for certain rich poetical qualities, above everything else that he has done, are eminently dramatic. But I do not find much that I should call dramatic in "The Portrait of a Lady," while I do find in it an amount of analysis which I should call super-abundance if it were not all such good literature. The novelist's main business is to possess his reader with a due conception of his characters and the situations in which they find themselves. If he does more or less than this he equally fails. I have sometimes thought that Mr. James's danger was to do more, but when I have been ready to declare this excess an error of his method I have hesitated. Could anything be superfluous that had given me so much pleasure as I read?

Certainly from only one point of view, and this is a rather narrow, technical one. It seems to me that an enlightened criticism will recognize in Mr. James's fiction a metaphysical genius working to æsthetic results, and will not be disposed to deny it any method it chooses to employ. No other novelist, except George Eliot, has dealt so largely in analysis of motive, has so fully explained and commented upon the springs of action in the persons of the drama, both before and after the facts. These novelists are more alike than any others in their processes, but with George Eliot an ethical purpose is dominant, and with Mr. James an artistic purpose. I do not know just how it should be stated of two such noble and generous types of character as Dorothea and Isabel Archer, but I think that we sympathize with the former in grand aims that chiefly concern others, and with the latter in beautiful dreams that primarily concern herself.

Both are unselfish and devoted women, sublimely true to a mistaken ideal in their marriages; but, though they come to this common martyrdom, the original difference in them remains. Isabel has her great weaknesses, as Dorothea had; but these seem to me, on the whole, the most nobly imagined and the most nobly intentioned women in modern fiction; and I think Isabel is the more subtly divined of the two. If we speak of mere characterization, we must not fail to acknowledge the perfection of Gilbert Osmond. It was a profound stroke to make him an American by birth. No European could realize so fully in his own life the ideal of a European *dilettante* in all the meaning of that cheapened word; as no European could so deeply and tenderly feel the sweetness and loveliness of the English past as the sick American, Searle, in "The Passionate Pilgrim."—From "Henry James, Jr.," in "The Century Magazine" (November, 1882).

FROM "THE NATION"

It has long been evident that Mr. James's powers of

observation are not only remarkably keen, but sleepless as well. But "The Portrait of a Lady" would not be what it is if it did not possess a *fond* of moral seriousness, in addition to and underlying its extraordinary interest of purely intellectual curiosity. There is a specific lesson for the American girl in the first place; there are others, more general, which accompany every imaginative work of large importance. That these are nowhere distinctly stated is now nothing new in fiction even of a distinctly moral purpose. But Mr. James has carried suggestiveness in this regard further than any rival novelist, and though, unless one has ears to hear, it is entirely possible to miss the undertone of his book, to an appreciative sense there is something exquisite in the refinement with which it is conveyed. Refinement in this respect cannot be carried too far. In strictly literary matters Mr. James's fastidiousness may be objected to, perhaps, if one chooses; he has carried the method of the essayist into the domain of romance: its light touch, its reliance on suggestiveness, its weakness for indirect statement, its flattering presupposition of the reader's perceptiveness, its low tones, its polish.

Upon occasion, where the circumstances really seem to warrant a little fervor, you only get from the author of "The Portrait of a Lady" irreproachability. Objection to this may easily be carried too far, however; and those who do thus carry it too far, and argue that no people ever spoke and acted with the elegance and precision of the personages here portrayed, must of necessity pay the penalty of ultra-literalness and miss the secret of Mr. James's success. To characterize this secret with adequate fulness would require far more than the space at our disposal; but it may be sufficiently indicated by calling it the imaginative treatment of reality. In this unquestionably lies Mr. James's truly original excellence. "The Portrait of a Lady" is the most original example we have thus far had of realistic art in fiction *á outrance,* because its substance is thoroughly, and at times profoundly, real and at the same time its presentation is imaginative. On the one hand, wilfulness and fantasticality are avoided, and on the other, prose and flatness. One may even go further, and say that the book succeeds in the difficult problem of combining a scientific value with romantic interest and artistic merit.—From a review in "The Nation" (February 2, 1882).

The List of Mr. James's novels are a long one, and his short stories are very numerous; and among them all there is not one with a perfunctory or desultory inspiration. Why is it that they in no sense constitute a *comédie humaine?* They are very populous; why is it that the characters that people them have so little relief? Taken together they constitute the least successful element of his fiction. Partly this is because, as I say, they possess so little typical quality. But why also do they possess so little personal interest? They have, seemingly, astonishingly little, even for their creator.

So far from knowing the sound of their voices, as Thackeray said of his, he is apparently less pre-occupied with them than about the situation—the "predicament," he would aptly say—in which he places them. Apparently he is chiefly concerned with what they are to do when confronted with the complications his ingenuity devises for them—how they are to "pull it off." These complications are sometimes very slight, in order to show, or at least showing, what trifles control destinies; sometimes they are very grave, and exhibit the conflict of the soul with warring desires and distracting perplexities. And they are never commonplace—any more than the characters themselves, each one of which is intimately observed and thoroughly respected as an individuality. But their situation rather than themselves is what constitutes the claim, the *raison d'être,* of the book in which they figure.

The interest in the book, accordingly, becomes analogous to that of a game in which the outcome rather than the pieces monopolizes the attention. It cannot be said that the pieces are not attentively described—some of them, indeed, are very artistically and even beautifully carved—but it is the moves that count most of all. Will Densher give a plausible solution to the recondite problem of how to combine the qualities of a cad and of a gentleman? Will Maisie decide for or against Sir Claude? What decision will Sir Claude himself make? Has Vanderbank ideality enough to marry Nanda? Will Chad

Newsome go back to Woollett? The game is very well, often exquisitely, played; and the result, which, nevertheless, from all we know of the characters, we can rarely foresee, wears—when we argue it out in retrospect as the author clearly has done in advance—the proper artistic aspect of a foregone conclusion. Mr. James rarely seems to impose it himself; except on the few occasions when, as in "The Princess Casamassima" or "The Other House," he deals in melodrama, in which he almost never succeeds in being convincing, his rectitude is so strong a reliance as to exclude all impression of perversity or wilfulness and convey the agreeable sense of sufficiently fatalistic predestination. Meantime you find out about the characters from the result. Since it has turned out in this way, they must have been such and such persons.

In other words, they have not been characterized very vividly, have not been presented very completely as human beings. At least they do not people one's memory, I think, as the personages of many inferior artists do. When one thinks of the number of characters that Mr. James has created, each, as I have said, carefully individualized, and none of them replicas—an amazing world they certainly compose in their originality and variety—it is odd what an effort it is to recall even their names. The immortal Daisy Miller, the sensitive and highly organized Ralph Touchett, the robust and thoroughly national Christopher Newman, the gentle Miss Pynsent, and a number of others that do remain in one's memory, mainly belong to the earlier novels and form but a small proportion of the great number of their author's creations. Different readers, however, would no doubt answer this rather crude test differently, and in any case it is not because they fail in precision that Mr. James's personages lose distinctness as their story, like all stories, fades from the recollection. They have a sharp enough outline, but they are not completely enough characterized.

Why? Why is it that when the American heroine of one of his stories, beautifully elaborated in detail, a perfect specimen of Dutch *intarsia,* kills herself because her English husband publishes a savage book about her country, we find ourselves perfectly unprepared for this *dénouement?* Why is it that with all the pains expended on the portrait of the extraordinary Mrs. Headway of "The Siege of London," we never quite get *his* point of view, but are kept considering the social duty of the prig who passes his valuable time in observing her attempts at rehabilitation and—no doubt most justly—exposes her in the end? There is nothing to complain of in the result, the problem is worked out satisfactorily enough, but Mrs. Headway herself does not count for us, does not hang together, in the way in which Augier's Aventurière does, or even Dumas's Baronne d'Ange. It would be difficult, for example, for this reason, to make a play of "The Siege of London."

The answer to this query, the explanation of this incompleteness of characterization in Mr. James's nevertheless very precise personages, consists, I think, in the fact that he rather pointedly neglects the province of the heart. This has been from the first the natural peril of the psychological novelist, the neglect of what in the Scripture view constitutes "the whole man," just as the neglect of the mind—which discriminates and defines personalities once constituted—was the defect of the psychological novelist's predecessor. But for Mr. James this peril has manifestly no terrors. The province of the heart seems to him, perhaps, so much to be taken for granted as to be on the whole rather negligible, so far as romantic exploitation is concerned. Incidentally, one may ask, if all the finest things in the world are to be assumed, what is there left for exploitation? Matter for curiosity mainly—the curiosity which in Mr. James is so sharp and so fruitful. The realm of the affections is that which—*ex vi termini,* one may say—most engages and attaches. Are we to be interested in fiction without liking it? And are we to savor art without experiencing emotion?

The fact that few reread Mr. James means that his form, however adequate and effective, is not in itself agreeable. But it means still more that his "content" is not attaching. When Lockhart once made some remark to Scott about poets and novelists looking at life as mere material for art, the "veteran Chief of Letters" observed: "I fear you have some very young ideas in your head. We shall never learn to feel and respect our real calling, unless we have taught ourselves to consider everything as moonshine compared with the education of the heart." Is it possible that Mr. James's controlling idea is a "young one"? Is his undoubted originality, after all, the exploitation of what seemed to so wise a practitioner as Scott, "moonshine"? That would account, perhaps, for the pallid light that often fills his canvas when his characters are grouped in a scene where "the human heart"—insight into which used to be deemed the standard of the novelist's excellence—has a part of any prominence to play. The voluntary abandonment by the novelist of such a field of interest as the province of the heart is witness, at all events, of an asceticism whose compensations ought in prudence to be thoroughly assured. Implied, understood—this domain! Very well, one may reply, but what a field of universal interest you neglect, what a rigorously puritanic sacrifice you make!...

He has, however, chosen to be an original writer in a way that precludes him from being, as a writer, a great one. Just as his theory of art prevents his more important fiction from being a rounded and synthetic image of life seen from a certain centralizing point of view, and makes of it an essay at conveying the sense and illusion of life by following, instead of focussing, its phenomena, so his theory of style prevents him from creating a texture of expression with any independent interest of its own. The interest of his expression consists solely in its correspondence to the character of what it endeavors to express. So concentrated upon this end is he that he very rarely gives scope to the talent for beautiful and effective expression which occasional lapses from his rigorous practice show him to possess in a distinguished degree. There are entire volumes of his writings that do not contain a sentence like, for example, this from a brief essay on Hawthorne: "His beautiful and light imagination is the wing that on the autumn evening just brushes the dusky pane."

Of a writer who has this touch, this capacity, in his equipment, it is justifiable to lament that his theory of art has so largely prevented his exercise of it. The fact that his practice has not atrophied the faculty—clear enough from a rare but perfect exhibition of it from time to time—only increases our regret. We do not ask of Mr. James's fastidiousness the purple patch of poetic prose, any more than we expect from him any kind of mediocrity whatever. But when a writer, who shows us unmistakably now and then that he could give us frequent equivalents of such episodes as the death of Ralph. Touchett, rigorously refrains through a long series of admirable books from producing anything of greater extent than a sentence or a paragraph that can be called classic, that has the classic "note," we may, I think, legitimately complain that his theory of art is exasperatingly exacting.—From "American Prose Masters" (1909).

And so again, if we take a modern author of a very different type, such a one as Henry James, whose concern it is to state life, with a view to throwing into relief the finer shades, we shall observe that most of his work is characterised by a kind of *intensive* culture, as opposed to that *extensive* method which, through lack of form, was abused in Dickens, and through obedience to form was satisfactorily applied by the poet Swinburne at his best. We may safely say that when Swinburne was at his best, when he was "himself," his world was a world of rhythmical energy, of impetuous freedom and sensuous activity which, translated into poetry, was expressed through the symbols of love and sea-foam and battle; to be true to the genius which was central to himself, he required no pregnancy or subtle suggestiveness of phrase; he needed no more than rhyme, rhythm, and onomatopœic words, and with these he gave all he had to give—the sense of energy remembered, the sensuous delight of physical activity, a world of divinely glorified sensation.

Mature readers do not seek him often, for there are only a few moods which he can satisfy. A writer such as Mr. Henry James stands at the exactly opposite pole. It is the proper business of such a man as Swinburne merely to affirm sensation, and he could do it perfectly. It is the proper business of Mr. James, not to affirm sensation or any experience—he could not do it with sincerity—but to question sensation, to question emotion and sentiment; it is his proper business to examine experience with the amused, searching gaze of one who expects the unexpected. It is his business to make experience interesting, not, like Swinburne, by multiplication, but rather by division—by the method of the microscope, which reveals in a fly's wing some unsuspected fineness of pattern and variegated brilliance of colour.

He himself is fond of the word "curiosity"; it defines something that is central to his personality; this, brought into activity by the "representational impulse" (which in his opinion is the one justification for the artist), takes form in the intricate and delicately woven patterns of human temperament which are the objects of his curiosity.—From "Literature as a Fine Art," in "The English Review" (April, 1913).

Chapter 8

Ivan Turgenev (1818-1883)

There is perhaps no novelist of alien race who more naturally than Ivan Turgenev inherits a niche in a Library for English readers; and this not because of any advance or concession that in his peculiar artistic independence he ever made, or could dream of making, such readers, but because it was one of the effects of his peculiar genius to give him, even in his lifetime, a special place in the regard of foreign publics. His position is in this respect singular; for it is his Russian savor that as much as anything has helped generally to domesticate him. Born in 1818, at Orel in the heart of Russia, and dying in 1883, at Bougival near Paris, he had spent in Germany and France the latter half of his life; and had incurred in his own country in some degree the reprobation that is apt to attach to the absent—the penalty they pay for such extension or such beguilement as they may have happened to find over the border.

He belonged to the class of large rural proprietors of land and of serfs; and with his ample patrimony, offered one of the few examples of literary labour achieved in high independence of the question of gain—a character that he shares with his illustrious contemporary Tolstoy, who is of a type in other respects so different. It may give us an idea of his primary situation to imagine some large Virginian or Carolinian slaveholder, during the first half of the century, inclining to 'Northern' views; and becoming (though not predominantly under pressure of these, but rather by the operation of an exquisite genius) the great American novelist—one of the great novelists of the world. Born under a social and political order sternly repressive, all Turgenev's deep instincts, all his moral passion, placed him on the liberal side; with the consequence that early in life, after a period spent at a German university, he found himself, through the accident of a trifling public utterance, under such suspicion in high places as to be sentenced to a term of tempered exile—confinement to his own estate.

It was partly under these circumstances perhaps that he gathered material for the work from the appearance of which his reputation dates—*A Sportsman's Sketches*, published in two volumes in 1852.

This admirable collection of impressions of homely country life, as the old state of servitude had made it, is often spoken of as having borne to the great decree of Alexander II the relation borne by Mrs. Beecher Stowe's famous novel to the emancipation of the Southern slaves. Incontestably, at any rate, Turgenev's rustic studies sounded, like *Uncle Tom's Cabin,* a particular hour: with the difference, however, of not having at the time produced an agitation—of having rather presented the case with an art too insidious for instant recognition, an art that stirred the depths more than the surface.

The author was designated promptly enough, at any rate, for such influence as might best be exercised at a distance: he travelled, he lived abroad; early in the sixties he was settled in Germany; he acquired property at Baden-Baden, and spent there the last years of the prosperous period—in the history of the place—of which the Franco-Prussian War was to mark the violent term. He cast in his lot after that event mainly with the victims of the lost cause; setting up a fresh home in Paris—near which city he had, on the Seine, a charming alternate residence—and passing in it, and in the country, save for brief revisitations, the remainder of his days.

His friendships, his attachments, in the world of art and of letters, were numerous and distinguished; he never married; he produced, as the years went on, without precipitation or frequency; and these were the years during which his reputation gradually established itself as, according to the phrase, European—a phrase denoting in this case, perhaps, a public more alert in the United States even than elsewhere. Tolstoy, his junior by ten years, had meanwhile come to fruition; though, as in fact happened, it was not till after Turgenev's death that the greater fame of *War and Peace* and of *Anna Karenina* began to be blown about the world.

One of the last acts of the elder writer, performed on his deathbed, was to address to the other (from whom for a considerable term he had been estranged by circumstances needless to reproduce) an appeal to return to the exercise of the genius that Tolstoy had already so lamentably, so monstrously forsworn. 'I am on my death-bed; there is no possibility of my recovery. I write you expressly to tell you how happy I have been to be your contemporary, and to utter my last, my urgent prayer.

Come back, my friend, to your literary labors. That gift came to you from the source from which all comes to us. Ah, how happy I should be could I think you would listen to my entreaty! My friend, great writer of our Russian land, respond to it, obey it!' These words, among the most touching surely ever addressed by one great spirit to another, throw an indirect light—perhaps I may even say a direct one—upon the nature and quality of Turgenev's artistic temperament; so much so that I regret being without opportunity, in this place, to gather such aid for a portrait of him as might be supplied by following out the unlikeness between the pair.

It would be too easy to say that Tolstoy was, from the Russian point of view, for home consumption, and Turgenev for foreign: *War and Peace* has probably had more readers in Europe and America than *A House of Gentlefolk* or *On the Eve* or *Smoke*—a circumstance less detrimental than it may appear to my claim of our having, in the Western world, supremely adopted the author of the latter works. Turgenev is in a peculiar degree what I may call the novelists' novelist—an artistic influence extraordinarily valuable and ineradicably established. The perusal of Tolstoy—a wonderful mass of life—is an immense event, a kind of splendid accident, for each of us: his name represents nevertheless no such eternal spell of method, no such quiet irresistibility of presentation, as shines, close to us and lighting our possible steps, in that of his precursor. Tolstoy is a reflector as vast as a natural lake; a monster harnessed to his great subject—all human life!—as an elephant might be harnessed, for purposes of traction, not to a carriage, but to a coach-house. His own case is prodigious, but his example for others dire: disciples not elephantine he can only mislead and betray.

One by one, for thirty years, with a firm, deliberate hand, with intervals and patiences and waits, Turgenev pricked in his sharp outlines. His great external mark is probably his concision: an ideal he never threw over—it shines most perhaps even when he is least brief—and that he often applied with a rare felicity. He has masterpieces of a few pages; his perfect things are sometimes his least prolonged. He abounds in short tales, episodes clipped as by the scissors of Atropos; but for a direct translation of the whole we have still to wait—depending meanwhile upon the French and German versions, which have been, instead of the original text (thanks to the paucity among us of readers of Russian), the source of several published in English.

For the novels and *A Sportsman's Sketches* we depend upon the nine volumes (1897) of Mrs. Garnett. We touch here upon the remarkable side, to our vision, of the writer's fortune—the anomaly of his having constrained to intimacy even those who are shut out from the enjoyment of his medium, for whom that question is positively prevented from existing. Putting aside extrinsic intimations, it is impossible to read him without the conviction of his being, in the vividness of his own tongue, of the strong type of those made to bring home to us the happy truth of the unity, in a generous talent, of material and form—of their being inevitable faces of the same medal; the type of those, in a word, whose example deals death to the perpetual clumsy assumption that subject and style are—aesthetically speaking, or in the living work—different and separable things. We are conscious, reading him in a language not his own, of not being reached by his personal tone, his individual accent.

It is a testimony therefore to the intensity of his presence, that so much of his particular charm does reach us; that the mask turned to us has, even without his expression, stills so much beauty. It is the beauty (since we must try to formulate) of the finest presentation of the familiar. His vision is of the world of character and feeling, the world of the relations life throws up at every hour and on every spot; he deals little, on the whole, in the miracles of chance—the hours and spots over the edge of time and space; his air is that of the great central region of passion and motive, of the usual, the inevitable, the intimate—the intimate for weal or woe.

No theme that he ever chooses but strikes us as full; yet with all have we the sense that their animation comes from within, and is not pinned to their backs like the pricking objects used of old in the horse-races of the Roman carnival, to make the animals run. Without a patch of 'plot' to draw blood, the story he mainly tells us, the situation he mainly gives, runs as if for dear life. His first book was practically full evidence of what, if we have to specify, is finest in him—the effect, for the commonest truth, of an exquisite envelope of poetry. In this medium of feeling—full, as it were, of all the echoes and shocks of the universal danger and need—everything in him goes on; the sense of fate and folly and pity and wonder and beauty. The tenderness, the humour, the variety of *A Sportsman's Sketches* revealed on the spot an observer with a rare imagination.

These faculties had attached themselves, together, to small things and to great: to the misery, the simplicity, the piety, the patience, of the unemancipated peasant; to all the natural wonderful life of earth and air and winter and summer and field and forest; to queer apparitions of country neighbors, of strange local eccentrics; to old-world practices and superstitions; to secrets gathered and types disinterred and impressions absorbed in the long, close contacts with man and nature involved in the passionate pursuit of game. Magnificent in stature and original vigour, Turgenev, with his love of the chase, or rather perhaps of the inspiration he found in it, would have been the model of the mighty hunter, had not such an image been a little at variance with his natural mildness, the softness that often accompanies the sense of an extraordinary reach of limb and play of muscle. He was in person the model rather of the strong man at rest: massive and towering, with the voice of innocence and the smile almost of childhood. What seemed still more of a contradiction to so much of him, however, was that his work was all delicacy and fancy, penetration and compression.

If I add, in their order of succession, *Rudin, Fathers and Children, Spring Floods,* and *Virgin Soil,* to the three novels I have (also in their relation of time) named above, I shall have indicated the larger blocks of the compact monument, with a base resting deep and interstices well filled, into which that work disposes itself. The list of his minor productions is too long to draw out: I can only mention, as a few of the most striking—*A Correspondence, The Wayside Inn, The Brigadier, The Dog, The Jew, Visions, Mumu, Three Meetings, A First Love, The Forsaken, Assia, The Journal of a Superfluous Man, The Story of Lieutenant Yergunov, A King Lear of the Steppe.* The first place among his novels would be difficult to assign: general opinion probably hesitates between *A House of Gentlefolk* and *Fathers and Children.* My own predilection is great for the exquisite *On the Eve;* though I admit that in such a company it draws no supremacy from being exquisite. What is less contestable is that *Virgin Soil*—published shortly before his death, and the longest of his fictions—has, although full of beauty, a minor perfection.

Character, character expressed and exposed, is in all these things what we inveterately find. Turgenev's sense of it was the great light that artistically guided him; the simplest account of him is to say that the mere play of it constitutes in every case his sufficient drama. No one has had a closer vision, or a hand at once more ironic and more tender, for the individual figure. He sees it with its minutest signs and tricks—all its heredity of idiosyncrasies, all its particulars of weakness and strength, of ugliness and beauty, of oddity and charm; and yet it is of his essence that he sees it in the general flood of life, steeped in its relations and contacts, struggling or submerged, a hurried particle in the stream. This gives him, with his quiet method, his extraordinary breadth; dissociates his rare power to particularize from dryness or hardness, from any peril of caricature. He understands so much that we almost wonder he can express anything; and his expression is indeed wholly in absolute projection, in illustration, in giving of everything the unexplained and irresponsible specimen.

He is of a spirit so human that we almost wonder at his control of his matter; of a pity so deep and so general that we almost wonder at his curiosity. The element of poetry in him is constant, and yet reality stares through it without the loss of a wrinkle. No one has more of that sign of the born novelist which resides in a respect unconditioned for the freedom and vitality, the absoluteness when summoned, of the creatures he invokes; or is more superior to the strange and second-rate policy of explaining or presenting them by reprobation or apology—of taking the short cuts and anticipating the emotions and judgments about them that should be left, at the best, to the perhaps not most intelligent reader. And yet his system, as it may summarily be called, of the mere particularized report, has a lucidity beyond the virtue of the cruder moralist.

If character, as I say, is what he gives us at every turn, I should speedily add that he offers it not in the least as a synonym, in our Western sense, of resolution and prosperity. It wears the form of the almost helpless detachment of the short-sighted individual soul; and the perfection of his exhibition of it is in truth too often but the intensity of what, for success, it just does not produce. What works in him most is the question of the will; and the most constant induction he suggests, bears upon the sad figure that principle seems mainly to make among his countrymen. He had seen—he suggests to us—its collapse in a thousand quarters; and the most general tragedy, to his view, is that of its desperate adventures and disasters, its inevitable abdication and defeat. But if the men, for the most part, let it go, it takes refuge in the other sex; many of the representatives of which, in his pages, are supremely strong—in wonderful addition, in various cases, to being otherwise admirable.

This is true of such a number—the younger women, the girls, the 'heroines' in especial—that they form in themselves, on the ground of moral beauty, of the finest distinction of soul, one of the most striking groups the modern novel has given us. They are heroines to the letter, and of a heroism obscure and undecorated: it is almost they alone who have the energy to determine and to act.

Elena, Lisa, Tatyana, Gemma, Marianna— we can write their names and call up their images, but I lack space to take them in turn. It is by a succession of the finest and tenderest touches that they live; and this, in all Turgenev's work, is the process by which he persuades and succeeds.

It was his own view of his main danger that he sacrificed too much to detail; was wanting in composition, in the gift that conduces to unity of impression. But no novelist is closer and more cumulative; in none does distinction spring from a quality of truth more independent of everything but the subject, but the idea itself.

This idea, this subject, moreover—a spark kindled by the innermost friction of things—is always as interesting as an unopened telegram. The genial freedom—with its exquisite delicacy—of his approach to this 'innermost' world, the world of our finer consciousness, has in short a side that I can only describe and commemorate as nobly disinterested; a side that makes too many of his rivals appear to hold us in comparison by violent means, and introduce us in comparison to vulgar things. When the mortal remains of Ivan Turgenev were about to be transported from Paris for interment in his own country, a short commemorative service was held at the Gare du Nord.

Ernest Renan and Edmond About, standing beside the train in which his coffin had been placed, bade farewell in the name of the French people to the illustrious stranger who for so many years had been their honoured and grateful guest. M. Renan made a beautiful speech, and M. About a very clever one, and each of them characterised, with ingenuity, the genius and the moral nature of the most touching of writers, the most lovable of men. "Turgenev," said M. Renan, "received by the mysterious decree which marks out human vocations the gift which is noble beyond all others: he was born essentially impersonal."

The passage is so eloquent that one must repeat the whole of it. "His conscience was not that of an individual to whom nature had been more or less generous: it was in some sort the conscience of a people. Before he was born he had lived for thousands of years; infinite successions of reveries had amassed themselves in the depths of his heart. No man has been as much as he the incarnation of a whole race: generations of ancestors, lost in the sleep of centuries, speechless, came through him to life and utterance." I quote these lines for the pleasure of quoting them; for while I see what M. Renan means by calling Turgenev impersonal, it has been my wish to devote to his delightful memory a few pages written under the impression of contact and intercourse. He seems to us impersonal, because it is from his writings almost alone that we of English, French, and German speech have derived our notions—even yet, I fear, rather meagre and erroneous—of the Russian people. His genius for us is the Slav genius; his voice the voice of those vaguely-imagined multitudes whom we think of more and more to-day as waiting their turn, in the arena of civilisation, in the grey expanses of the North.

There is much in his writings to encourage this view, and it is certain that he interpreted with wonderful vividness the temperament of his fellow-countrymen. Cosmopolite that he had become by the force of circumstances, his roots had never been loosened in his native soil. The ignorance with regard to Russia and the Russians which he found in abundance in the rest of Europe—and not least in the country he inhabited for ten years before his death—had indeed the effect, to a certain degree, to throw him back upon the deep feelings which so many of his companions were unable to share with him, the memories of his early years, the sense of wide Russian horizons, the joy and pride of his mother-tongue. In the collection of short pieces, so deeply interesting, written during the last few years of his life, and translated into German under the name of "Senilia," I find a passage—it is the last in the little book—which illustrates perfectly this reactionary impulse: "In days of doubt, in days of anxious thought on the destiny of my native land, thou alone art my support and my staff, O great powerful Russian tongue, truthful and free! If it were not for thee how should man not despair at the sight of what is going on at home? But it is inconceivable that such a language has not been given to a great people." This Muscovite, home-loving note pervades his productions, though it is between the lines, as it were, that we must listen for it.

None the less does it remain true that he was not a simple conduit or mouthpiece; the inspiration was his own as well as the voice. He was an individual, in other words, of the most unmistakable kind, and those who had the happiness to know him have no difficulty to-day in thinking of him as an eminent, responsible figure. This pleasure, for the writer of these lines, was as great as the pleasure of reading the admirable tales into which he put such a world of life and feeling: it was perhaps even greater, for it was not only with the pen that nature had given Turgenev the power to express himself.

He was the richest, the most delightful, of talkers, and his face, his person, his temper, the thoroughness with which he had been equipped for human intercourse, make in the memory of his friends an image which is completed, but not thrown into the shade, by his literary distinction. The whole image is tinted with sadness: partly because the element of melancholy in his nature was deep and constant—readers of his novels have no need to be told of that; and partly because, during the last years of his life, he had been condemned to suffer atrociously. Intolerable pain had been his portion for too many months before he died; his end was not a soft decline, but a deepening distress. But of brightness, of the faculty of enjoyment, he had also the large allowance usually made to first-rate men, and he was a singularly complete human being.

The author of these pages had greatly admired his writings before having the fortune to make his acquaintance, and this privilege, when it presented itself, was highly illuminating. The man and the writer together occupied from that moment a very high place in his affection. Some time before knowing him I committed to print certain reflections which his tales had led me to make; and I may perhaps, therefore, without impropriety give them a supplement which shall have a more vivifying reference. It is almost irresistible to attempt to say, from one's own point of view, what manner of man he was. It was in consequence of the article I just mentioned that I found reason to meet him, in Paris, where he was then living, in 1875. I shall never forget the impression he made upon me at that first interview. I found him adorable; I could scarcely believe that he would prove—that any man could prove—on nearer acquaintance so delightful as that. Nearer acquaintance only confirmed my hope, and he remained the most approachable, the most practicable, the least unsafe man of genius it has been my fortune to meet.

He was so simple, so natural, so modest, so destitute of personal pretension and of what is called the consciousness of powers, that one almost doubted at moments whether he were a man of genius after all. Everything good and fruitful lay near to him; he was interested in everything; and he was absolutely without that eagerness of self-reference which sometimes accompanies great, and even small, reputations. He had not a particle of vanity; nothing whatever of the air of having a part to play or a reputation to keep up. His humour exercised itself as freely upon himself as upon other subjects, and he told stories at his own expense with a sweetness of hilarity which made his peculiarities really sacred in the eyes of a friend. I remember vividly the smile and tone of voice with which he once repeated to me a figurative epithet which Gustave Flaubert (of whom he was extremely fond) had applied to him—an epithet intended to characterise a certain expansive softness, a comprehensive indecision, which pervaded his nature, just as it pervades so many of the characters he has painted.

He enjoyed Flaubert's use of this term, good-naturedly opprobrious, more even than Flaubert himself, and recognised perfectly the element of truth in it. He was natural to an extraordinary degree; I do not think I have ever seen his match in this respect, certainly not among people who bear, as he did, at the same time, the stamp of the highest cultivation. Like all men of a large pattern, he was composed of many different pieces; and what was always striking in him was the mixture of simplicity with the fruit of the most various observation. In the little article in which I had attempted to express my admiration for his works, I had been moved to say of him that he had the aristocratic temperament: a remark which in the light of further knowledge seemed to me singularly inane. He was not subject to any definition of that sort, and to say that he was democratic would be (though his political ideal was a democracy) to give an equally superficial account of him. He felt and under stood the opposite sides of life; he was imaginative, speculative, anything but literal. He had not in his mind a grain of prejudice as large as the point of a needle, and people (there are many) who think this a defect would have missed it immensely in Ivan Sergueitch. (I give his name, without attempting the Russian orthography, as it was uttered by his friends when they addressed him in French.)

Our Anglo-Saxon, Protestant, moralistic, conventional standards were far away from him, and he judged things with a freedom and spontaneity in which I found a perpetual refreshment. His sense of beauty, his love of truth and right, were the foundation of his nature; but half the charm of conversation with him was that one breathed an air in which cant phrases and arbitrary measurements simply sounded ridiculous. I may add that it was not because I had written a laudatory article about his books that he gave me a friendly welcome; for in the first place my article could have very little importance for him, and in the second it had never been either his habit or his hope to bask in the light of criticism. Supremely modest as he was, I think he attached no great weight to what might happen to be said about him; for he felt that he was destined to encounter a very small amount of intelligent appreciation, especially in foreign countries. I never heard him even allude to any judgment which might have been passed upon his productions in England.

In France he knew that he was read very moderately; the "demand" for his volumes was small, and he had no illusions whatever on the subject of his popularity. He had heard with pleasure that many intelligent persons in the United States were impatient for everything that might come from his pen; but I think he was never convinced, as one or two of the more zealous of these persons had endeavoured to convince him, that he could boast of a "public" in America. He gave me the impression of thinking of criticism as most serious workers think of it—that it is the amusement, the exercise, the subsistence of the critic (and, so far as this goes, of immense use); but that though it may often concern other readers, it does not much concern the artist himself. In comparison with all those things which the production of a considered work forces the artist little by little to say to himself, the remarks of the critic are vague and of the moment; and yet, owing to the large publicity of the proceeding, they have a power to irritate or discourage which is quite out of proportion to their use to the person criticised. It was not, moreover (if this explanation be not more gross than the spectre it is meant to conjure away), on account of any esteem which he accorded to my own productions (I used regularly to send them to him) that I found him so agreeable, for to the best of my belief he was unable to read them.

As regards one of the first that I had offered him he wrote me a little note to tell me that a distinguished friend, who was his constant companion, had read three or four chapters aloud to him the evening before and that one of them was written *de main de maître!* This gave me great pleasure, but it was my first and last pleasure of the kind. I continued, as I say, to send him my fictions, because they were the only thing I had to give; but he never alluded to the rest of the work in question, which he evidently did not finish, and never gave any sign of having read its successors. Presently I quite ceased to expect this, and saw why it was (it interested me much) that my writings could not appeal to him. He cared, more than anything else, for the air of reality, and my reality was not to the purpose. I do not think my stories struck him as quite meat for men. The manner was more apparent than the matter; they were too *tarabiscoté,* as I once heard him say of the style of a book—had on the surface too many little flowers and knots of ribbon. He had read a great deal of English, and knew the language remarkably well—too well, I used often to think, for he liked to speak it with those to whom it was native, and, successful as the effort always was, it deprived him of the facility and raciness with which he expressed himself in French.

I have said that he had no prejudices, but perhaps after all he had one. I think he imagined it to be impossible to a person of English speech to converse in French with complete correctness. He knew Shakespeare thoroughly, and at one time had wandered far and wide in English literature. His opportunities for speaking English were not at all frequent, so that when the necessity (or at least the occasion) presented itself, he remembered the phrases he had encountered in books. This often gave a charming quaintness and an unexpected literary turn to what he said. "In Russia, in spring, if you enter a beechen grove"—those words come back to me from the last time I saw him.

He continued to read English books and was not incapable of attacking the usual Tauchnitz novel. The English writer (of our day) of whom I remember to have heard him speak with most admiration was Dickens, of whose faults he was conscious, but whose power of presenting to the eye a vivid, salient figure he rated very high. In the young French school he was much interested; I mean, in the new votaries of realism, the grandsons of Balzac. He was a good friend of most of them, and with Gustave Flaubert, the most singular and most original of the group, he was altogether intimate. He had his reservations and discriminations, and he had, above all, the great back-garden of his Slav imagination and his Germanic culture, into which the door constantly stood open, and the grandsons of Balzac were not, I think, particularly free to accompany him. But he had much sympathy with their experiment, their general movement, and it was on the side of the careful study of life as the best line of the novelist that, as may easily be supposed, he ranged himself. For some of the manifestations of the opposite tradition he had a great contempt. This was a kind of emotion he rarely expressed, save in regard to certain public wrongs and iniquities; bitterness and denunciation seldom passed his mild lips. But I remember well the little flush of conviction, the seriousness, with which he once said, in allusion to a novel which had just been running through the *Revue des Deux Mondes,* "If I had written anything so bad as that I should blush for it all my life."

His was not, I should say, predominantly, or even in a high degree, the artistic nature, though it was deeply, if I may make the distinction, the poetic. But during the last twelve years of his life he lived much with artists and men of letters, and he was eminently capable of kindling in the glow of discussion. He cared for questions of form, though not in the degree in which Flaubert and Edmond de Goncourt cared for them, and he had very lively sympathies. He had a great regard for Madame George Sand, the head and front of the old romantic tradition; but this was on general grounds, quite independent of her novels, which he never read, and which she never expected him, or apparently any one else, to read. He thought her character remarkably noble and sincere. He had, as I have said, a great affection for Gustave Flaubert, who returned it; and he was much interested in Flaubert's extraordinary attempts at bravery of form and of matter, knowing perfectly well when they failed.

During those months which it was Flaubert's habit to spend in Paris, Turgenev went almost regularly to see him on Sunday afternoon, and was so good as to introduce me to the author of "Madame Bovary," in whom I saw many reasons for Turgenev's regard. It was on these Sundays, in Flaubert's little salon, which, at the top of a house at the end of the Faubourg Saint-Honoré, looked rather bare and provisional, that, in the company of the other familiars of the spot, more than one of whom [Maxime Du Camp, Alphonse Daudet, Emile Zola] have commemorated these occasions, Turgenev's beautiful faculty of talk showed at its best. He was easy, natural, abundant, more than I c an describe, and everything that he said was touched with the exquisite quality of his imagination. What was discussed in that little smoke-clouded room was chiefly questions of taste, questions of art and form;

and the speakers, for the most part, were in æsthetic matters radicals of the deepest dye. It would have been late in the day to propose among them any discussion of the relation of art to morality, any question as to the degree in which a novel might or might not concern itself with the teaching of a lesson. They had settled these preliminaries long ago, and it would have been primitive and incongruous to recur to them. The conviction that held them together was the conviction that art and morality are two perfectly different things, and that the former has no more to do with the latter than it has with astronomy or embryology.

The only duty of a novel was to be well written; that merit included every other of which it was capable. This state of mind was never more apparent than one afternoon when *ces messieurs* delivered themselves on the subject of an incident which had just befallen one of them. "L'Assommoir" of Emile Zola had been discontinued in the journal through which it was running as a serial, in consequence of repeated protests from the subscribers. The subscriber, as a type of human imbecility, received a wonderful dressing, and the Philistine in general was roughly handled. There were gulfs of difference between Turgenev and Zola, but Turgenev, who, as I say, understood everything, understood Zola too, and rendered perfect justice to the high solidity of much of his work. His attitude, at such times, was admirable and I could imagine nothing more genial or more fitted to give an idea of light, easy, human intelligence. No one could desire more than he that art should be art; always, ever, incorruptibly, art. To him this proposition would have seemed as little in need of proof, or susceptible of refutation, as the axiom that law should always be law or medicine always medicine.

As much as any one he was prepared to take note of the fact that the demand for abdications and concessions never comes from artists themselves, but always from purchasers, editors, subscribers. I am pretty sure that his word about all this would have been that he could not quite see what was meant by the talk about novels being moral or the reverse; that a novel could no more propose to itself to be moral than a painting or a symphony, and that it was arbitrary to lay down a distinction between the numerous forms of art. He was the last man to be blind to their unity. I suspect that he would have said, in short, that distinctions were demanded in the interest of the moralists, and that the demand was indelicate, owing to their want of jurisdiction. Yet at the same time that I make this suggestion as to his state of mind, I remember how little he struck me as bound by mere neatness of formula, how little there was in him of the partisan or the pleader. What he thought of the relation of art to life his stories, after all, show better than anything else. The immense variety of life was ever present to his mind, and he would never have argued the question I have just hinted at in the interest of particular liberties—the liberties that were apparently the dearest to his French *confrères.*

It was this air that he carried about with him of feeling all the variety of life, of knowing strange and far-off things, of having an horizon in which the Parisian horizon—so familiar, so wanting in mystery, so perpetually *exploité*—easily lost itself, that distinguished him from these companions. He was not all there, as the phrase is; he had something behind, in reserve. It was Russia, of course, in a large measure; and, especially before the spectacle of what is going on there to-day, that was a large quantity. But so far as he was on the spot, he was an element of pure sociability. I did not intend to go into these details immediately, for I had only begun to say what an impression of magnificent manhood he made upon me when I first knew him. That impression, indeed, always remained with me, even after it had been brought home to me how much there was in him of the quality of genius. He was a beautiful intellect, of course, but above all he was a delightful, mild, masculine figure. The combination of his deep, soft, lovable spirit, in which one felt all the tender parts of genius, with his immense, fair Russian physique, was one of the most attractive things conceivable. He had a frame which would have made it perfectly lawful, and even becoming, for him to be brutal; but there was not a grain of brutality in his composition.

He had always been a passionate sportsman; to wander in the woods or the steppes, with his dog and gun, was the pleasure of his heart. Late in life he continued to shoot, and he had a friend in Cambridgeshire for the sake of whose partridges, which were famous, he used sometimes to cross the Channel. It would have been impossible to imagine a better representation of a Nimrod of the north. He was exceedingly tall, and broad and robust in proportion. His head was one of the finest, and though the line of his features was irregular, there was a great deal of beauty in his face. It was eminently of the Russian type—almost everything in it was wide. His expression had a singular sweetness, with a touch of Slav languor, and his eye, the kindest of eyes, was deep and melancholy. His hair, abundant and straight, was as white as silver, and his beard, which he wore trimmed rather short, was of the colour of his hair. In all his tall person, which was very striking wherever it appeared, there was an air of neglected strength, as if it had been a part of his modesty never to remind himself that he was strong. He used sometimes to blush like a boy of sixteen. He had very few forms and ceremonies, and almost as little manner as was possible to a man of his natural *prestauce.*

His noble appearance was in itself a manner; but whatever he did he did very simply, and he had not the slightest pretension to not being subject to rectification. I never saw any one receive it with less irritation. Friendly, candid, unaffectedly benignant, the impression that he produced most strongly and most generally was, I think, simply that of goodness. When I made his acquaintance he had been living, since his removal from Baden-Baden, which took place in consequence of the Franco-Prussian war, in a large detached house on the hill of Montmartre, with his friends of many years, Madame Pauline Viardot and her husband, as his fellow-tenants. He occupied the upper floor, and I like to recall, for the sake of certain delightful talks, the aspect of his little green sitting-room, which has, in memory, the consecration of irrecoverable hours. It was almost entirely green, and the walls were not covered with paper, but draped in stuff. The *portières* were green, and there was one of those immense divans, so indispensable to Russians, which had apparently been fashioned for the great person of the master, so that smaller folk had to lie upon it rather than sit. I remember the white light of the Paris street, which came in through windows more or less blinded in their lower part, like those of a studio. It rested, during the first years that I went to see Turgenev, upon several choice pictures of the modern French school, especially upon a very fine specimen of Théodore Rousseau, which he valued exceedingly. He had a great love of painting, and was an excellent critic of a picture.

The last time I saw him—it was at his house in the country—he showed me half a dozen large copies of Italian works, made by a young Russian in whom he was interested, which he had, with characteristic kindness, taken into his own apartments in order that he might bring them to the knowledge of his friends. He thought them, as copies, remarkable; and they were so, indeed, especially when one perceived that the original work of the artist had little value. Turgenev warmed to the work of praising them, as he was very apt to do; like all men of imagination, he had frequent and zealous admirations. As a matter of course there was almost always some young Russian in whom he was interested, and refugees and pilgrims of both sexes were his natural clients. I have heard it said by persons who had known him long and well that these enthusiasms sometimes led him into error, that he was apt to *se monter la tête* on behalf of his protégés.

He was prone to believe that he had discovered the coming Russian genius; he talked about his discovery for a month, and then suddenly one heard no more of it. I remember his once telling me of a young woman who had come to see him on her return from America, where she had been studying obstetrics at some medical college, and who, without means and without friends, was in want of help and of work. He accidentally learned that she had written something, and asked her to let him see it. She sent it to him, and it proved to be a tale in which certain phases of rural life were described with striking truthfulness. He perceived in the young lady a great natural talent; he sent her story off to Russia to be printed, with the conviction that it would make a great impression, and he expressed the hope of being able to introduce her to French readers. When I mentioned this to an old friend of Turgenev he smiled, and said that we should not hear of her again, that Ivan Sergueitch had already discovered a great many surprising talents, which, as a general thing, had not borne the test. There was apparently some truth in this, and Turgenev's liability to be deceived was too generous a weakness for me to hesitate to allude to it, even after I have insisted on the usual certainty of his taste. He was deeply interested in his young Russians; they were what interested him most in the world. They were almost always unhappy, in want and in rebellion against an order of things which he himself detested.

The study of the Russian character absorbed and fascinated him, as all readers of his stories know. Rich, unformed, undeveloped, with all sorts of adumbrations, of qualities in a state of fusion, it stretched itself out as a mysterious expanse in which it was impossible as yet to perceive the relation between gifts and weaknesses. Of its weaknesses he was keenly conscious, and I once heard him express himself with an energy that did him honour and a frankness that even surprised me (considering that it was of his countrymen that he spoke), in regard to a weakness which he deemed the greatest of all—a weakness for which a man whose love of veracity was his strongest feeling would have least toleration. His young compatriots, seeking their fortune in foreign lands, touched his imagination and his pity, and it is easy to conceive that under the circumstances the impression they often made upon him may have had great intensity.

The Parisian background, with its brilliant sameness, its absence of surprises (for those who have known it long), threw them into relief and made him see them as he saw the figures in his tales, in relations, in situations which brought them out. There passed before him in the course of time many wonderful Russian types. He told me once of his having been visited by a religious sect. The sect consisted of but two persons, one of whom was the object of worship and the other the worshipper. The divinity apparently was travelling about Europe in company with his prophet. They were intensely serious, but it was very handy, as the term is, for each. The god had always his altar, and the altar had (unlike some altars) always its god. In his little green salon nothing was out of place; there were none of the odds and ends of the usual man of letters, which indeed Turgenev was not; and the case was the same in his library at Bougival, of which I shall presently speak. Few books even were visible; it was as if everything had been put away.

The traces of work had been carefully removed. An air of great comfort, an immeasurable divan and several valuable pictures—that was the effect of the place. I know not exactly at what hours Turgenev did his work; I think he had no regular times and seasons, being in this respect as different as possible from Anthony Trollope, whose autobiography, with its candid revelation of intellectual economies, are so curious. It is my impression that in Paris Turgenev wrote little; his times of production being rather those weeks of the summer that he spent at Bougival, and the period of that visit to Russia which he supposed himself to make every year. I say "supposed himself," because it was impossible to see much of him without discovering that he was a man of delays. As on the part of some other Russians whom I have known, there was something Asiatic in his faculty of procrastination. But even if one suffered from it a little, one thought of it with kindness, as a part of his general mildness and want of rigidity. He went to Russia, at any rate, at intervals not infrequent, and he spoke of these visits as his best time for production. He had an estate far in the interior, and here, amid the stillness of the country and the scenes and figures which give such a charm to the "Sketches of a Sportsman," he drove his pen without interruption.

It is not out of place to allude to the fact that he possessed considerable fortune; this is too important in the life of a man of letters. It had been of great value to Turgenev, and I think that much of the fine quality of his work is owing to it. He could write according to his taste and his mood; he was never pressed nor checked (putting the Russian censorship aside) by considerations foreign to his plan, and never was in danger of becoming a hack. Indeed, taking into consideration the absence of a pecuniary spur and that complicated indolence from which he was not exempt, his industry is surprising, for his tales are a long list.

In Paris, at all events, he was always open to proposals for the midday breakfast. He liked to breakfast *au cabaret*, and freely consented to an appointment. It is not unkind to add that, at first, he never kept it. I may mention without reserve this idiosyncrasy of Turgenev's, because in the first place it was so inveterate as to be very amusing—it amused not only his friends but himself; and in the second, he was as sure to come in the end as he was sure not to come in the beginning.

After the appointment had been made or the invitation accepted, when the occasion was at hand, there arrived a note or a telegram in which Ivan Sergueitch excused himself, and begged that the meeting might be deferred to another date, which he usually himself proposed. For this second date still another was sometimes substituted; but if I remember no appointment that he exactly kept, I remember none that he completely missed.

His friends waited for him frequently, but they never lost him. He was very fond of that wonderful Parisian *déjeûner*—fond of it I mean as a feast of reason. He was extremely temperate, and often ate no breakfast at all; but he found it a good hour for talk, and little, on general grounds, as one might be prepared to agree with him, if he was at the table one was speedily convinced.

I call it wonderful, the *déjeûner* of Paris, on account of the assurance with which it plants itself in the very middle of the morning. It divides the day between rising and dinner so unequally, and opposes such barriers of repletion to any prospect of ulterior labours, that the unacclimated stranger wonders when the fertile French people do their work. Not the least wonderful part of it is that the stranger himself likes it, at last, and manages to piece together his day with the shattered fragments that survive. It was not, at any rate, when one had the good fortune to breakfast at twelve o'clock with Turgenev that one was struck with its being an inconvenient hour.

Any hour was convenient for meeting a human being who conformed so completely to one's idea of the best that human nature is capable of. There are places in Paris which I can think of only in relation to some occasion on which he was present, and when I pass them the particular things I heard him say there come back to me. There is a café in the Avenue de l'Opéra—a new, sumptuous establishment, with very deep settees, on the right as you leave the Boulevard—where I once had a talk with him, over an order singularly moderate, which was prolonged far into the afternoon, and in the course of which he was extraordinarily suggestive and interesting, so that my memory now reverts affectionately to all the circumstances.

It evokes the grey damp of a Parisian December, which made the dark interior of the café look more and more rich and hospitable, while the light faded, the lamps were lit, the habitués came in to drink absinthe and play their afternoon game of dominoes, and we still lingered over our morning meal. Turgenev talked almost exclusively about Russia, the nihilists, the remarkable figures that came to light among them, the curious visits he received, the dark prospects of his native land.

When he was in the vein, no man could speak more to the imagination of his auditor. For myself, at least, at such times, there was something extraordinarily vivifying and stimulating in his talk, and I always left him in a state of "intimate" excitement, with a feeling that all sorts of valuable things had been suggested to me; the condition in which a man swings his cane as he walks, leaps lightly over gutters, and then stops, for no reason at all, to look, with an air of being struck, into a shop window where he sees nothing. I remember another symposium, at a restaurant on one of the corners of the little *place* in front of the Opéra Comique, where we were four, including Ivan Sergueitch, and the two other guests were also Russian, one of them uniting to the charm of this nationality the merit of a sex that makes the combination irresistible. The establishment had been a discovery of Turgenev's—a discovery, at least as far as our particular needs were concerned—and I remember that we hardly congratulated him on it.

The dinner, in a low entresol, was not what it had been intended to be, but the talk was better even than our expectations. It was not about nihilism but about some more agreeable features of life, and I have no recollection of Turgenev in a mood more spontaneous and charming. One of our friends had, when he spoke French, a peculiar way of sounding the word *adorable,* which was frequently on his lips, and I remember well his expressive prolongation of the *a* when, in speaking of the occasion afterwards, he applied this term to Ivan Sergueitch. I scarcely know, however, why I should drop into the detail of such reminiscences, and my excuse is but the desire that we all have, when a human relationship is closed, to save a little of it from the past—to make a mark which may stand for some of the happy moments of it.

Nothing that Turgenev had to say could be more interesting than his talk about his own work, his manner of writing. What I have heard him tell of these things was worthy of the beautiful results he produced; of the deep purpose, pervading them all, to show us life itself. The germ of a story, with him, was never an affair of plot—that was the last thing he thought of: it was the representation of certain persons. The first form in which a tale appeared to him was as the figure of an individual, or a combination of individuals, whom he wished to see in action, being sure that such people must do something very special and interesting. They stood before him definite, vivid, and he wished to know, and to show, as much as possible of their nature. The first thing was to make clear to himself what he did know, to begin with; and to this end, he wrote out a sort of biography of each of his characters, and everything that they had done and that had happened to them up to the opening of the story.

He had their *dossier,* as the French say, and as the police has that of every conspicuous criminal. With this material in his hand he was able to proceed; the story all lay in the question, What shall I make them do? He always made them do things that showed them completely; but, as he said, the defect of his manner and the reproach that was made him was his want of "architecture"—in other words, of composition. The great thing, of course, is to have architecture as well as precious material, as Walter Scott had them, as Balzac had them. If one reads Turgenev's stories with the knowledge that they were composed—or rather that they came into being—in this way, one can trace the process in every line. Story, in the conventional sense of the word—a fable constructed, like Wordsworth's phantom, "to startle and waylay"—there is as little as possible.

The thing consists of the motions of a group of selected creatures, which are not the result of a preconceived action, but a consequence of the qualities of the actors. Works of art are produced from every possible point of view, and stories, and very good ones, will continue to be written in which the evolution is that of a dance—a series of steps, the more complicated and lively the better, of course, determined from without and forming a figure. This figure will always, probably, find favour with many readers, because it reminds them enough, without reminding them too much, of life. On this opposition many young talents in France are ready to rend each other, for there is a numerous school on either side.

We have not yet in England and America arrived at the point of treating such questions with passion, for we have not yet arrived at the point of feeling them intensely, or indeed, for that matter, of understanding them very well. It is not open to us as yet to discuss whether a novel had better be an excision from life or a structure built up of picture-cards, for we have not made up our mind as to whether life in general may be described. There is evidence of a good deal of shyness on this point—a tendency rather to put up fences than to jump over them. Among us, therefore, even a certain ridicule attaches to the consideration of such alternatives. But individuals may feel their way, and perhaps even pass unchallenged, if they remark that for them the manner in which Turgenev worked will always seem the most fruitful. It has the immense recommendation that, in relation to any human occurrence it begins, as it were, further back. It lies in its power to tell us the most about men and women. Of course it will but slenderly satisfy those numerous readers among whom the answer to this would be, "Hang it, we don't care a straw about men and women: we want a good story!"

And yet, after all, "Elena" is a good story, and "Lisa" and "Virgin Soil" are good stories. Reading over lately several of Turgenev's novels and tales, I was struck afresh with their combination of beauty and reality. One must never forget, in speaking of him, that he was both an observer and a poet. The poetic element was constant, and it had great strangeness and power. It inspired most of the short things that he wrote during the last few years of his life, since the publication of "Virgin Soil," things that are in the highest degree fanciful and exotic. It pervades the frequent little reveries, visions, epigrams of the "Senilia."

It was no part of my intention, here, to criticise his writings, having said my say about them, so far as possible, some years ago. But I may mention that in re-reading them I find in them all that I formerly found of two other elements—their richness and their sadness. They give one the impression of life itself, and not of an arrangement, a *réchauffé* of life. I remember Turgenev's once saying in regard to Homais, the little Norman country apothecary, with his pedantry of "enlightened opinions," in "Madame Bovary," that the great strength of such a portrait consisted in its being at once an individual, of the most concrete sort, and a type. This is the great strength of his own representations of character; they are so strangely, fascinatingly particular, and yet they are so recognisably general. Such a remark as that a bout Homais makes me wonder why it was that Turgenev should have rated Dickens so high, the weakness of Dickens being in regard to just that point. If Dickens fail to live long, it will be because his figures are particular without being general; because they are individuals without being types; because we do not feel their continuity with the rest of humanity—see the matching of the pattern with the piece out of which all the creations of the novelist and the dramatist are cut. I often meant, but accidentally neglected, to put Turgenev on the subject of Dickens again, and ask him to explain his opinion. I suspect that his opinion was in a large measure merely that Dickens diverted him, as well he might. That complexity of the pattern was in itself fascinating. I have mentioned Flaubert, and I will return to him simply to say that there was something very touching in the nature of the friendship that united these two men. It is much to the honour of Flaubert, to my sense, that he appreciated Ivan Turgenev. There was a partial similarity between them. Both were large, massive men, though the Russian reached to a greater height than the Norman; both were completely honest and sincere, and both had the pessimistic element in their composition.

Each had a tender regard for the other, and I think that I am neither incorrect nor indiscreet in saying that on Turgenev's part this regard had in it a strain of compassion. There was something in Gustave Flaubert that appealed to such a feeling. He had failed, on the whole, more than he had succeeded, and the great machinery of erudition,—the great polishing process,—which he brought to bear upon his productions, was not accompanied with proportionate results. He had talent without having cleverness, and imagination without having fancy.

His effort was heroic, but, except in the case of "Madame Bovary," a masterpiece, he imparted something to his works (it was as if he had covered them with metallic plates) which made them sink rather than sail. He had a passion for perfection of form and for a certain splendid suggestiveness of style. He wished to produce perfect phrases, perfectly interrelated, and as closely woven together as a suit of chain-mail. He looked at life altogether as an artist, and took his work with a seriousness that never belied itself. To write an admirable page—and his idea of what constituted an admirable page was transcendent—seemed to him something to live for. He tried it again and again, and he came very near it; more than once he touched it, for " Madame Bovary" surely will live. But there was something ungenerous in his genius. He was cold, and he would have given everything he had to be able to glow.

There is nothing in his novels like the passion of Elena for Inssaroff, like the purity of Lisa, like the anguish of the parents of Bazaroff, like the hidden wound of Tatiana; and yet Flaubert yearned, with all the accumulations of his vocabulary, to touch the chord of pathos. There were some parts of his mind that did not "give," that did not render a sound. He had had too much of some sorts of experience and not enough of others. And yet this failure of an organ, as I may call it, inspired those who knew him with a kindness. If Flaubert was powerful and limited, there is something human, after all, and even rather august in a strong man who has not been able completely to express himself.

After the first year of my acquaintance with Turgenev I saw him much less often. I was seldom in Paris, and sometimes when I was there he was absent. But I neglected no opportunity of seeing him, and fortune frequently assisted me. He came two or three times to London, for visits provokingly brief. He went to shoot in Cambridgeshire, and he passed through town in arriving and departing. He liked the English, but I am not sure that he liked London, where he had passed a lugubrious winter in 1870-71. I remember some of his impressions of that period, especially a visit that he had paid to a "bishopess" surrounded by her daughters, and a description of the cookery at the lodgings which he occupied. After 1876 I frequently saw him as an invalid. He was tormented by gout, and sometimes terribly besieged; but his account of what he suffered was as charming—I can apply no other word to it—as his description of everything else. He had so the habit of observation, that he perceived in excruciating sensations all sorts of curious images and analogies, and analysed them to an extraordinary fineness. Several times I found him at Bougival, above the Seine, in a very spacious and handsome chalet—a little unsunned, it is true—which he had built alongside of the villa occupied by the family to which, for years, his life had been devoted. The place is delightful; the two houses are midway up a long slope, which descends, with the softest inclination, to the river, and behind them the hill rises to a wooded crest. On the left, in the distance, high up and above an horizon of woods, stretches the romantic aqueduct of Marly. It is a very pretty domain. The last time I saw him, in November, 1882, it was at Bougival. He had been very ill, with strange, intolerable symptoms, but he was better, and he had good hopes. They were not justified by the event. He got worse again, and the months that followed were cruel.

His beautiful serene mind should not have been darkened and made acquainted with violence; it should have been able to the last to take part, as it had always done, in the decrees and mysteries of fate. At the moment I saw him, however, he was, as they say in London, in very good form, and my last impression of him was almost bright. He was to drive into Paris, not being able to bear the railway, and he gave me a seat in the carriage. For an hour and a half he constantly talked, and never better.

When we got into the city I alighted on the Boulevard Extérieur, as we were to go in different directions. I bade him goodbye at the carriage window, and never saw him again. There was a kind of fair going on, near by, in the chill November air beneath the denuded little trees of the Boulevard, and a Punch and Judy show, from which nasal sounds proceeded. I almost regret having accidentally to mix up so much of Paris with this perhaps too complacent enumeration of occasions, for the effect of it may be to suggest that Ivan Turgenev had been Gallicised. But this was not the case; the French capital was an accident for him, not a necessity. It touched him at many points, but it let him alone at many others, and he had, with that great tradition of ventilation of the Russian mind, windows open into distances which stretched far beyond the *banlieue.* I have spoken of him from the limited point of view of my own acquaintance with him, and unfortunately left myself little space to allude to a matter which filled his existence a good deal more than the consideration of how a story should be written—his hopes and fears on behalf of his native land. He wrote fictions and dramas, but the great drama of his life was the struggle for a better state of things in Russia.

In this drama he played a most distinguished part, and the splendid obsequies that, simple and modest as he was, have unfolded themselves over his grave, sufficiently attest the recognition of it by his countrymen. His funeral, restricted and officialised, was none the less a magnificent "manifestation."

I have read the accounts of it, however, with a kind of chill, a feeling in which assent to the honours paid him bore less part than it ought. All this pomp and ceremony seemed to lift him out of the range of familiar recollection, of valued reciprocity, into the majestic position of a national glory. And yet it is in the presence of this obstacle to social contact that those who knew and loved him must address their farewell to him now. After all, it is difficult to see how the obstacle can be removed. He was the most generous, the most tender, the most delightful, of men; his large nature overflowed with the love of justice: but he also was of the stuff of which glories are made.

Chapter 9

Review of Passages from the French and Italian Note-Books

MR. Hawthorne is having a posthumous productivity almost as active as that of his lifetime. Six volumes have been compounded from his private journals, an unfinished romance is doings duty as a "serial," and a number of his letters, with other personal memorials, have been given to the world. These liberal excisions from the privacy of so reserved and shade-seeking a genius suggest forcibly the general question of the proper limits of curiosity as to that passive personality of an artist of which the elements are scattered in portfolios and table-drawers. It is becoming very plain, however, that whatever the proper limits may be, the actual limits will be fixed only by a total exhaustion of matter.

There is much that is very worthy and signally serviceable to art itself in this curiosity, as well as much that is idle and grossly defiant of the artist's presumptive desire to limit and define the ground of his appeal to fame. The question is really brought to an open dispute between this instinct of self-conservatism and the general fondness for squeezing an orange dry. Artists, of course, as time goes on, will be likely to take the alarm, empty their table-drawers, and level the approaches to their privacy. The critics, psychologists, and gossip-mongers may then glean amid the stubble.

Our remarks are not provoked by any visible detriment conferred on Mr. Hawthorne's fame by these recent publications. He has very fairly withstood the ordeal; which, indeed, is as little as possible an ordeal in his case, owing to the superficial character of the documents. His journals throw but little light on his personal feelings, and even less on his genius *per se.* Their general effect is difficult to express. They deepen our sense of that genius, while they singularly diminish our impression of his general intellectual power. There can be no better proof of his genius than that these common daily scribblings should unite so irresistible a charm with so little distinctive force. They represent him, judged with any real critical rigor, as superficial, uninformed, incurious, inappreciative; but from beginning to end they cast no faintest shadow upon the purity of his peculiar gift. Our own sole complaint has been not that they should have been published, but that there are not a dozen volumes more.

The truth is that Mr. Hawthorne belonged to the race of magicians, and that his genius took its nutriment as insensibly—to our vision—as the flowers take the dew. He was the last man to have attempted to explain himself, and these pages offer no adequate explanation of him. They show us one of the gentlest, lightest, and most leisurely of observers, strolling at his ease among foreign sights in blessed intellectual irresponsibility, and weaving his chance impressions into a tissue as smooth as fireside gossip. Mr. Hawthorne had what belongs to genius—a style individual and delightful; he seems to have written as well for himself as he did for others—to have written from the impulse to keep up a sort of literary tradition in a career singularly devoid of the air of professional authorship; but, as regards substance, his narrative flows along in a current as fitfully diffuse and shallow as a regular correspondence with a distant friend—a friend familiar but not intimate—sensitive but not exacting.

With all allowance for suppressions, his entries are never confidential; the author seems to have been reserved even with himself. They are a record of things slight and usual. Some of the facts noted are incredibly minute; they imply a peculiar *leisure* of attention. How little his journal was the receptacle of Mr. Hawthorne's deeper feelings is indicated by the fact that during a long and dangerous illness of his daughter in Rome, which he speaks of later as "a trouble that pierced into his very vitals," he never touched his pen. These volumes of Italian notes, charming as they are, are on the whole less rich and substantial than those on England. The theme, in this case, is evidently less congenial. "As I walked by the hedges yesterday," he writes at Siena, "I could have fancied that the olive trunks were those of apple-trees, and that I were in one or other of the two lands that I love better than Italy." There are in these volumes few sentences so deeply sympathetic as that in which he declares that "of all the lovely closes that I ever beheld, that of Peterborough Cathedral is to me the most delightful; so quiet is it, so solemnly and nobly cheerful, so verdant, so sweetly shadowed, and so presided over by the stately minster and surrounded by the ancient and comely habitations of Christian men."

The book is full, nevertheless, of the same spirit of serene, detached contemplation; equally full of refined and gently suggestive description. Excessively detached Mr. Hawthorne remains, from the first, from Continental life, touching it throughout mistrustfully, shrinkingly, and at the rare points at which he had, for the time, unlearnt his nationality. The few pages describing his arrival in France betray the irreconcilable foreignness of his instincts with a frank simplicity which provokes a smile. "Nothing really thrives here," he says of Paris; "man and vegetables have but an artificial life, like flowers stuck in a little mould, but never taking root."

The great city had said but little to him; he was deaf to the Parisian harmonies. Just so it is under protest, as it were, that he looks at things in Italy. The strangeness, the remoteness, the Italianism of manners and objects, seem to oppress and confound him. He walks about bending a puzzled, ineffective gaze at things, full of a mild, genial desire to apprehend and penetrate, but with the light wings of his fancy just touching the surface of the massive consistency of fact about him, and with an air of good-humored confession that he is too simply an idle Yankee *flaneur* to conclude on such matters.

The main impression produced by his observations is that of his simplicity. They spring not only from an unsophisticated, but from an excessively natural mind. Never, surely, was a man of literary genius less a man of letters. He looks at things as little as possible in that composite historic light which forms the atmosphere of many imaginations. There is something extremely pleasing in this simplicity, within which the character of the man rounds itself so completely and so firmly. His judgments abound in common sense; touched as they often are by fancy, they are never distorted by it.

His errors and illusions never impugn his fundamental wisdom; even when (as is almost the case in his appreciation of works of art) they provoke a respectful smile, they contain some saving particle of sagacity. Fantastic romancer as he was, he here refutes conclusively the common charge that he was either a melancholy or a morbid genius. He had a native relish for the picturesque greys and browns of life; but these pages betray a childlike evenness and clearness of intellectual temper. Melancholy lies deeper than the line on which his fancy moved. Toward the end of his life, we believe, his cheerfulness gave way; but was not this in some degree owing to a final sense of the inability of his fancy to grope with fact?—fact having then grown rather portentous and overshadowing.

It was in midwinter of 1858 that Mr. Hawthorne journeyed from England to Italy. He went by sea from Marseilles to Civita Vecchia, and arrived at Rome weary, homeless, dejected, and benumbed. "Ah! that was a dismal time!" he says with a shudder, alluding to it among the happier circumstances of his second visit. His imagination, dampened and stiffened by that Roman cold of which he declares himself unable to express the malignity, seems to have been slow to perceive its opportunities. He spent his first fortnight shivering over his fire, venturing out by snatches, and longing for an abode in the tepid, stagnant, constant climate—as one may call it—of St. Peter's. There seems from the first to have been nothing inflammable in his perception of things; there was a comfortable want of eagerness in his mind. Little by little, however, we see him thaw and relent, and in his desultory strolls project a ray of his gentle fancy, like a gleam of autumnal American sunshine, over the churches, statues, and ruins. From the first he is admirably honest. He never pretends to be interested unless he has been really touched; and he never attempts to work himself into a worshipful glow because it is expected of a man of fancy.

He has the tone of expecting very little of himself in this line, and when by chance he is pleased and excited, he records it with modest surprise. He confesses to indifference, to ignorance and weariness, with a sturdy candor which has far more dignity, to our sense, than the merely mechanical heat of less sincere spirits. Mr. Hawthorne would assent to nothing that he could not understand; his understanding on the general aesthetic line was not comprehensive; and the attitude in which he figures to the mind's eye throughout the book is that of turning away from some dusky altar-piece with a good-humored shrug, which is not in the least a condemnation of the work, but simply an admission of personal incompetency.

The pictures and statues of Italy were a heavy burden upon his conscience; though indeed, in a manner, his conscience bore them lightly—it being only at the end of three months of his Roman residence that he paid his respects to the "Transfiguration," and a month later that he repaired to the Sistine Chapel. He was not, we take it, without taste; but his taste was not robust. He is "willing to accept Raphael's violin-player as a good picture"; but he prefers "Mr. Brown," the American landscapist, to Claude. He comes to the singular conclusion that "the most delicate, if not the highest, charm of a picture is evanescent, and that we continue to admire pictures prescriptively and by tradition, after the qualities that first won them their fame have vanished."

The "most delicate charm" to Mr. Hawthorne was apparently simply the primal freshness and brightness of paint and varnish, and—not to put too fine a point upon it—the new gilding of the frame. "Mr. Thompson," too, shares his admiration with Mr. Brown: "I do not think there is a better painter . . . living—among Americans at least; not one so earnest, faithful, and religious in his worship of art. I had rather look at his pictures than at any, except the very old masters; and taking into consideration only the comparative pleasure to be derived, I would not except more than one or two of those." From the statues, as a general thing, he derives little profit. Every now and then he utters a word which seems to explain his indifference by the Cis-Atlantic remoteness of his point of view.

He remains unreconciled to the nudity of the marbles. "I do not altogether see the necessity of our sculpturing another nakedness. Man is no longer a naked animal; his clothes are as natural to him as his skin, and we have no more right to undress him than to flay him." This is the sentiment of a man to whom sculpture was a sealed book; though, indeed, in a momentary "burst of confidence," as Mr. Dickens says, he pronounces the Pompey of the Spada Palace "worth the whole sculpture gallery of the Vatican"; and when he gets to Florence, gallantly loses his heart to the Venus de' Medici and pays generous tribute to Michael Angelo's Medicean sepulchres.

He has indeed, throughout, that mark of the man of genius that he may at any moment surprise you by some extremely happy "hit," as when he detects at a glance, apparently, the want of force in Andrea del Sarto, or declares the Florentine cathedral that "any little Norman church in England would impress me as much and more. There is something, I do not know what, but it is in the region of the heart, rather than in the intellect, that Italian architecture, of whatever age or style, never seems to reach." It is in his occasional sketches of the persons—often notabilities—whom he meets that his perception seems finest and firmest. We lack space to quote, in especial, a notice of Miss Bremer and of a little tea-party of her giving, in a modest Roman chamber overhanging the Tarpeian Rock, in which in a few kindly touches the Swedish romancer is herself suffused with the atmosphere of romance, and relegated to quaint and shadowy sisterhood with the inmates of the "House of the Seven Gables."

Mr. Hawthorne left Rome late in the spring, and travelled slowly up to Florence in the blessed fashion of the days when, seen through the open front of a crawling *vettura*, with her glamorous beggars, her black-walled mountain-towns, the unfolding romance of her landscape, Italy was seen as she really needs and deserves to be seen. Mr. Hawthorne's minute and vivid record of this journey is the most delightful portion of these volumes, and, indeed, makes well-nigh as charming a story as that of the enchanted progress of the two friends in the Marble Faun from Monte Beni to Perugia. He spent the summer in Florence—first in town, where he records many talks with Mr. Powers, the sculptor, whom he invests, as he is apt to do the persons who impress him, with a sort of mellow vividness of portraiture which deepens what is gracious in his observations, and gains absolution for what is shrewd; and afterwards at a castellated suburban villa—the original of the dwelling of his Donatello. This last fact, by the way, is a little of a disenchantment, as we had fancied that gentle hero living signorial-wise in some deeper Tuscan rurality. Mr. Hawthorne took Florence quietly and soberly—as became the summer weather; and bids it farewell in the gravity of this sweet-sounding passage, which we quote as one of many:

"This evening I have been on the tower-top star-gazing and looking at the comet which waves along the sky like an immense feather of flame. Over Florence there was an illuminated atmosphere, caused by the lights of the city gleaming upward into the mists which sleep and dream above that portion of the valley as well of the rest of it. I saw dimly, or fancied I saw, the Hill of Fiesole, on the other side of Florence, and remembered how ghostly lights were seen passing thence to the Duomo on the night when Lorenzo the Magnificent died. From time to time the sweet bells of Florence rang out, and I was loath to come down into the lower world, knowing that I shall never again look heavenward from an old tower-top, in such a soft calm evening as this."

Mr. Hawthorne returned to Rome in the autumn, spending some time in Siena his way. His pictures of the strange, dark little mountain-cities of Radicofani and Bolsena, on his downward journey, are masterpieces of literary etching. It is impossible to render better that impression as of a mild nightmare which such places make upon the American traveller. "Rome certainly draws itself into my heart," he writes on his return, "as I think even London, or even Concord itself, or even old sleepy Salem never did and never will." The result of this increased familiarity was the mature conception of the romance of his "Marble Faun." He journalizes again, but at rarer intervals, though his entries retain to the last a certain appealing charm which we find it hard to define.

It lies partly perhaps in what we hinted at above—in the fascination of seeing so potent a sovereign in his own fair kingdom of fantasy so busily writing himself simple, during such a succession of months, as to the dense realities of the world. Mr. Hawthorne's, however, was a rich simplicity. These pages give a strong impression of moral integrity and elevation. And, more than in other ways, they are interesting from their strong national flavour. Exposed late in life to European influences, Mr. Hawthorne was but superficially affected by them—far less so than would be the case with a mind of the same temper growing up among us to-day. We seem to see him strolling through churches and galleries as the last pure American—attesting by his shy responses to dark canvas and cold marble his loyalty to a simpler and less encumbered civilization. This image deepens that tender personal regard which it is the constant effect of these volumes to produce.

Chapter 10

Review on Our Mutual Friend

Our Mutual Friend is, to our perception, the poorest of Mr Dickens's works. And it is poor with the poverty not of momentary embarrassment, but of permanent exhaustion. It is wanting in inspiration. For the last ten years it has seemed to us that Mr Dickens has been. Unmistakably forcing himself *Bleak House* was forced; *Little Dorrit* was labored; the present work is dug out as with a spade and pickaxe. Of course — to anticipate the usual argument — who but Dickens could have written it? Who, indeed? Who else would have established a lady in business in a novel on the admirably solid basis of her always putting on gloves and tieing a handkerchief round her head in moments of grief, and of her habitually addressing her family with 'Peace! hold!' It is needless to say that Mrs Reginald Wilfer is first and last the occasion of considerable true humour. When, after conducting her daughter to Mrs Boffin's carriage, in sight of all the envious neighbors, she is described as enjoying her triumph during the next quarter of an hour by airing herself on the door-step 'in a kind of splendidly serene trance,' we laugh with as uncritical a laugh as could be desired of us.

We pay the same tribute to her assertions, as she narrates the glories of the society she enjoyed at her father's table, that she has known as many as three copper-plate engravers exchanging the most exquisite Sallies and retorts there at one time. But when to these we have added a dozen more happy examples of the humour which was exhaled from every line of Mr Dickens's earlier writings, we shall have closed the list of the merits of the work before us. To say that the conduct of the story, with all its complications, betrays a long-practised hand, is to pay no compliment worthy the author. If this were, indeed, a compliment, we should be inclined to carry it further, and congratulate him on his success in what we should call the manufacture of fiction; for in so doing we should express a feeling that has attended us throughout the book. Seldom, we reflected, had we read a book so intensely *written*, so little seen, known, or felt.

In all Mr Dickens's works the fantastic has been his great resource; and while his fancy was lively and vigorous it accomplished great things. But the fantastic, when the fancy is dead, is a very poor business. The movement of Mr Dickens's fancy in Mrs Wilfer and Mr Boffin and Lady Tippins, and the Lammles and Miss Wren, and even in Eugene Wrayburn, is, to our mind, a movement lifeless, forced, mechanical. It is the letter of his old humour without the spirit. It is hardly too much to say that every character here put before us is a mere bundle of eccentricities, animated by no principle of nature whatever. In former days there reigned in Mr Dickens's extravagances a comparative consistency; they were exaggerated statements of types that really existed. We had, perhaps, never known a Newman Noggs, nor a Pecksniff, nor a Micawber; but we had known persons of whom these figures were but the strictly logical consummation.

But among the grotesque creatures who occupy the pages before us, there is not one whom we can refer to as an existing type. In all Mr Dickens's stories, indeed, the reader has been called upon, and has willingly consented, to accept a certain number of figures or creatures of pure fancy, for this was the author's poetry. He was, moreover, always repaid for his concession by a peculiar beauty or power in these exceptional characters. But he is now expected to make the same concession with a very inadequate reward. What do we get in return for accepting Miss Jenny Wren as a possible person? This young lady is the type of a certain class of characters of which Mr Dickens has made a speciality, and with which he has been accustomed to draw alternate smiles and tears, according as he pressed one spring or another. But this is very cheap merriment and very cheap pathos. Miss Jenny Wren is a poor little dwarf, afflicted, as she constantly reiterates, with a 'bad back' and 'queer legs,' who makes dolls' dresses, and is for ever pricking at those with whom she converses, in the air, with her needle, and assuring them that she knows their 'tricks and their manners.' Like all Mr Dickens's pathetic characters, she is a little monster; she is deformed, unhealthy, unnatural; she belongs to the troop of hunchbacks, imbeciles, and precocious children who have carried on the sentimental business in all Mr Dickens's novels; the little Nells, the Smikes, the Paul Dombeys.

Mr Dickens goes as far out of the way for his wicked people as he does for his good ones. Rogue Riderhood, indeed, in the present story, is villanous with a sufficiently natural villany; he belongs to that quarter of society in which the author is most at his ease. But was there ever such wickedness as that of the Lammles and Mr Fledgeby? Not that people have not been as mischievous as they; but was any one ever mischievous in that singular fashion? Did a couple of elegant swindlers ever take such particular pains to be aggressively inhuman? — for we can find no other word for the gratuitous distortions to which they are subjected. The word *humanity* strikes us as strangely discordant, in the midst of these pages; for, let us boldly declare it, there is no humanity here. Humanity is nearer home than the Boffins, and the Lammles, and the Wilfers, and the Veneerings. It is in what men have in common with each other, and not in what they have in distinction. The people just named have nothing in common with each other, except the fact that they have nothing in common with mankind at large.

What a world was this world if the world of *Our Mutual Friend* were an honest reflection of it! But a community of eccentrics is impossible. Rules alone are consistent with each other; exceptions are inconsistent. Society is maintained by natural sense and natural feeling. We cannot conceive a society in which these principles are not in some manner represented. Where in these pages are the depositaries of that intelligence without which the movement of life would cease? Who represents nature? Accepting half of Mr Dickens's persons as intentionally grotesque, where are those exemplars of sound humanity who should afford us the proper measure of their companions' variations? We ought not, injustice to the author, to seek them among his weaker — that is, his mere conventional — characters; in John Harmon, Lizzie Hexam, or Mortimer Lightwood; but we assuredly cannot find them among his stronger — that is, his artificial creations. Suppose we take Eugene Wrayburn and Bradley Headstone. They occupy a half-way position between the habitual probable of nature and the habitual impossible of Mr Dickens. A large portion of the story rests upon the enmity borne by Headstone to Wrayburn, both being in love with the same woman. Wrayburn is a gentleman, and Headstone is one of the people.

Wrayburn is well-bred, careless, elegant, sceptical, and idle: Headstone is a high-tempered, hard-working, ambitious young schoolmaster. There lay in the opposition of these two characters a very good story. But the prime requisite was that they should *be* characters: Mr Dickens, according to his usual plan, has made them simply figures, and between them the story that was to be, the story that should have been, has evaporated. Wrayburn lounges about with his hands in his pockets, smoking a cigar, and talking nonsense. Headstone strides about, clenching his fists and biting his lips and grasping his stick.

There is one scene in which Wrayburn chaffs the schoolmaster with easy insolence, while the latter writhes impotently under his well-bred sarcasm. This scene is very clever, but it is very insufficient. If the majority of readers were not so very timid in the use of words we should call it vulgar. By this we do not mean to indicate the conventional impropriety of two gentlemen exchanging lively personalities; we mean to emphasize the essentially small character of these personalities. In other words, the moment, dramatically, is great, while the author's conception is weak. The friction of two *men*, of two characters, of two passions, produces stronger sparks than Wrayburn's boyish repartees and Headstone's melodramatic commonplaces. Such scenes as this are useful in fixing the limits of Mr Dickens's insight. Insight is, perhaps, too strong a word; for we are convinced that it is one of the chief conditions of his genius not to see beneath the surface of things. If we might hazard a definition of his literary character, we should, accordingly, call him the greatest of superficial novelists.

We are aware that this definition confines him to an inferior rank in the department of letters which he adorns; but we accept this consequence of our proposition. It were, in our opinion, an offence against humanity to place Mr Dickens among the greatest novelists. For, to repeat what we have already intimated, he has created nothing but figure. He has added nothing to our understanding of human character. He is master of but two alternatives: he reconciles us to what is commonplace, and he reconciles us to what is odd. The value of the former service is questionable; and the manner in which Mr Dickens performs it sometimes conveys a certain impression of charlatanism. The value of the latter service is incontestable, and here Mr Dickens is an honest, an admirable artist. But what is the condition of the truly great novelist? For him there are no alternatives, for him there are no oddities, for him there is nothing outside of humanity.

He cannot shirk it; it imposes itself upon him. For him alone, therefore, there is a true and a false; for him alone it is possible to be right, because it is possible to be wrong. Mr Dickens is a great observer and a great humorist, but he is nothing of a philosopher. Some people may hereupon say, so much the better; we say, so much the worse. For a novelist very soon has need of a little philosophy. In treating of Micawber, and Boffin, and Pickwick, *et hoc genus omne*, he can, indeed, dispense with it, for this — we say it with all deference — is not serious writing. But when he comes to tell the story of a passion, a story like that of Headstone and Wrayburn, he becomes a moralist as well as an artist. He must know *man* as well as *men*, and to know man is to be a philosopher. The writer who knows men alone, if he have Mr Dickens's humour and fancy, will give us figures and pictures for which we cannot be too grateful, for he will enlarge our knowledge of the world.

But when he introduces men and women whose interest is preconceived to lie not in the poverty, the weakness, the drollery of their natures, but in their complete and unconscious subjection to ordinary and healthy human emotions, all his humour, all his fancy, will avail him nothing, if, out of the fulness of his sympathy, he is unable to prosecute those generalizations in which alone consists the real greatness of a work of art. This may sound like very subtle talk about a very simple matter; it is rather very simple talk about a very subtle matter. A story based upon those elementary passions in which alone we seek the true and final manifestation of character must be told in a spirit of intellectual superiority to those passions. That is, the author must understand what he is talking about. The perusal of a story so told is one of the most elevating experiences within the reach of the human mind. The perusal of a story which is not so told is infinitely depressing and unprofitable.

Chapter 11

Events in His Life

The events of Mr. James's life—as we agree to understand events—may be told in a very few words. His race is Irish on his father's side and Scotch on his mother's, to which mingled strains the generalizer may attribute, if he likes, that union of vivid expression and dispassionate analysis which has characterized his work from the first. There are none of those early struggles with poverty, which render the lives of so many distinguished Americans monotonous reading, to record in his case: the cabin hearth-fire did not light him to the youthful pursuit of literature; he had from the start all those advantages which, when they go too far, become limitations.

He was born in New York city in the year 1843, and his first lessons in life and letters were the best which the metropolis—so small in the perspective diminishing to that date—could afford. In his twelfth year his family went abroad, and after some stay in England made a long sojourn in France and Switzerland. They returned to America in 1860, placing themselves at Newport, and for a year or two Mr. James was at the Harvard Law School, where, perhaps, he did not study a great deal of law. His father removed from Newport to Cambridge in 1866, and there Mr. James remained till he went abroad, three years later, for the residence in England and Italy which, with infrequent visits home, has continued ever since.

But that artistic impartiality which puzzled so many in the treatment of Daisy Miller is one of the qualities most valuable in the eyes of those who care how things are done, and I am not sure that it is not Mr. James's most characteristic quality. As "frost performs the effect of fire," this impartiality comes at last to the same result as sympathy. We may be quite sure that Mr. James does not like the peculiar phase of our civilization typified in Henrietta Stackpole; but he treats her with such exquisite justice that he lets US like her. It is an extreme case, but I confidently allege it in proof. His impartiality is part of the reserve with which he works in most respects, and which at first glance makes us say that he is wanting in humour. But I feel pretty certain that Mr. James has not been able to disinherit himself to this degree. We Americans are terribly in earnest about making ourselves, individually and collectively; but I fancy that our prevailing mood in the face of all problems is that of an abiding faith which can afford to be funny.

He has himself indicated that we have, as a nation, as a people, our joke, and every one of us is in the joke more or less. We may, some of us, dislike it extremely, disapprove it wholly, and even abhor it, but we are in the joke all the same, and no one of us is safe from becoming the great American humorist at any given moment. The danger is not apparent in Mr. James's case, and I confess that I read him with a relief in the comparative immunity that he affords from the national facetiousness. Many of his people are humorously imagined, or rather humorously SEEN, like Daisy Miller's mother, but these do not give a dominant colour; the business in hand is commonly serious, and the droll people are subordinated. They abound, nevertheless, and many of them are perfectly new finds, like Mr. Tristram in "The American," the bill-paying father in the "Pension Beaurepas," the anxiously Europeanizing mother in the same story, the amusing little Madame de Belgarde, Henrietta Stackpole, and even Newman himself. But though Mr. James portrays the humorous in character, he is decidedly not on humorous terms with his reader; he ignores rather than recognizes the fact that they are both in the joke.

If we take him at all we must take him on his own ground, for clearly he will not come to ours. We must make concessions to him, not in this respect only, but in several others, chief among which is the motive for reading fiction. By example, at least, he teaches that it is the pursuit and not the end which should give us pleasure; for he often prefers to leave us to our own conjectures in regard to the fate of the people in whom he has interested us. There is no question, of course, but he could tell the story of Isabel in "The Portrait of a Lady" to the end, yet he does not tell it. We must agree, then, to take what seems a fragment instead of a whole, and to find, when we can, a name for this new kind in fiction. Evidently it is the character, not the fate, of his people which occupies him; when he has fully developed their character he leaves them to what destiny the reader pleases.

The analytic tendency seems to have increased with him as his work has gone on. Some of the earlier tales were very dramatic: "A Passionate Pilgrim," which I should rank above all his other short stories, and for certain rich poetical qualities, above everything else that he has done, are eminently dramatic. But I do not find much that I should call dramatic in "The Portrait of a Lady," while I do find in it an amount of analysis which I should call superabundance if it were not all such good literature. The novelist's main business is to possess his reader with a due conception of his characters and the situations in which they find themselves. If he does more or less than this he equally fails. I have sometimes thought that Mr. James's danger was to do more, but when I have been ready to declare this excess an error of his method I have hesitated. Could anything be superfluous that had given me so much pleasure as I read?

Certainly from only one point of view, and this a rather narrow, technical one. It seems to me that an enlightened criticism will recognize in Mr. James's fiction a metaphysical genius working to aesthetic results, and will not be disposed to deny it any method it chooses to employ. No other novelist, except George Eliot, has dealt so largely in analysis of motive, has so fully explained and commented upon the springs of action in the persons of the drama, both before and after the facts. These novelists are more alike than any others in their processes, but with George Eliot an ethical purpose is dominant, and with Mr. James an artistic purpose. I do not know just how it should be stated of two such noble and generous types of character as Dorothea and Isabel Archer, but I think that we sympathize with the former in grand aims that chiefly concern others, and with the latter in beautiful dreams that primarily concern herself.

Both are unselfish and devoted women, sublimely true to a mistaken ideal in their marriages; but, though they come to this common martyrdom, the original difference in them remains. Isabel has her great weaknesses, as Dorothea had, but these seem to me, on the whole, the most nobly imagined and the most nobly intentioned women in modern fiction; and I think Isabel is the more subtly divined of the two.

If we speak of mere characterization, we must not fail to acknowledge the perfection of Gilbert Osmond. It was a profound stroke to make him an American by birth. No European could realize so fully in his own life the ideal of a European dilettante in all the meaning of that cheapened word; as no European could so deeply and tenderly feel the sweetness and loveliness of the English past as the sick American, Searle, in "The Passionate Pilgrim."

What is called the international novel is popularly dated from the publication of "Daisy Miller," though "Roderick Hudson" and "The American" had gone before; but it really began in the beautiful story which I have just named. Mr. James, who invented this species in fiction, first contrasted in the "Passionate Pilgrim" the New World and Old World moods, ideals, and prejudices, and he did it there with a richness of poetic effect which he has since never equalled.

I own that I regret the loss of the poetry, but you cannot ask a man to keep on being a poet for you; it is hardly for him to choose; yet I compare rather discontentedly in my own mind such impassioned creations as Searle and the painter in "The Madonna of the Future" with "Daisy Miller," of whose slight, thin personality I also feel the indefinable charm, and of the tragedy of whose innocence I recognize the delicate pathos.

Looking back to those early stories, where Mr. James stood at the dividing ways of the novel and the romance, I am sometimes sorry that he declared even superficially for the former. His best efforts seem to me those of romance; his best types have an ideal development, like Isabel and Claire Belgarde and Bessy Alden and poor Daisy and even Newman. But, doubtless, he has chosen wisely; perhaps the romance is an outworn form, and would not lend itself to the reproduction of even the ideality of modern life.

I myself waver somewhat in my preference—if it is a preference—when I think of such people as Lord Warburton and the Touchetts, whom I take to be all decidedly of this world. The first of these especially interested me as a probable type of the English nobleman, who amiably accepts the existing situation with all its possibilities of political and social change, and insists not at all upon the surviving feudalities, but means to be a manly and simple gentleman in any event. An American is not able to pronounce as to the verity of the type; I only know that it seems probable and that it is charming. It makes one wish that it were in Mr. James's way to paint in some story the present phase of change in England.

A titled personage is still mainly an inconceivable being to us; he is like a goblin or a fairy in a storybook. How does he comport himself in the face of all the changes and modifications that have taken place and that still impend? We can hardly imagine a lord taking his nobility seriously; it is some hint of the conditional frame of Lord Warburton's mind that makes him imaginable and delightful to us. It is not my purpose here to review any of Mr. James's books; I like better to speak of his people than of the conduct of his novels, and I wish to recognize the fineness with which he has touched-in the pretty primness of Osmond's daughter and the mild devotedness of Mr. Rosier. A masterly hand is as often manifest in the treatment of such subordinate figures as in that of the principal persons, and Mr. James does them unerringly. This is felt in the more important character of Valentin Belgarde, a fascinating character in spite of its defects,—perhaps on account of them—and a sort of French Lord Warburton, but wittier. and not so good. "These are my ideas," says his sister-in-law, at the end of a number of inanities. "Ah, you call them ideas!" he returns, which is delicious and makes you love him. He, too, has his moments of misgiving, apparently in regard to his nobility, and his acceptance of Newman on the basis of something like "manhood suffrage" is very charming.

It is of course difficult for a remote plebeian to verify the pictures of legitimist society in "The American," but there is the probable suggestion in them of conditions and principles, and want of principles, of which we get glimpses in our travels abroad; at any rate, they reveal another and not impossible world, and it is fine to have Newman discover that the opinions and criticisms of our world are so absolutely valueless in that sphere that his knowledge of the infamous crime of the mother and brother of his betrothed will have no effect whatever upon them in their own circle if he explodes it there. This seems like aristocracy indeed! and one admires, almost respects, its survival in our day.

But I always regretted that Newman's discovery seemed the precursor of his magnanimous resolution not to avenge himself; it weakened the effect of this, with which it had really nothing to do. Upon the whole, however, Newman is an adequate and satisfying representative of Americanism, with his generous matrimonial ambition, his vast good-nature, and his thorough good sense and right feeling.

We must be very hard to please if we are not pleased with him. He is not the "cultivated American" who redeems us from time to time in the eyes of Europe; but he is unquestionably more national, and it is observable that his unaffected fellow-countrymen and women fare very well at Mr. James's hand always; it is the Europeanizing sort like the critical little Bostonian in the "Bundle of Letters," the ladies shocked at Daisy Miller, the mother in the "Pension Beaurepas" who goes about trying to be of the "native" world everywhere, Madame Merle and Gilbert Osmond, Miss Light and her mother, who have reason to complain, if any one has.

Doubtless Mr. James does not mean to satirize such Americans, but it is interesting to note how they strike such a keen observer. We are certainly not allowed to like them, and the other sort find somehow a place in our affections along with his good Europeans. It is a little odd, by the way, that in all the printed talk about Mr. James—and there has been no end of it—his power of engaging your preference for certain of his people has been so little commented on. Perhaps it is because he makes no obvious appeal for them; but one likes such men as Lord Warburton, Newman, Valentin, the artistic brother in "The Europeans," and Ralph Touchett, and such women as Isabel, Claire Belgarde, Mrs. Tristram, and certain others, with a thoroughness that is one of the best testimonies to their vitality.

This comes about through their own qualities, and is not affected by insinuation or by downright petting, such as we find in Dickens nearly always and in Thackeray too often. The art of fiction has, in fact, become a finer art in our day than it was with Dickens and Thackeray. We could not suffer the confidential attitude of the latter now, nor the mannerism of the former, any more than we could endure the prolixity of Richardson or the coarseness of Fielding. These great men are of the past—they and their methods and interests; even Trollope and Reade are not of the present.

The new school derives from Hawthorne and George Eliot rather than any others; but it studies human nature much more in its wonted aspects, and finds its ethical and dramatic examples in the operation of lighter but not really less vital motives. The moving accident is certainly not its trade; and it prefers to avoid all manner of dire catastrophes. it is largely influenced by French fiction in form; but it is the realism of Daudet rather than the realism of Zola that prevails with it, and it has a soul of its own which is above the business of recording the rather brutish pursuit of a woman by a man, which seems to be the chief end of the French novelist.

This school, which is so largely of the future as well as the present, finds its chief exemplar in Mr. James; it is he who is shaping and directing American fiction, at least. It is the ambition of the younger contributors to write like him; he has his following more distinctly recognizable than that of any other English-writing novelist. Whether he will so far control this following as to decide the nature of the novel with us remains to be seen. Will the reader be content to accept a novel which is an analytic study rather than a story, which is apt to leave him arbiter of the destiny of the author's creations? Will he find his account in the unflagging interest of their development? Mr. James's growing popularity seems to suggest that this may be the case; but the work of Mr. James's imitators will have much to do with the final result. In the meantime it is not surprising that he has his imitators. Whatever exceptions we take to his methods or his results, we cannot deny him a very great literary genius.

To me there is a perpetual delight in his way of saying things, and I cannot wonder that younger men try to catch the trick of it. The disappointing thing for them is that it is not a trick, but an inherent virtue. His style is, upon the whole, better than that of any other novelist I know; it is always easy, without being trivial, and it is often stately, without being stiff; it gives a charm to everything he writes; and he has written so much and in such various directions, that we should be judging him very incompletely if we considered him only as a novelist.

His book of European sketches must rank him with the most enlightened and agreeable travelers; and it might be fitly supplemented from his uncollected papers with a volume of American sketches. In his essays on modern French writers he indicates his critical range and grasp; but he scarcely does more, as his criticisms in "The Atlantic" and "The Nation" and elsewhere could abundantly testify.

There are indeed those who insist that criticism is his true vocation, and are impatient of his devotion to fiction; but I suspect that these admirers are mistaken. A novelists he is not, after the old fashion, or after any fashion but his own; yet since he has finally made his public in his own way of story-telling—or call it character-painting if you prefer,—it must be conceded that he has chosen best for himself and his readers in choosing the form of fiction for what he has to say.

It is, after all, what a writer has to say rather than what he has to tell that we care for nowadays. In one manner or other the stories were all told long ago; and now we want merely to know what the novelist thinks about persons and situations. Mr. James gratifies this philosophic desire. If he sometimes forbears to tell us what he thinks of the last state of his people, it is perhaps because that does not interest him, and a large-minded criticism might well insist that it was childish to demand that it must interest him.

I am not sure that any criticism is sufficiently large-minded for this. I own that I like a finished story; but then also I like those which Mr. James seems not to finish.

This is probably the position of most of his readers, who cannot very logically account for either preference. We can only make sure that we have here an annalist, or analyst, as we choose, who fascinates us from his first page to his last, whose narrative or whose comment may enter into any minuteness of detail without fatiguing us, and can only truly grieve us when it ceases.

Chapter 12

Note on Henry James Jr

Twenty-five years ago, walking on a beach one summer morning in Atlantic City, I thought of writing about Justice Oliver Wendell Holmes and his friends Henry and William James. Without knowing very much about them, it seemed to me that the two families were admirable representatives of what one might call the male and female poles of culture. Holmes, the famously hard-minded materialist soldier and judge, I had come to admire in law school; the James boys were artists and men of letters, and while I didn't know much about them, they seemed to represent a different strand of America thought.

William James was perhaps the brightest the star, intellectually speaking, in the liberal political firmament, and Holmes was a hero to many political conservatives; Henry was a motherly nursemaid of culture. Together, the three friends lived through the fashioning of post-Civil-War America and helped to create its government, its literature, its thought, its place in the world. Much had been written about these famous men; it seemed to me that I might write some brief, graceful reflection about their complementary characters and their often adversarial friendship.

Although much had ben written about Holmes, there was nothing like the adequate biography I felt I needed, however. After his death, Holmes's letters and journals were collected at the Harvard Law School, where Mark DeWolfe Howe was given exclusive access to them; Prof. Howe did remarkable work in assembling and preparing many of Holmes's letters for publication, but he regrettably died before getting beyond the early years of the biography. The law school appointed another "authorized" biographer, but he too died without having advanced the project very much; another prospective biographer gave up the notion of writing Holmes's biography when he took his seat on a federal court. I wandered in at that moment to have a look at the Holmes papers and found that the Harvard law faculty had surrendered its protective grip on the archive. It was now open to all comers, and I accordingly sat down to write the first complete biography of Holmes: *Honorable Justice: The Life of Oliver Wendell Holmes.*

My biography was well received, and I was encouraged to write another. Henry James attracted me more than William as a subject, and I had learned in my research on Holmes that the canonical account by Leon Edel was oddly partial and omitted what seemed to me important aspects of James's life and thought — omitted indeed the life-long friendships with Henry and William James that so interested me. I did not then know how limited Edel's access to James materials had been, nor the constraints under which he was working. (I have said a few words about Edel and the work of other James scholars in an epilogue to my own book, posted elsewhere on this Web site.)

Life intervened, as it will, and years elapsed before I was able to complete the two volumes of my biography of Henry James. As I was finishing with Henry, an admirable life of William appeared (Linda Simon's *Genuine Reality: A Life of William James*) and I no longer had any excuse for postponing my effort to write some brief, graceful work that puts the three men into fruitful opposition. But my original notion seemed too simple, now.

Others have lookd at the same period and the same figures, and seen a different moment. The late Felix Frankfurter seemed to have been the first to focus on the "Mataphysical Club," a short-lived and informal conversation club that included Holmes, the James brothers, Charles Sanders Peirce and one or two others, and that met briefly and irregularly in 1871 or 1872 under the benign and tolerant patronage of Harvard Professor Chauncey Wright. The club had its name because the principal topic of discussion was the great metaphysical question of the day, the would-be scientific materialism that was having a fashion in the world of letters. Holmes and Wright were materialists, and spoke of evolution; in later years it was Wright's influence that Holmes remembered. Henry and William James were traditional idealists. William especially had argued metaphyscs with Holmes — the traces of their late-night debates can be found in their still unpublished letters — and their arguments were the beginning of the club. Henry was often present at those discussions in Holmes's and the Jameses' bedrooms, of which he later recorded fond memories.

Frankfurter used the Metaphysical Club to give a somewhat misleading impression of Holmes as a pragmatic, early New Dealer, however, and it seems to have been Frankfurter who prompted Catherine Drinker Bowen to give a long fictional account of the club, complete with pages of imagined conversation, in her best-selling *Yankee from Olympus* (1943). Bowen's account of the club although fictional was highly persuasive, and seems to have influenced later accounts of intellectual history. Mark Howe and others who later gained access to the Holmes papers discredited Bowen's account and doubted the influence of the club, but the story of pragmatism's supposed birth in the 1870s has recently been revived, and seems to have taken on the life of an attractive fable. Contemperaneous writings of Holmes and the James brothers didn't reflect any discussion of pragmatism. (Holmes's few pragmatic notions were published before the club came into existence.) About twenty-five years later, in the 1890s, Peirce — having fallen on hard times — claimed that he had first brought forward in those early conversations the epistemology that was then being developed by him, and independently by others, seeking to establish a priority in the new discipline.

Peirce, John Dewey and others went on to propose a new sort of philosophy which William called "pragmatism," generously giving Peirce the priority for which he asked. William became its best-known champion, however, with the publication of his best-selling *Pragmatism*. William James's version never established itself among philosophers, although it has greatly influenced literary and historical criticism. Tempting as it always is to see the past as a more innocent version of the present, none of the other young men of the Metaphysical Club (perhaops including Peirce himself) had anything like Peirce's later ideas in mind in the early 1870s. They did have in common a fascination with science and its wild discoveries; but science was ambiguous (as it always is) on the great questions of spirt and meaning. The "magnetic ether" seemed to be the ground stuf of thought and spirit; the survival of the personality after the death of the body a natural phenomenon; mesmerism an application of scientific idealism. Henry and William James were raised in an atmosphere of scientific investigation of religious truths; Ernest Renan's best-selling *Life of Jesus* was an example of careful empirical study of the historical truths embedded in the New Testament; his investigations of language and culture seemed to establish an idealist taxonomy of races — one that was to have tragic reverberations in the twentieth century.

Now we have come around at last to Henry Jame's place in this conversation. Henry, too, was entranced by fact. To an idealist, indeed, the great miracles of existence are not the seeming truths of morality and religion, which are commonplace, but their numinous embodiments. The beauty of a human face, the intense experience of an embrace, is rendered with mysterious intensity in James's work. Like Michelangelo's portrayals of nude saints, James's novels are essays in the theology of the body. Not that he was precisely religious, in the usual sense. James never expressed a belief in God. When late in life he wrote of his tentative willingness to believe in the survival of the personality after death, he spoke of this (as William had) as a natural phenemonen; he described seances and other supposed manifestations of the spirit world as possible examples of thought transference, of the communication (always somewhat mysterious) between minds. Like William, Henry had a profound distrust of systems and absolutes, and felt drawn to his brother's own expression of "pragmatism" when it came late in their joint lives. But he never lost his deep sense of the firm reality of moral principles, and of the continuity of human life and thought over the centuries, which he characterized sometimes as a secret letter passed on from hand to hand, and sometimes as the Word whose embodiment he saw portrayed in Titian's portraits of young men.

How this Word was to be carried forward in an age of democratic revolution was one of his themes. In Henry novel's, it is the ideal young American woman who is "the heir of all the ages," and carries forward the accumlated moral wisdom of the human race. Henry criticizes American men for leaving this task all to unaided women, and he notably takes it upon himself to carry forward his own share, and more, of the treasures of civilization. The institutions of feudal Europe, founded as they were upon violence and injustice, nevertheles are vehicles in which civilization is to be carried forward, and James labors throughout his long life to marry (sometimes literally) the beauties and continuities of material European life with the moral spontaneity of that most highly evolved organism, the young American. I should not like to give up Holmes's hard-minded materialism, which I share to some degree. But Henry James was right, within limits.

Democracy, however necessary, is not enough for a civilization; we can't share masterwork paintings by cutting each into a thousand pieces. There are many things, including human rights and personal privacy, that cannot be voted upon. He had great hopes for museums, universities, and other charitable public enterprises, that he thought could take the place of landed family estates and established churches in carrying forward, into a democratic future, what was worth preserving and necessary to keep of the old civilizations of Europe. While he was a democrat and a republican in his politics, therefore, he admired the surviving institutions of royalty and aristocracy, rendered non-violent and powerless in the American republic. Constitutional monarchy on the British and Dutch models seemed valuable to him, he famously regreted their absence in American life, and at the end of his own life he became a British subject and swore an oath of loyalty to the king. He was a complex man, not easily categorized, but well worth listening to. These are some of thoughts that occur to me now; perhaps I shall yet write that essay about Holmes and the James brothers, and this in any case is a start.

THE SACRED FOUNT

I've long had an aversion to the prose of Henry James. (How I prefer his brother, "the adorable William James," as Whitehead calls him). There is just something so smug about Henry James' prose, creepy and self-congratulatory and fussy and self-important and filled with hideous phrases like "in fine," and "I daresay," and "she hung fire." I often think of Henry James as the polar opposite of Proust (who is my favourite author of all time). James is all about the subtle folds and crevices of consciousness, where Proust is about those aspects of our emotional life where consciousness fails to reach (like "involuntary memory"). James fetishizes a narrow, instrumental "intelligence"; Proust is all about the limitations and failures, and ultimately the irrelevance, of such an intelligence. James' characters are always calculating, always jousting for advantage, always manipulating one another, while Proust tracks the movements of passion, for good and for ill, in generosity and in cruelty, that are beyond calculation. James and Proust are both snobs; but where James takes his snobbery complacently for granted, Proust subjects it to lacerating self-analysis. And so on.

But Nightspore has been after me for ages to read James' little-known novel *The Sacred Fount*, and his recent post quoting Rebecca West's hilarious description of the novel (she writes that James "records how a week-end visitor spends more intellectual force than Kant can have used on The Critique of Pure Reason in an unsuccessful attempt to discover whether there exists between certain of his fellow-guests a relationship not more interesting among these vacuous people that it is among sparrows") finally persuaded me to do so.

Well, I have to admit that *The Sacred Fount* really is quite something. It's James' parody (intentional or not, I'm not quite sure) and *reductio ad absurdum* of his entire aesthetic and method. Significantly, the novel features James' only first-person narrator; and this very Jamesian narrator spends the entire novel discerning subtleties that simply aren't there, 'reading' his fellows entirely incorrectly, congratulating himself for his own mistaken insights, and constructing a "theory" of human behaviour that finally collapses into a black hole of irrelevance and inaccuracy (or collapses like a house of cards, to use one of the novel's own metaphors). The ultra-subtle discernment of James' prose turns out to be nothing but projection and interpretive paranoia; the novel's seeming exploration of intersubjectivity is unmasked as a wishful solipsistic fantasy. Thus, the narrator goes to great lengths to describe to the reader his silent unspoken sympathy and commiseration with a ravaged woman, filled with desperation, at the end of her rope, her life blasted by passion, on the verge of total breakdown, courageously and beyond her own strength struggling to hold herself together only a few moments longer... only it turns out the woman is none of these things, but rather just a witty and skittish flirt.

What's more, you can't even say the narrator *learns* anything at the end, when the full extent of his folly is revealed to him. He sort of shrugs it off, admitting a kind of defeat, but with his faith in his own intelligence and discernment largely unshaken. The entire content of the novel, including everything that makes any of the characters potentially interesting, is withdrawn at the end, leaving nothing but a void. *The Sacred Fount* is so wonderfully crazy and pointless a book, so extreme an exercise in style (albeit one that makes me cringe) devoid of any meaningful content, so dazzling a display of writing without any reason to write, an act of pure expression without anything whatsoever to express, that it won me over in spite of myself.

THE MYSTERY OF HENRY JAMES'S TESTICLES

A long time ago, I heard a rumor that Henry James had injured his testicles. In my novel *The Extra Man*, I used this rumor in the following bit of dialogue between the characters Louis Ives and Henry Harrison (the first speaker is Louis; he is also the narrator):

"It's really very strange that I'll be moving to New York. It's all because I was looking at the cover of Henry James's Washington Square and I thought I should be in New York."

"I can't stand James!" Henry proclaimed. "He's unreadable."

"I know what you mean." I was worried that I had said the wrong thing, but then I stood up for myself and James a little bit by saying, "But the earlier books are quite good, like Daisy Miller, or Washington Square."

"Yes, that's true, his style did change. I wonder why. He burned himself, you know. Sat on a stove and shriveled his testicles. That may account for the change in style."

I then recycled this rumor in my next book, my so-called memoir *What's Not to Love?*:

In my small East Village apartment, the bathtub is in the kitchen. I can't shower in my tub, but attached to the faucet is a hose with a showerhead, and I use this to rinse off while I sit there . . .

Last Sunday morning, I was in the tub and I was working on my head with my scalp invigorator. The rubber hose was lying coiled at the bottom of the tub like a snake; water was jetting out of the showerhead, warming my ankles. Then I nudged the snake and at that precise moment something happened to the building's cold-water supply — it was cut off — and the nudging moved the showerhead so that it was aimed not at my ankles, but at my testicles. My tiny balls were then scalded and I screamed and threw the scalp invigorator into the air. I quickly shut off the water and stared down at myself. Was I going to have to call 911 for singed testicles? I had heard many stories over the years of children burned in their bathtubs, and then I thought of Henry James and the myth that his testicles had been burned, or punctured on a fence, and this had caused his legendary asexuality — was this to be my fate?

Well, a few months ago a young scholar named Michael

Wood wrote to me after reading *The Extra Man* and *What's Not to Love?* and asked me if I had any proof to back up this Henry James testicle rumor. I did not have any proof, but I asked him if he could look into it for me, for *us*. It was my hope that he would discover just what the hell happened to Henry James. Well, the following extraordinary essay, on this very important literary matter, is the result. (You can find Michael Wood's bio and a list of his sources at the end of this document.)

Another thing that should put us on our guard with James is that, more than most writers, he tended to live and make fiction behind a mask. In spite of the Herculean labors of Leon Edel, our image of James remains in many respects precisely the image he designed for us.

He was very careful to doctor certain facts about his life and to conceal others. He sifted and destroyed documents [...] Many surviving family letters allude by date to others that are no longer extant; some of this missing correspondence undoubtedly requested the recipient to burn the letter after reading it. [...] Furthermore, many of these missing letters date from certain critical periods in the lives of one or more of the Jameses. There are many ambiguities about Henry James that we cannot sort out, and there are probably many important facts we do not even suspect

-Alfred Habegger, *Henry James and the "Woman Business"* (p.8)

I was talking with a couple of friends about sex and art and one of them mentioned *The Great Gatsby*. "Nick," he said, "is totally gay." As evidence, he read to us - emphasizing with gusto every suggestive phrase - the end of Chapter II, in which Nick (drunk for only the second time in his life) leaves Tom and Mrs. Wilson's party with Mr. McKee - who he had previously wiped some shaving lather off of - "a pale, feminine male":

'Come to lunch,' he suggested, as we groaned down in the elevator.

'Where?'

'Anywhere.'

'Keep your hands off the lever,' snapped the elevator boy.

'I beg your pardon,' said Mr McKee with dignity, 'I didn't know I was touching it.'

'All right,' I agreed, 'I'll be glad to.'

...I was standing besides his bed and he was sitting up between the sheets, clad in his underwear, with a great portfolio in his hands.

'Beauty and the Beast...Loneliness...Old Grocery Horse...Brook'n Bridge...'

Then I was lying half asleep in the cold lower level of the Pennsylvania Station, staring at the morning Tribune, and waiting for the four o'clock train.

I hadn't read *Gatsby* for years and when I had, I hadn't noticed any homosexual undertones; then, as I thought about it, I realized it made perfect sense and I had been a fool to have missed it. And then, as my mind was reeling over this development an image started to form in my head and when it became clear, what I saw in my mind's eye was Henry James, impeccably dressed in a three piece suit and bow tie, hoisting his testicles onto a white hot stove. I knew this was somehow relevant to our discussion but my prudery got the best of me and all I could offer was that I'd heard a story about *The Portrait of a Lady* author sitting on a stove, because he thought he deserved it, and that that must mean something.

"He thought he deserved to burn his bum?"

"I've never heard that."

"Yeah, it was definitely something like that. I think it had something to do with, yeah - you know?" I was hoping that one of them would jump in with details of the story but that wasn't happening. I was racking my head for an elegant way to suggest that it was the gonads, not the buttocks that had been the focus of the scorching when it hit me where I'd read about the incident: it wasn't from a biography on James, but from a novel called *The Extra Man* by Jonathan Ames. I realized that if something had happened to Henry James' testicles that my friends didn't know about it, because if they did, it'd just be weird that they didn't mention it - given what we were talking about. And I thought this was sort of neat because one of my friends had done his Ph.D. on James, and even he didn't know about the guy's self-castration! I instantly resolved to solve the mystery.

"Look," I said, exited now, "I'm pretty sure something happened down there, so I'm going to check it out. And when I do find out - "

"You'll let us know.

"We'll look forward to it."

I think it was the personal nature of Ames writing which made me feel comfortable in e-mailing him. In his essays he addressed such topics as his poo-ing misadventures in France, his late puberty, and his Oedipal complex. I knew about his first sexual encounter, (which was with a prostitute,) so why would I be embarrassed about contacting him? Ames seemed like the kind of author who would bother to write back when a fan asked a sexually specific question; true to my suspicions, he responded quickly to my query:

I alluded to this rumor in both 'the extra man' and in 'what's not to love?'. I heard it somewhere, don't know if it's fact, but I'm pretty sure something did happen to Henry James's testicles. He may have gotten them spiked on a fence or something. please find out the real story and report back.

It was exiting to hear back from Ames and the fence rumor (had puncturing been involved?) coupled with his exhortation to "find out the real story" sent a shot of adrenaline through my body.

After sorting through the mishmash an internet search for "Henry James + testicles" revealed, I came upon the first of several literary feuds I would encounter during the course of my investigation: In the 1950's, Leon Edel published his five volume biography of James; Edel also edited the equally massive *Henry James: Letters* as well as writing and editing many other works on James. In 1996 Sheldon Novick published *Henry James: The Young Master*, a biography which refuted many of Edel's ideas. The two got catty in a couple of articles published in 'Slate', Edel striking first, with his piece 'Oh Henry! What Henry James didn't do with Oliver Wendell Holmes (or anyone else)'. Edel takes issue with Novick's claim that James and the Supreme Court Justice were lovers. "It upsets," he writes, "a century of scholarship that seems to have clearly shown James was a firm bachelor with a 'low amatory coefficient,' as one of his doctors put it in 1905 in New York." Edel goes on:

Another bit of imaginative projection upon James' life can be found in Ernest Hemingway's letters. This novelist, on learning that Brooks [Van Wyck Brooks, author of *The Pilgrimage of Henry James*] had written that James was 'prevented by an accident from taking part in the Civil War,' immediately incorporated this into his nearly finished novel, '*The Sun Also Rises*'. In Chapter 12, Jake Barnes refers to his World War I accident, and Gorton says, 'That's the sort of thing that can't be spoken of. That's what you ought to work up into a mystery. Like Henry's bicycle.' Barnes replies it wasn't a bicycle; 'he was riding horseback.' (In his memoirs, James spoke of having had a 'horrid' but 'obscure hurt.' He had strained his back during a stable fire while serving as a volunteer fireman.) Hemingway had originally inserted James' name in the novel, but Scribner's editor, Maxwell Perkins, vetoed this. Hemingway insisted. They finally compromised on the 'Henry' alone. F. Scott Fitzgerald wrote to Brooks, 'Why didn't you touch more on James'impotence (physical) and its influence?'

Novick (a Professor of Law at The University of Vermont) responded to Edel's attack in the form of a letter directed at Edel himself:

I was startled to find in SLATE last week your intemperate and rather personal diatribe about my book *Henry James: The Young Master*. Whatever your reasons, you have allowed yourself to be provoked into saying outrageous things, and I have no choice but to answer plainly. Your remarks focus obsessively on Henry James' sexuality. This is your obsession, not mine. You dwell on a single sexual encounter that takes no more than a page in my book and is not referred to again. What I do say in my book, and give considerably more prominence—and what you fail to mention—is that your own biography of James is no longer useful. For a modern reader, it badly distorts the record of the novelist's life. I point out numerous errors and outright inventions in your work, mistakes you give a fair sample of in your SLATE story. [...] As you will see if you read it, my book is devoted largely to a discussion of James' intellectual development and his stories, novels, and critical essays. James' sexual orientation is necessarily portrayed, and I take it for granted—as most scholars do now—that he was a closeted gay man. I don't think you have ever really disputed this, but you now seem to be shying away from its implications. In your story you hint that James was impotent, and you quote a bizarre, homophobic pronouncement by a doctor who examined James once when he was ill and away from home, then announced to a breathless world that the famous novelist was badly hung.

What I like best about Novick's response is how he chides Edel for not admitting that much of his life's work, "is no longer useful". As I read Novick's article, I instantly accepted his picture of Leon Edel as a crusty old man, ensconced in the ways of the past and unwilling to confront James' sexuality.

As far as the original mystery went, I had some clues, but nothing definite. Had the accident James suffered as a fireman involved flames, or a fence? Was this what I was after? And was this Pre-Civil War accident connected to the "bizarre, homophobic" report in 1905 by James' doctor? I was also intrigued by the Hemingway-Fitzgerald connection because Ames, in numerous essays, had professed a strong affection for both these writers; perhaps what he'd done in *The Extra Man* was an intentional echo of the reference in *The Sun Also Rises*. But if this was so, why hadn't he told me? Either he hadn't thought it worth mentioning, or he didn't know about it - which would mean that he and Hemingway had each independently decided to include what was to both men only gossip about Henry James' sex organs into their fiction. What was it about James' genitalia which inspired generations of writers?

I knew that if I was going to solve this caper I would have to broaden my investigatory techniques, and so, in a series of trips to the New York Public Library's Main Branch, and it's less glamorous neighbour, the Mid-Manhattan Branch I delved into the lore of Henry James - or at least that lore connected to his private parts.

At this point I'm going to tell you what happened to Henry James' testicles: basically, he hurt them on a fence, helping put out a fire. Well, he definitely hurt his back - how much he hurt the testicles is open to debate; but the story Edel mentions in his 'Slate' article is definitely the basis not only for the rumor Hemingway heard, but also Ames (who says he was unaware of the reference in *The Sun Also Rises*).

As I learned more about the case I constantly picked up interesting tangential information: every impotence rumor quashed would reveal another literary fight, or another incredible coincidence. I would e-mail Ames progress reports and he was always enthusiastic and encouraging, though I wondered if, privately, he wasn't at all disturbed my increasingly long and minutia-filled communiqué. While I knew that what I was finding out was news to Ames and me I was also aware that, as much as I liked to play the gumshoe, tracking down clues and solving the insolvable, that that's not what was going on. And how could it? All the information I was getting was from books that were already published; the testicles' story (and all the stories it connects to) aren't exactly State secrets. Plus, I'm a complete idiot.

In narrowing my search from the infinitely fertile ground of topics related to Henry James, I decided to zero in on following areas:

- The testicles story
- Any sex stuff (particularly insinuations of homosexuality)
- Literary back stabbings

Here's what I found out:

In 1914, James' *Notes on A Son and Brother* was published. In it, he writes of the 1861 accident he had as a volunteer fireman. During the blaze, the eighteen year old Henry James was:

Jammed into the acute angle between two high fences, where the rhythmic play of my arms, in tune with that of several other pairs, but at a dire disadvantage of positions, induced a rural, a rusty, a quasi-extemporised old engine to work and saving the stream to flow, I had done myself a horrid even if obscure hurt; and what was interesting from the first was my not doubting in the least its duration - though what seemed equally clear was that I needn't as a matter of course adopt and appropriate it, so to speak, or place it for increase of interest on exhibition.

The above is just a small part of James' recount of the saga; James stretches the story to many pages, recalling his sensations and motivations without revealing exactly what happened. Elsewhere he writes of seeing a doctor about the pain:

I have little forgotten how I felt myself, the warning absent, treated but to a comparative pooh-pooh - an impression I long looked back to as a sharp parting of the ways, with an adoption of the wrong one distinctly determined.

In summarizing James' account various critics have tackled the challenge of condensing and making clear James' famously circumlocutory, flowery and often opaque prose. Leon Edel does a relatively good job in the first volume of his biography, in capturing the spirit of the story and in chronicling the brouhaha which ensued:

The hurt is 'horrid' but it is also 'obscure.' It is a 'catastrophe,' but it is in the very same phrase only a 'difficulty.' It is a passage of history 'most entirely personal' yet apparently not too personal to be broadcast to the world in his memoirs[...]It is also 'extraordinarily intimate' and at the same time 'awkwardly intimate.'[...] His readers were to imagine the worst.

What, after all is the most odious, horrid, intimate, thing that can happen to a man? However much different men might have different answers, in the case of Henry James critics tended to see a relationship between the accident and his celibacy, his apparent avoidance of involvements with women and the absence of overt sexuality in his work. Thus there emerged a 'theory' - promptly converted into a rumor - that the novelist suffered a hurt, during those 'odious twenty minutes' which amounted to castration. In the April-June 1934

House & Hound issue, devoted entirely to James, Glenway Wescott reported it almost as a fact: "Henry James, expatriation and castration. . . . Henry James it is rumored, could not have had a child. But if he was as badly hurt, in the pre-Civil War accident as that - since he triumphed over other authors of his epoch - perhaps the injury was a help to him." Stephen Spender quotes this passage in *The Destructive Element* and suggests that "Castration, or the fear of castration, is supposed to preoccupy the mind with ideas about suicide and death."

He goes on to show how this is true of many of James's characters. Mr. Spender, however does have a second thought and adds in a footnote: "The rumor of castration seems exaggerated and improbable, but it seems likely that James sustained a serious injury." In the above, you will notice, I am quoting Edel, who quotes Wescott and Spender, and the part of Westcott that Edel quotes is the same part of the Wescott that Spender quotes. In my research I saw this sort of thing happening a lot: one person writes something, then someone else quotes it and adds their two cents to it, then someone quotes that person, and on and on until you get a shmuck like me quoting Edel. One might think this would lead to an increase in the universe's store of knowledge, but as far as I can tell, what happens as often as not is we get a bunch of critics playing telephone.

Edel chooses not to quote Spender when Spender writes erroneously:

There is another reference to the accident in Miss Rebecca West's little book on James. Apparently he was called on as a volunteer to help with a fire engine to put out a bad fire. There was an accident, in which he was very severely scalded. What is spurious is not that Rebecca West references the incident, but that James was burned. In his 1996 'Slate' piece, Edel again doesn't mention West when he could have, an omission resulting in a misstatement of fact: "Novick's attempt to find love affairs in James' life reminds me of the 1920's, when there were no biographies of James".

In fact, Rebecca West's *Henry James* was published in 1916

- just two years after *Notes on A Son and Brother* - when West was twenty-three years old. Her reference is the earliest example that I've been able to find of an author mentioning the episode, and speculating on its significance:

In 1861 the Civil War broke out; and had it not been for an accident the whole character of Mr. James' genius would have been altered. If he had seen America by the light of bursting shells and flaming forest he might never have taken his eyes off her again, he might have watched her fascinated through all the changes of tone and organisation which began at the close of the war, he might have been the Great American Novelist in subject as well as origin. But it happened, in that soft spring when he and every other young man of the North realised that there was a crisis at hand in which their honour was concerned and they must answer Lincoln's appeal for recruits, that he was one day called to help putting out a fire. In working the fire-engine he sustained an injury so serious that he could never hope to share the Northern glory, that there were before him years of continuous pain and weakness, that ultimately he formed a curious and on the whole mischievous conception of himself.

West's comments are interesting as much for what they say, as for what they don't. She suggests that the accident changed James, but not because it may have left him impotent or castrated. She doesn't mention (as far as I've read) the exact nature of the accident and unless she does it means that Spender was sloppy for assuming that the accident James suffered helping put out a fire involved his being burned. If West does say that fire was the culprit, than both she and I are guilty of poor reportage, and Spender's statement is more excusable. It's also possible that West (as I suspect) doesn't write that James was burned but someone in the twenty-one years between when West and Spender wrote did make that assumption and that's the story Spender heard. However, considering that James clearly states that it was a fence issue and no roasting was involved, it's fair to say that Spender made an avoidable mistake.

This charge (and worse) was leveled against Van Wyck

Brooks almost immediately after *The Pilgrimage of Henry James* appeared in 1925. As Leon Edel writes:

Edna Kenton, a devoted Jamesian in Greenwich Village, demonstrated in a biting review in *The Bookman* that Brooks used important James quotations out of context. Years later, Brooks confessed to having nightmares "in which Henry James turned great luminous menacing eyes upon me."

In *The Legacy of Van Wyck Brooks; A Study of Maladies and Motives,* William Wasserstrom quotes from an amusing letter written by the then seventeen year old Brooks:

I don't know much about Henry James, except that he's a brother of Prof. James, of Harvard, is an infernal snob, and *does* know how to write English. His books are very psychological, aren't they? His brother is the greatest psychologist in the world. I think Henry James is the reprobate who wrote Daisy Miller. Read that and you won't think much of him. He lives in Europe in a sort of Williams-Waldorf-Astor style.

My own experience with *The Pilgrimage of Henry James* was rather pleasant. Brooks' voice is excitable and dramatic; he uses exclamation marks a lot, (which I have a soft spot for) as when he writes:

Was he not, for comprehensible reasons, the prey of that "fear of life" to which Flaubert also confessed himself a victim? Undoubtedly; and to this may be traced perhaps the deep longing for security, privacy, ceremony that was to mark his later years. But to return from the ultimate to the immediate, what a light this fact seems to throw upon the great "renunciation" with which his career opened!

While I was generally charmed by Brooks' prose style, I wondered where he got the chutzpah to write his introductory note. I'm tempted to think I'm misreading what he's saying, because what I think he's saying is so blatant and weird:

Readers who are familiar with Henry James will observe that many phrases and even long passages from his writings have been incorporated in the text of this book, usually without any indication of their source. The author has resorted to this expedient because he knows of no other means of conveying with strict accuracy at moments what he conceives to have been James's thoughts and feelings.

If we read the above without the phrase, "usually without any indication of their source" it kind of makes sense: Brooks is telling us that in his book he quotes James a lot, because he's found that it's a quick and accurate way of communicating what James thinks. Fair enough. But the inclusion of the phrase makes it seem as if Brooks thinks that it is his *not* including the source of his quotations which will make his account of James even more precise. Is the "expedient" quoting James, or quoting James without a source? It's confusing. As you'll remember, F. Scott Fitzgerald wrote to Brooks, asking, "Why didn't you touch more on James' impotence (physical) and its influence?"

It's cute that in Fitzgerald's letter he mentions Hemingway, and in Hemingway's he mentions, "Scott". Their friendship has been examined in numerous books and in reading these accounts it is always fun to imagine this wonderfully odd couple traipsing around 1920's France. In *Fitzgerald and Hemingway: A Dangerous Friendship*, Matthew J. Broccoli chronicles the history of the relationship, asking such questions as: How did they affect one another as people? To what degree did they influence each others writing? To what extent did the fact that they didn't want to be influenced by each other affect their work? It should go without saying that I'm just going to talk about the speculation that they were gay lovers.

In Nancy Milford's biography of Zelda Fitzgerald, she writes on page 153:

On a boat to Europe Zelda had mentioned to Scott that she thought a friend from the ballet was homosexual. Now, desperately uncertain of herself, she accused Scott of a homosexual liaison with Ernest Hemingway. Scott, who had gone without Zelda to have a drink one evening with Hemingway and his wife, had returned home intoxicated and had fallen into a deep sleep. In his sleep he murmured, "no more baby," which was taken by Zelda as absolute proof of her suspicions.

Milford also mentions the following letter Fitzgerald wrote to Perkins about accusations made by the American writer Robert McAlmon:

By the way McAlmon is a bitter rat and I'm not surprised at anything he does or says. He's failed as a writer and tries to fortify himself by tying up to the big boys like Joyce and Stein and despising everything else. Part of his quarrel with Ernest some years ago was because he assured Ernest that I was a fairy - God knows he shows more creative imagination in his malice than in his work. Next he told Callaghan that Ernest was a fairy. He's a pretty good person to avoid.

We sense, I think, in Fitzgerald's words, an overly defensive posture. Scott Donaldson quotes Fitzgerald as writing in his notebooks of Hemingway:

I really loved him, but of course it wore out like a love affair. The fairies have spoiled all that.

What are we to make Fitzgerald's words? And more, how does all of this relate to Nick Carraway's sexuality? A clue can possibly be found in looking at the draft of *Gatsby* which Fitzgerald sent to Perkins in 1924. In examining this version we find that the end of Chapter II is *nearly* identical to that which was published the next year:

...I was standing besides his bed and he was sitting up between the sheets, *still* clad in his underwear, *and* with a great portfolio in his hands.

The additional "and" seems unimportant, but the "still" is interesting, suggesting different scenarios. Does it imply that McKee is soon to be separated from his underwear? Perhaps it suggests that Nick had attempted to dislodge McKee from the underwear, but had been unsuccessful. In this reading, the "and" could be seen as emphasising Nick's frustration: 'Not only wasn't he naked, but he had this massive portfolio in his hands.' On the other hand, we could read Nick's words in as an effusive denial (much like Fitzgerald's) of any homosexual shenanigans: 'Hey look, he still had his on the underwear - nothing happened.' Or maybe Nick had intended to access McKee's genitals, but had second thoughts before McKee was denuded. - However we interpret what Nick and

McKee are meant to have done between the time McKee is described as underwear-clad and Nick's ending up in Penn Station, it is clear that they *did not* make love within the period marked by the ellipses, a possibility which does exist in *Gatsby*. Therefore, it is possible that "still" was removed to allow for more gay sex.

It seems clear to me that 1) F. Scott Fitzgerald was gay, but completely paranoid about people finding this out 2) Nick Carraway is also gay, and so therefore 3) Fitzgerald used Carraway's homosexuality – never explicitly stated – as a surrogate and mask for his own sexuality, a sexuality he could never reveal, could in fact, only obliquely hint at through the vessel of his fiction. Either that, or he was straight and really hated gays.

Now, by an incredible coincidence, at the same time that Wells was having his *Boon* induced-spat with James, he was also in the midst of what was to be a ten year affair with Henry James's biographer, Rebecca West. The two met after West wrote a not entirely favorable review of Wells' *Marriage* - the book James praises so enthusiastically in the above letter. So: Wells was forty-six years old and married when he wrote *Marriage,* which was published in 1911. West (who was nineteen at the time) didn't like *Marriage,* but Henry James did. By 1913 however, it was West, not James, who was sleeping with H.G. Wells. In 1914 they had a son (Wells was still married) and the next year *Boon* was published. 1916 saw the first appearance of West's James-friendly *Henry James* as well as the last appearance of Henry James, who died in February of that year.

To return to the fence incident (and the possible testicle crushing it resulted in) when, we justly ask, did this accident take place? In Edel claims a victory in solving this mystery:

It is clear that Henry James's blurring of the date of the hurt (the same dark hour" as the outbreak of the Civil War) served to, minimize his failure during the first six months to spring to the colors with other young men. To take his timing literally would fix the hurt as occurring in April or perhaps May of 1861. Had it occurred that spring, however, it is doubtful whether he would have climbed mountains in New Hampshire with T.S. Perry during July. Fortunately it is no longer necessary to speculate, since Perry comes to our assistance with specific dates. In a letter to James's nephew and executor, written shortly after publication of *Notes of a Son and Brother*, alluding directly to the "obscure hurt" passage, Perry wrote that "the fire at West Stables was in the night of Oct. 28, '61."

Edel goes on to give a description of the fire, based on newspaper records and the "official report written by one of the firemen" which is great, if we concur on the date he fixes for the fire. Sheldon Novick doesn't, and in a note in his book, he explains why:

Edel claimed that the strain occurred at a fire in a stable in October 1861, which was reported in the local press. Edel has psychoanalytic reasons for linking HJ's sense of injury to a fire very much like the one in which HJ Sr. lost his leg; but the evidence makes the coincidence extremely unlikely. There is no evidence HJ was at the fire in October, to begin with. HJ visited his brother William in Cambridge three days later, without apparent difficulty. William's letter home describing the visit says nothing about Harry's supposed back injury. In a family that monitored their own and each other's health as closely as the Jameses, it is not credible that Harry could have visited William, shortly after injuring his back, without provoking comment.

Like the exact nature of the accident, it seems the date will be forever shrouded in controversy. For my part, I'd like to offer what I think is a comprehensive list of the possibilities which exist with regard to the outcome of the accident and James' sexuality. I'm not going to comment on how each scenario might be seen to change how we "approach James' work": if James was a gay man who died an impotent virgin, you can read into that whatever you think is appropriate. Here's what came up with:

Let's say James was heterosexual: during the accident he was either left impotent, or he wasn't. If he was impotent this explains the lack of relations with women. If he wasn't rendered impotent, we can infer that either he just wasn't very lucky with the ladies, he did have sex with women (and we just don't know about it) or he choose to live a chaste life. Or maybe he was a straight man who had sex (or didn't) with women, but also fooled around with a few guys.

Now, if James was gay, than this explains the dearth of female companionship in his life. If he wasn't impotent then he could have had sex with Oliver Wendell Holmes or any other guys, and maybe a few gals. He could have also been physically able to engage in the sex act, but unwilling to do so, for whatever reason; in this instance, he would have died a gay, potent, virgin. Or maybe he was a gay man who only experimented sexually with women. Or maybe he was impotent but was still coupled with men (and women), giving oral pleasure, and/or taking it. This last conjecture is as far as I know, completely original to the canon of criticism on Henry James. Here's another theory I've been working on: the earliest dated reference I've seen of the impotence theory comes from Fitzgerald's letter to Van Wyck Brooks. What if the whole story was cooked up by Fitzgerald and Ernest Hemingway? It wouldn't have had to have been an intentionally deceitful thing. Maybe they were in bed together and Scott couldn't perform. This would have been caused by his internal turmoil about acting on his homosexual desires.

"Jesus," Ernest would say, "you really are like Henry James."

"I didn't know James was a fairy?"

"He wasn't. But didn't you ever hear about that accident he had? I think was a bicycle or something. . ."

As you know, libraries are hotbeds of sexual tension. I would sit with my books and look at the cuties and sometimes I thought they were smiling back at me. One time this old geezer sat down across from me. I looked his way and he smiled. Then he put on his shades. Then he tilted his head down so I could see his eyes and he smiled again. I don't know if he was making a pass but it made me realize that maybe the girls I was looking at thought I was creepy. I got up, in part to escape his penetrating gaze, and headed to the letters/

biographies section. I was going to look up some of Hemingway's and Fitzgerald's letters - by a lovely coincidence these books are ordered back to back - but when I got there, the books were gone! In all the time I'd been working, none of the books I'd wanted had been missing!

It occurred to me that perhaps not the entire library's other patrons were researching the genitals of famous authors. But if that was the case then what on earth were they doing? Why else would you need these books? I pondered this, but no answers were forthcoming and a thought hit me: A day or two earlier I had emailed Ames with information on the Hemingway connection; what if Ames was in the library, checking my handiwork? I was buzzed and I did a quick 360, checking out the immediate area. I pictured Ames keeping an eye on the shelf where the precious volumes were housed, so that if I came along, he'd know. I didn't know if he'd bolt when he saw me, or if he'd say hello. I walked briskly around the third floor, then raced up the stairs to the fifth floor, though I knew that if Ames had removed the books from the third floor, he would be in flagrant violation of library regulations. My plan was to make a pass on each floor and then go to the one below. Unless Ames was in the toilet I would spot him; if it wasn't him with the books I would get a look at whoever it was, and through that undoubtedly work out their motivation.

The fifth floor proved fruitless, though twice I thought I spotted him - but in both instances it turned out to be Asian men. (Ames is white.) I recognized a mustachioed Russian library worker who had been eager to assist me at an earlier visit, but I didn't think this was a case where he could help. As I walked around the fourth and then the third floor again, I wondered if I would even recognize Ames if I saw him. All I had to go on were the pictures on the back of his books. What if he looked different in real life? It occurred to me that that a metaphor for life.

The second floor was a bust too; this time the red herring was a black man reading the newspaper. I knew the first floor would be fruitless as there are no desks and few places to sit; Ames would have only used this area for his study if he was going out of his way to avoid being detected by me! The whole hunt had me high; the library didn't close for another few hours and I considered sticking around and waiting for Ames (or whoever it was) to return the books, but I knew that would mean crossing some line of weirdness I wasn't ready for.

Ames didn't take out the dumb books. What would he waste his time with that for? He had me to provide him with all the stupid testicle news he could possibly hope for. I left the library without seeing Ames and pretty sure he hadn't been there.

But heading home it occurred to me that I should have left some note in the spot where the books go, just in case. That would have been the thing to do, what they would have done in a movie. In the movie version I would have left a note and it would have said, "Enjoy the books, MR. J.AMES?"

Chapter 13

Cult of the Master

The story of Henry James's fruitless flirtation with the theater has been so often told that it has become folkloric, invoked and repeated by generations of marveling Jamesians. Everyone knows the tale of the first night, in London, of his historical play *Guy Domville* (1895) —how the nervous playwright spent the evening down the road at the Wildely successful new play *An Ideal Husband*, by James's despised rival, the "mechanical Oscar"; how he finally slipped into his own theater just as the performance was ending; how he was led on stage by the play's actor-manager, ostensibly to enjoy the curtain call but in reality to receive the boos and jeers of a large proportion of the audience; how a few moments earlier, when this same actor-manager had declaimed from the stage, "I'm the *last*, my lord, of the Domvilles!," a cry had come from the seats: "It's a bloody good thing y'are!"

Leon Edel, who tells this story well in his five-volume biography of James, fails to mention only one detail: that James's play was preceded in the same programme by a one-act comedy written by a certain Julian Field, titled *Too Happy By Half*. That tells us, in four words, what the mandarin moralist was up against in his quixotic campaign amid the lights of the West End; he had about as much chance with his audience as Don Quixote had with his gang of convicts. *Guy Domville* was his only original play to make it to the boards. He had loaded it with all his longing for popular success. He was never seriously involved in the theater again.

Few writers have been as reliably amnestied as Henry James. From the 1940s to the 1970s he was steadily enshrined as both the greatest American novelist and the most solid object of academic study. There was something cultish about the way modern American critics talked about "the Master" and his exquisite refinements; it was palpably painful for them to admit that James ever blotted a line. Edel's biography was the breviary of that cult, and it was Edel who—with some help from James himself—converted James's disastrous pursuit of theatrical success into a narrative of the novelist's failing at success but ultimately succeeding at failure. James, it was argued, took from his many wasted years of playwriting a new style of novel writing: one based on what he called the "divine principle of the Scenario." Plundering his own efforts at stagecraft, he began to cut away all extraneous detail, to write only in dramatic scenes, and to make his dialogue wholly germane to the thematic forwarding of the story.

The most glorious results of this late, post-theater period are the last novels: *The Wings of the Dove* (1902), *The Ambassadors* (1903), and *The Golden Bowl* (1904). But the immediate results, the first fruits, are *The Spoils of Poynton*, *What Maisie Knew*, and *The Awkward Age*, written from 1895 to 1899 and now collected, with *The Other House* (1896), in a useful single volume by The Library of America.

There is some justice in the idea that the theatrical experiment "rescued" James at a pivotal moment in his life. He had been interested for many years both in the theater and in certain popular novelists, especially those who wrote extensively in dialogue. "I have worked like a horse—far harder than anyone will ever know—over the whole mystery of 'technique,'" he wrote to William James, referring to his intense study of questions of dramaturgy. In 1882 he had turned *Daisy Miller* into a play, though it was never produced. In the early 1890s he was led toward Ibsen, whom he admired, though with the usual precise flutter of Jamesian qualifications: "so dry a view of life, so indifferent a vision of the comedy of things." Ibsen, he felt, wrote "moral tales in dialogue." James, one feels, wanted to write novels in dialogue and then stage them.

But it is still an open question—isn't it?—whether James

was a great writer of dialogue. He rightly complained that all Wilde's characters spoke like Wilde; but many of James's characters, especially in the late work, sound like James. The particular difficulty, and the difficult reward, of late James is the way in which he transfers his own acute sensitivity to verbal calibration onto his characters: they become Chief Justices of the word, forever raising to moral scrutiny certain anointed terms and phrases. This is what gives late James its strongly philosophical flavour.

Most readers learn not to read this speech as realistic dialogue and instead consider it as essentially continuous with all the other language that surrounds it on the page—a borderless region of inquiry. His fictional dialogue needs his fictional nondialogue to apologize for it, as it were. One can sense this just by looking at the way that James, even in the supposedly "dramatic" novels collected in this volume, is always restlessly confirming his characters' speech: "she passionately asseverated" (this is at one of the most obviously passionate moments of *What Maisie Knew*, when Maisie is clearly asseverating); "[she] wonderingly moaned"; "she helplessly wailed"; "she then simply ejaculated."

Orphaned from its larger family of prose, the dialogue in James's plays can seem precious, a silken music for cloth ears. Whatever the reason, popular success in the theater was never to come his way. In 1894 he published four unproduced plays—something of an admission of failure for a writer as distinguished and famous as James then was. By February of 1895, a month after the *Guy Domville* collapse, James had abandoned the theater and was beginning to speculate about how he might turn his recently acquired knowledge to fresh use. He wrote *The Spoils of Poynton* over the next several months and immediately afterward began work on *The Other House*, which was developed from a discarded play scenario. *What Maisie Knew* followed a year later, *The Turn of the Screw* (not part of this collection) in 1898, and *The Awkward Age* in 1899.

The four novels in this collection are indeed peculiar ones—and very peculiar ones to come from Flaubert's great (if critical) disciple, because they are distinctly anti-Flaubertian. Exposition, for example, is starved to a thin dramatic minimum, though people—or certain people—are flamboyantly and sharply described. The formidable and morally questionable women who dominate most of these novels—Mrs. Gereth in *The Spoils of Poynton,* Maisie's mother and stepmother in *What Maisie Knew,* and Mrs. Brookenham in *The Awkward Age* —are painted with fitting luridity. But James has hardly any interest here in setting up characters in the usual visual way, by piling details of clothing and gesture and face on top of one another. Instead he selects one or two attributes and then works them until a strange, grotesque essence is achieved.

He was clearly influenced in this by Dickens's genius for caricature, though he affected to have little time for Dickens. Thus Maisie's mother, Ida Farange, is seized, descriptively, by her eyes: "like Japanese lanterns swung under festive arches." Later in the book we read that "her huge eyes, her red lips, the intense marks in her face formed an illumination as distinct and public as a lamp set in a window."

One of her lovers, the unfortunate, heavily moustached Mr. Perriam, is seen as a Dickensian gargoyle: "He seemed also to have moustaches over his eyes, which, however, by no means prevented these polished little globes from rolling round the room as if they had been billiard-balls impelled by Ida's celebrated stroke." (Ida is known in society for her skill at billiards.)

If James's characters are allowed the odd descriptive donation, his settings are not. As in a play, most of them are domestic rooms, and these rooms are hardly mentioned. Only when an object, such as a picture, is important to the action is it included in the visual sweep.

Poynton, a great house full of immaculate treasures, has hardly any physical presence in the novel; we have to infer the beauty and preciousness of these "spoils" from the intensity with which the characters battle over them. In *What Maisie Knew,* Maisie is taken to the great Exhibition at Earl's Court, an event that Flaubert would have researched, as he researched the agricultural fair in *Madame Bovary*, to get the many details exactly right.

But James tosses off the entire spectacle in one sentence, as "a collection of extraordinary foreign things, in tremendous gardens, with illuminations, bands, elephants, switchbacks and side-shows." That's it, essentially. He is interested in what his subjects make of this show, not in what he, the writer, can make of it.

The result—for all that James's late style is thought of as a braided nest of interminable additions and qualifications—is in fact an art of great purification. It is striking just how much the novels do without. Focus is all, and the focus is only on what James once called (in his notebook) "something important ... something intimate, something vital." This is an art of the essence.

The reader, used to being fattened by Flaubert and Zola on big visual spreads, is forced to become a lean decipherer who must imagine the various visual contexts, using the characters as clues. The modernism of this style lies in its frank intellectualism, in its admission that reading has now become hermeneutic. If one mark of modernism is that it reveals the fragmentary, these novels sneakily inaugurate modernism in English.

Yet how good are they as novels? If it was difficult for the James cult of the 1950s to find fault with the Master, contemporary scholars are simply not interested in value judgment at all (they have smaller fish to fry), and the two sides are therefore oddly allied in obscuring a proper adjudication.

The old side winces to judge; the new side winces at those who do judge—and the field is left open to those complainers who simply find all of late James "unreadable" or "not worth the effort." Of the novels collected here, only *What Maisie Knew* seems a really great book.

The Other House is an unworthy melodrama; James himself somewhat disdained it. It has an uncharacteristic cruelty about it—quite the opposite atmosphere of the other three books, which represent tender arguments in defence of innocence. *The*

Awkward Age offers a powerful satire on the callousness of London society, and has at its centre a striking creation, the beautiful, striving, terrible Mrs. Brookenham.

But it lacks the relentless precision of *What Maisie Knew*. *The Spoils of Poynton*, a work of real penetration, is marred, I think, by an inadequate sense of the motivations of its heroine, Fleda Vetch.

Fleda, a young woman of considerable insight and intellect, is the new friend of Mrs. Gereth, the owner of Poynton. James got the idea for this novel—what he habitually called the *donnée*—at a dinner party; he dined out frequently and used these evenings to truffle for rich stories. His neighbour at the table had told him about a "small and ugly matter" in which a Scottish widow was suing her son over the fine furniture he had inherited, which she would not let him have.

Mrs. Gereth, like the Scottish widow, has become embroiled in a struggle with her son, Owen, who is about to marry the vulgar, nouveau riche Mona Brigstock. Under English law, once Owen marries, he and his wife will become master and mistress of Poynton.

In general, James's characters divide into gentle but weak men; formidable and finally monstrous manipulators (mostly women, but sometimes men); and those whose innocence needs to be protected (sometimes young women, sometimes young men, sometimes children). Mrs. Gereth is one of the manipulators, like Madame Merle in *The Portrait of a Lady* and Aunt Maud in *The Wings of the Dove*. She cannot bear the idea of the brash Mona in charge of her beautiful *objets*, and determines to act.

Her weapon—at first unwitting, and then unwilling—will be young Fleda, whom she takes under her wing. Mrs. Gereth becomes excited when she hears that Owen and Mona have not yet agreed on a date for the wedding, and assumes that something is amiss with this detestable union. She sees that Fleda is attracted to her son, and soon hears that Owen returns the attraction. She decides to use Fleda as a wedge between Owen and Mona, so that he might eventually marry the malleable Fleda. The spoils would then be in safe hands once again.

But goodness always works dialectically in James, forcing ironic reversals. Fleda is very bright and very good; precisely because she comes to Owen, and Owen to her, she feels she must resist Mrs. Gereth's machinations. Fleda declares that she will accept Owen only if Mona releases him from his bond. She has a hunch—a moral hunch—that Owen does not love her as freely as he says he does, that he is making a fuss over her in part because of the pressure from his mother. And indeed, given a free choice, Owen, a weak, bumbling, honorable fellow, does return to Mona, and Fleda, once so near to what she desires (she truly adores Owen), loses it forever.

The Spoils of Poynton, *What Maisie Knew*, and *The Awkward Age* all close with acts of apparent renunciation, in which the heroines reject happiness in favor of good. In *What Maisie Knew* this gesture has a truly paradoxical power. We feel that Maisie's innocence is very much worth defending, and has already been so badly damaged that any bargain that might salvage it—even at the cost of her obvious and immediate happiness—is worth accepting. But Fleda is a contradictory moral presence. She is supposed to be clever, sensitive, the proper point of view of the novel. Yet she is in thrall to wickedness.

Though James is critical of Mrs. Gereth's materialism (her treasures are, after all, called *spoils*), in the end he and the novel seem too ready to agree with Mrs. Gereth's sense that the spoils merit the commotion that ensued. The highly moral Fleda consistently—like the novel itself—conflates mere acquisitiveness (Mrs. Gereth's good taste) with virtuous behaviour. She reflects that "To have created such a place was to have had dignity enough; when there was a question of defending it the fiercest attitude was the right one." And later: "[Owning the spoils] was not the crude love of possession; it was the need to be faithful to a trust and loyal to an idea. The idea was surely noble."

One view might be that James wants us to see Fleda as somewhat naive, duped by her very virtuousness into becoming the agent of stealthy wickedness. But this is hard to square with the powerful intelligence and tact those Fleda otherwise shows in her analysis of the situation. And if James is perhaps inviting us to judge, even to disapprove of, Fleda's final renunciation (I doubt it, but the notion is worth entertaining), then it is still hard to read it as tragic, given our dim view of her earlier surrender to Mrs. Gereth. Many of James's heroes and heroines almost destroy themselves in their strenuous efforts at moral self-cleansing. But we feel that Fleda should have been bright enough, and good enough, to resist getting so dirty in the first place.

Early in 1896 James complained of pain in his right (writing) wrist, and in February of the next year he hired a stenographer, William MacAlpine. A lot has been said about the connection between James's dictation to MacAlpine at the typewriter and his famous late sentences—those beautiful, maddening, loaded convoys.

Leon Edel wrote that James's friends swore they could identify the very chapter in *What Maisie Knew* that marked his new method of writing. But *The Spoils of Poynton,* written before MacAlpine's arrival, has its share of fairly appalling sentences ("I may not perhaps too much diminish the merit of that generosity if I mention that it could take the flight we are considering just because really, with the telescope of her long thought, Fleda saw what might bring her out of the wood"), and the speedy and compact *What Maisie Knew* in fact has very few.

What Maisie Knew is both deeply affecting and technically remarkable, a novel whose plot races ahead like a drawing-room comedy's but leaves a wake of grief wherever it goes. Like *The Awkward Age,* it is a scathing swipe at London high society, here figured in the dreadful husband and wife—now divorced—Beale and Ida Farange. The novel (also powered by a dinner-party *donnée*) opens with the couple's divorce and their decision, enforced by the court, to share custody of their daughter. Young Maisie (who is seven or eight) must spend six months a year at each parent's London house, back and forth. The arrangement is complicated by the parents' loathing of each other and by the moral irregularity of their households; Beale and Ida pile up lovers like dirty dishes.

James tells the story in what seems like conventional third-person narration but is really a way of seeing everything through Maisie's wide eyes. The effort to be faithful to a young girl's vision prompts James to create extraordinary and wonderful effects. Each parent's household is seen as if on the canvas of a German Expressionist. Her father's house is a blurred picture of men with cigarettes and bared teeth, who are forever pinching and patting Maisie: "Her features had somehow become prominent; they were so perpetually nipped by the gentlemen who came to see her father and the smoke of whose cigarettes went into her face." Her mother's is characterized by endless "shrieks" from Ida's friends, and by secrecy: "Everything had something behind it: life was like a long, long corridor with rows of closed doors."

Maisie's life becomes even harder when her father and mother both remarry. Ida marries the gentle and wise Sir Claude; Beale marries Maisie's glamorous governess, Miss Overmore. Maisie is fond of both of these new additions. But relationships last no longer than a chapter or two in this novel, and before long Sir Claude and Miss Overmore have left their respective spouses and have fallen in love with each other. Throughout the novel adults use Maisie for their own purposes, even while congratulating themselves on not doing just that. Sir Claude and Miss Overmore promise to look after Maisie as neither her mother nor her father can. But Maisie rightly suspects (like Fleda, she has a moral hunch) that Sir Claude and his lover really care more for each other than they do for her.

Maisie, abandoned by her parents, finally has to choose between this handsome and apparently loving couple and the dowdy, self-righteous Mrs. Wix, her new governess, who strongly disapproves of the liaison between Sir Claude and Miss Overmore (they are not yet married), and who longs to take Maisie away from the moral dishevelment she has witnessed. Very subtly, James makes Mrs. Wix noble but unlikeable. She is lower-class, dresses poorly, and knows very little, yet she is the only character in the novel who loves Maisie as a *mother* would—and that is because she lost her own little daughter, Clara Matilda, in a road accident years earlier. Maisie feels that Mrs. Wix is safe, "as safe as Clara Matilda, who was in heaven and yet, embarrassingly, also in Kensal Green, where they had been together to see her little huddled grave."

That last sentence is a perfect example of James's mastery of technique. What appears to be third-person storytelling is in fact much closer to first-person narration, so saturated is it with Maisie's language and vision. "Embarrassingly." Whose adverb is that? It is the word Maisie would have used to herself, dragged by poor Mrs. Wix to visit her daughter's grave.

The technical term for this kind of thing, in which the author inflects third-person narration with the language of a particular character, is "free indirect style," and James uses it systematically and devastatingly throughout this novel, to keep close to Maisie's knowledge and Maisie's sensibility. Nothing is more powerful in this novel than the moment when Maisie, out walking one day with Sir Claude, sees her mother in the park with a strange man, clearly a new lover, identified only as the Captain.

As Sir Claude and Ida talk, the Captain eventually leads Maisie to a couple of chairs under a tree. He assures her that it is not as bad as it looks, that her mother has had a hard life, that above all she is "true." Maisie is deeply moved, and seizes on this word. Tears fill her eyes, and she says to the Captain, "Oh, do you love her?" The Captain assures her stiffly that he does. It was an almost incredible balm—it soothed so her impression of danger and pain. She sank back in her chair; she covered her face with her hands. "Oh, mother, mother, mother!" she sobbed ... "Say you love her, Mr. Captain; say it, say it!" she implored.

The Captain again assures her that he loves her mother. "Then don't do it only for just a little," begs this extraordinary and damaged child. A moment later she has returned to Sir Claude's side and is cheerfully denying that anything much took place between her and the Captain. Maisie knows what she knows—and in a world of secrets, she knows how to keep her own. When she chooses to spend the rest of her childhood with Mrs. Wix, the reader rejoices.

This Library of America selection, impeccably edited by Myra Jehlen, presents just the texts themselves, with a minimum of notes and no introduction. The enterprise, like Henry James's charge into the West End, seems quixotic; it suggests a faith in the interests, not to mention the capacities, of the common reader that may turn out to be sweetly superstitious.

We shall see. Still, it is welcome, and adds permanence to permanence, enshrining these now canonical works in this now canonical library.

Chapter 14

On The Turn of the Screw

Any history of the criticism of The Turn of the Screw should begin with a discussion of Henry James's own statements about what is arguably his most enigmatic and controversial work.

The first point to be made is that James did not come down unequivocally on one side or the other of the central controversy concerning The Turn of the Screw—focused by Edmund Wilson's famous assertion (in his 1934 essay) that "the ghosts are not real ghosts at all but merely the governess's hallucinations". Indeed, James's statements on that score are perhaps as enigmatic as the novella itself.

For example, in the Preface to Volume 12 of the New York Edition of The Novels and Tales of Henry James (the volume in which The Turn of the Screw appears in definitive form), James asserts his intention to avoid "the new type... [of ghost story], the mere modern 'psychical' case, washed clean of all queerness as by exposure to a flowing laboratory tap, and equipped with credentials vouching for this".

One problem with this quotation is the meaning of the word "psychical." The American Heritage Dictionary lists two quite different definitions of "psychic... Also psychical": "of or pertaining to the human mind or psyche"; and "of or pertaining to extraordinary, especially extrasensory and nonphysical, mental processes ... proceeding from, produced by, or responding to such processes."

Seizing on the latter definition and apparently oblivious of the former, Edmund Wilson — perhaps the Freudian non-apparitionist par excellence — in his 1934 essay argues that the ghosts of Quint and Jessel are not "those in cases of psychic research". Similarly, Leon Edel, who also reads the story psychoanalytically, in his Introduction to The Ghostly Tales of Henry James interprets this passage in James's Preface as a devaluation of any story "too closely resembling a case history out of psychical research" because such material would be "unusable to a literary artist". On the contrary, James's ghost stories, says Edel, "constitute a series of psychological case histories of disturbed and frightened people" — in this instance,

the testimony of a horrified little governess away from home for the first time in her life who has fantasies which may or may not be founded on reality, but which partake of reality as far as she is concerned. At the other end of the spectrum, Glen A. Reed, assuming the other definition of the word "psychical," cites the very same passage from James as evidence that the author of The Turn of the Screw would have opposed non-apparitionist readings:

if the evils and the ghosts are able to escape as mere hallucinations of the governess ... if we treat the story as a psychological study in sexual frustration, as Mr. Wilson suggests, then James is guilty of attempting to write the very type of modern 'psychical' case he scorned. The situation is further complicated by the fact that both Henry James and his brother William had a lifelong interest in both mental illness and paranormal phenomena — i.e., a lifelong interest in the "psychical" in each of the senses given.

Later, however, in the same Preface, James specifically discusses scientific investigations of paranormal phenomena. I had ... for instance simply to renounce all attempts to keep the kind and degree of impression I wished to produce on terms with the today so copious psychical record of cases of apparitions. This seems clear enough upon a first reading, yet upon further reflection difficulties arise.

James's main objection to the ghosts of psychical research seems to be their inactive and innocuous quality — i.e., they cannot terrify because they do so little. His remarks on this matter are worth citing at some length:

Different signs and circumstances, in the reports, mark these cases; different things are done—though on the whole very little appears to be—by the persons appearing; the point is, however, that some things are never done at all: this negative quality is large—certain reserves and proprieties and immobilities consistently impose themselves. Recorded and attested 'ghosts' are in other words as little expressive, as little dramatic, above all as little continuous and conscious and responsive, as is consistent with their taking the trouble—and an immense trouble they find it, we gather—to appear at all. Wonderful and interesting therefore at a given moment, they are inconceivable figures in an action—and The Turn of the Screw was an action, desperately, or it was nothing. I had to decide in fine between having my apparitions correct and having my story 'good'—that is producing my impression of the dreadful, my designated horror.

Good ghosts, speaking by book, make poor subjects, and it was clear that from the first my hovering prowling blighting presences, my pair of abnormal agents, would have to depart altogether from the rules. They would be agents in fact; there would be laid on them the dire duty of causing the situation to reek with an air of Evil. Their desire and their ability to do so, visibly measuring meanwhile their effect, together with their observed and described success—this was exactly my central idea; so that, briefly, I cast my lot with pure romance, the appearances conforming to the true type being so little romantic.

The meaning of this passage for the interpretation of the story is quite puzzling. Upon a first consideration James seems to be asserting that the ghosts are objective entities—not hallucinations—but entities different in kind from those studied by the Society for Psychical Research, of which his brother William was president for two years. However, as Francis X. Roellinger and E. A. Sheppard point out, Quint and Jessel are very much like the apparitions frequently studied by the Society. As a matter of fact, they particularly resemble the scientific apparitions in that "very little appear to be [done] by the persons appearing" in The Turn of the Screw. Quint and Jessel never speak, perform any noteworthy actions, or even approach the governess or the children; they each time simply appear and stare at the governess or at one of the children. For example, recall the governess's conversation with Mrs. Grose in chapter five immediately following the second appearance of Quint in chapter four. In their discussion of the first apparition, Mrs. Grose asks, "What was he doing on the tower?" The governess answers, "Only standing there and staring down at me".

Later, in chapter seven, describing to Mrs. Grose the first appearance of Jessel, the governess says, "She just appeared and stood there...". Indeed, it sometimes seems that one of the most eerie things about Quint is that he does so little. In relating her vision of Quint on the staircase just before dawn the governess goes out of her way to stress this point:

It was the dead silence of our long gaze at such close quarters that gave the whole horror, huge as it was, its only note of the unnatural. If I had met a murderer in such a place and at such an hour we still at least would have spoken. Something would have passed in life between us; if nothing had passed one of us would have moved.

Roellinger goes so far as to assert that Quint and Jessel "conform precisely" to the typical patterns found in psychical research:

In the majority of cases reported to the Society, the ghost does not appear at any known fixed time of day or year. It is usually seen distinctly 'in all kinds of light; from broad daylight to the faint light of dawn.' It is described in detail, and appears 'in such clothes as are now, or have recently been, worn by living persons.' ... Sudden death, 'often either murder or suicide, appears to be connected with the cause of the apparition' in many cases .... If several persons are together when the ghost appears, 'it will sometimes be seen by all and sometimes not, and failure to see it is not always merely the result of not calling attention to it'.

It is easy to see how closely Quint and Jessel fit the above criteria. The ghosts appear in both summer and fall and in various kinds of light. Quint appears on the tower near twilight, outside the parlor window in late afternoon (chapter four), on the staircase before dawn (chapter nine), and outside the dining room window while Miles and the governess are having their evening meal (chapter twenty- four). Miss Jessel appears by the lake twice in the middle of the afternoon (chapter six and chapter twenty), once in the schoolroom in the middle of the afternoon (chapter fifteen), and once on the staircase shortly before dawn (chapter ten). Quint's clothes are described in considerable detail, and it is partly on the basis of this description that Mrs. Grose is able to identify the man the governess claims to have seen.

Both Quint and Jessel have died recently and perhaps violently when the apparitions begin—Quint in an apparent accident which may have been a murder, and Miss Jessel possibly through suicide or as a result of complications of childbirth. Miss Jessel's final appearance is not seen by Mrs. Grose, even though the governess frantically calls her attention to the apparition, and the governess frequently suspects that Quint and Jessel are in the same room with herself and the children, unseen by the governess but in full communication with her "little charges."

"AGENTS IN FACT" AND THE "ACTION OF THE STORY"

How then are we to interpret the author's disclaimer that Quint and Jessel are ghosts of psychical research? In view of the above striking parallels, Roellinger suggests that James viewed the story as an interesting tour de force, an attempt to recreate ... 'a lost form,' and rouse, as he puts it, 'the dear old sacred horror' [sic] without departing any more than artistically necessary from the then current knowledge of psychical phenomena.

Since the ghosts are never seen to perform any extraordinary physical actions, the nature of this departure, it seems to me, and the source of the "dear old sacred terror" must be the effect the ghosts have on people—i.e., on the governess and on the children. The anguish of the governess, the moral deterioration of the children leading to Miles's expulsion from school and Flora's obscene ravings near the story's end—these are effects which might distinguish Quint and Jessel from "psychical case" ghosts whom they otherwise resemble. Thus, the destruction of the children is the central "action"—"The Turn of the Screw was an action, desperately, or it was nothing"—and, because the ghosts are responsible for this destruction, they are "agents in fact" and they fulfill their "dire duty of causing the situation to reek with an air of Evil."

Such a view is consistent with James's remarks about ghost stories in the Preface to Volume 17 of the New York Edition of The Novels and Tales of Henry James:

... the safest arena for the play of ... strange encounters, or whatever odd matters, is the field ... rather of their second than of their first exhibition. By which, to avoid obscurity, I mean nothing more cryptic than I feel myself show them best by showing almost exclusively the way they are felt, by recognizing as their main interest some impression strongly made by them and intensely received.

This is Glenn A. Reed's interpretation of James's insistence that the ghosts are "agents in fact": "... the ghosts carry the burden of creating an atmosphere of horror and of exerting the worst possible action on the children ...". Charles G. Hoffman, another apparitionist critic, comments thus on James's remarks on "psychical" apparitions:

Peter Quint and Miss Jessel are not 'stage' ghosts who clank chains and whirl across the stage in white sheets in order to frighten a character and thrill an audience. They are agents who create an atmosphere of evil. It is their evil effect, not their appearance, that is important ("Innocence and Evil" 102)

Likewise, Robert Heilman sees the central "action" of the story as "the children ... our sense of what is happening to them." He continues, What is happening to them is Quint and Jessel; the governess's awareness of the apparitions is her awareness of a change within the children; the shock of ghostly appearances is the shock of evil perceived unexpectedly, suddenly, after it has secretly made inroads ("Poem" 178).

Since Heilman reads the story as a moral and religious

allegory, he sees the ghosts as "symbolic ghosts". According to him, they differ form the ghosts of psychical research in that "we are never permitted to see the apparitions except as moral realities". We might assume, then, that—because of their similarities to the ghosts of the psychical research current at the end of the nineteenth century—Quint and Jessel are not hallucinations but objective entities, differing from the former type of apparitions in the evil effects they produce on the human beings who come in contact with them.

However, if the governess's visions resemble paranormal apparitions—as Roellinger and Sheppard have pointed out—they also resemble the hallucinations of mentally ill people—as Cranfill and Clark, Harold C. Goddard, M. Katan, M.D., C. Knight Aldrich, M.D., and Oscar Cargill have demonstrated in detail. All of these critics have pointed out the "intense hush" or abnormal silence that accompanies the visions and the fact that they seem to come in response to the governess's needs—e.g., she sees Quint for the first time while she is daydreaming about the employer; she sees Miss Jessel in the schoolroom when she is preparing to leave Bly after her disastrous confrontation with Miles on the way to church and is probably subconsciously looking for an excuse to stay; she sees Miss Jessel by the lake for the last time and Quint by the dining room window for the last time when she is doubting her own interpretation of the events at Bly and needs the ghosts for reassurance. Discussing her last vision of Miss Jessel, the governess tells us,

> She was there, and I was justified; she was there, and I was neither cruel nor mad ... I consciously threw out to her—with the sense that, pale and ravenous demon as she was, she would catch and understand it—an inarticulate message of gratitude.

And, before the final vision of Quint, the governess appears beset by anxiety and guilt which only some definitive proof of Miles's depravity—e.g., an appearance of Quint—can alleviate: "If he were innocent, what then on earth was I?". Cargill, in both of his studies, presents detailed analogies linking the history, psychology, and behaviour of the governess with one of Freud's case histories and also with the schizophrenic reaction of the author's sister, Alice James. The psychiatrist Katan compliments James for demonstrating in this story "an imagination which conceived a picture very close to the description of hallucinations as they occur in our patients".

Viewing the ghosts as hallucinations does not preclude our seeing them as "agents in fact" who fulfill the "dire duty of causing the situation to reek witn an air of Evil." Indeed, as we contemplate the disasters which end the story of Bly, we are "visibly measuring ... their effect, together with their observed and described success," for, if the children have been destroyed by an insane governess, certainly it can be said that Quint and Jessel—the "abnormal agents" of her diseased mind, the "hovering prowling blighting presences" of her hallucinations have succeeded in "causing the situation to reek with an air of evil."

Numerous critics have seen the "action" of the story—"The Turn of the Screw was an action, desperately, or it was nothing," —as the destruction of the children through the agency of an insane, possessed, or self-deluded governess. Harold C. Goddard, one of the pioneers of non-apparitionist Turn of the Screw criticism, considers the story "one of the most powerful ever written ... dreadful, but also beautiful." He asks, Are Peter Quint and Miss Jessel a whit less mysterious or less appalling because they are evoked by the governess's imagination? Are they a whit less real? Surely the human brain is as solid a fact as the terrestrial globe, and inhabitants of the former have just as authentic an existence as inhabitants of the latter.

John Lydenberg also holds that the "action" of the story is the destruction of the children through the agency of a deluded governess: "What is happening to the children is clearly and terribly the governess herself. Similarly, Oscar Cargill refers to "the central motif in his story, the horror of children betrayed by their protectress". Cargill considers Douglas's reference to "Griffin's ghost or whatever it was" to be an expression of doubt concerning the supernatural and an indication that his own story will be about ghosts of another kind—i.e., about creations of a hysterical mind.

We find, then, in James's critical remarks no clear and unequivocal stand concerning the nature of the apparitions which infect the atmosphere at Bly, "causing the situation to reek with an air of Evil." We cannot, however, dismiss the question as non-essential, for, while James has been primarily interested in their effect on the governess and the children—"I feel myself show them best by showing almost exclusively the way they are felt, by recognizing as their main interest some impression strongly made by them and intensely received"—almost any interpretation of the meaning of the story hinges on the question of the reality of the apparitions and their relationship to the governess. In Goddard's words,

This is the crucial point. Everything else is incidental. Believe that the children saw, and the tale is one thing. Believe that they did not see, and it is another—as different as light from darkness. The reader is called upon to respond to what has happened to the children and their governess, and the reader's response will vary, depending on whether the tale is perceived as "a tale of corrupted childhood" or "a tale of incorruptible childhood", depending on whether the governess is "an innocent mad woman" or as a "savior, not only in a general sense, but with certain Christian associations". The answers to these questions in turn depend on the answer to the prior question: Are the ghosts objectively real and evil entities, or do they exist only in the mind of the governess? To this question James gives no definite answer.

"A FAIRY TALE PURE AND SIMPLE"

James made several references to fairy tales in his discussions of The Turn of the Screw. In the Preface to Volume 17 of the New York Edition of The Novels and Tales of Henry James, James cites the "straight fairy tale" as the "ideal" type of story for "the creation of alarm and suspense and surprise and relief ... that blest faculty of wonder..." He then contends that the ghost story,' as we for conscience call it, has ever been for me the most possible form of the fairy tale. It enjoys, to my eyes, this honour by being so much the neatest—neat with that neatness without which representation, and therewith beauty, drops.

In the Preface to Volume 12 James terms The Turn of the Screw "a fairy tale pure and simple" and adds that it belongs to the sub-category of "the short and sharp and single, charged more or less with the compactness of anecdote (as to which let the familiar tales of our childhood, `Cinderella' and `Blue Beard' and `Hop o' My Thumb' and `Little Red Riding Hood' and many of the gems of the Brothers Grimm directly testify)," rather than to the other subcategory, the long and loose, the copious, the various, the endless, where, dramatically speaking, roundness is quite sacrificed—sacrificed to fullness, sacrificed to exuberance, if one will: witness at hazard almost any one of the Arabian Nights.

Finally, after the discussion of the insufficiencies of "psychical ghosts," James asserts that, Peter Quint and Miss Jessel are not `ghosts' at all, as we now know the ghost, but goblins, elves, imps, demons as loosely constructed as those of the old trials for witchcraft; if not, more pleasing, fairies of the legendary order, wooing their victims forth to see them dance under the moon. Like other Jamesian statements about The Turn of the Screw, these remarks about fairy tales can be variously interpreted. Glenn A. Reed, for example, cites these statements as evidence that James considered the apparitions to be real entities and the governess to be a reliable narrator of "objective horror with no attempt to explain it away."

According to Reed, There is hardly a fairy story that does not contain objective, pictorial evil—evil that is in the world for no good reason and that lures innocent victims to their doom. This interpretation makes it as unnecessary to explain the demons as psychological phenomena as it would be to explain in psychological terms how a wolf could dress up in woman's clothing and talk to Little Red Riding Hood. Reed admits that the story contains quite a bit of ambiguity and quite a few unanswered questions (for example, the reason for Miles's expulsion from school and the causes of Quint's and Jessel's deaths), but he sees in the story no justification for the critical controversies concerning the reliability of the governess.

There are, as in fairy stories, many questions left unanswered. James uses the technique of the fairy tale in leading the reader on step by step to accept impossible happenings without ever attempting a rational explanation of them. Thus if there is little possibility of ambiguity of interpretation regarding the governess, there is intentional and calculated lack of explicitness in identifying the evils that pervade the story. To James this obscurity was of the utmost importance in allowing the reader's imagination fertile ground in which to pullulate. Edmund Wilson, on the other hand, in his 1934 essay, chooses to emphasize James's remark that the story's supernatural entities are "as loosely constructed as those of the old trials for witchcraft."

Wilson seems to be comparing the governess to those fanatical witch hunters of the Inquisition and the seventeenth century Salem trials, for, in the next paragraph, he interprets James's statements that the governess has "`authority,' which is a good deal to have given her" as meaning that she is able to inflict on others "her somber and guilty visions" because of "the relentless English `authority' which enables her to put over on inferiors even purposes which are totally deluded and not at all in the other people's best interests". Leon Edel, in discussing the same remarks of James, points out that the fairy tales James specifically mentioned were all "psychological": "Little Red Riding Hood," "Hop o' My Thumb," "Cinderella," and "Blue Beard."

The governess is, like Cinderella, a "daydreaming daughter" who has "rivals in the family circle," and the employer is her Prince Charming. The sexually repressed governess is tortured by insatiable curiosity like Blue Beard's wife Fatima. Finally, although James did not specifically mention "Hansel and Gretel" in connection with The Turn of the Screw, Edel sees in the governess "some of the attributes of a witch." The orphaned children depend on the governess just as Hansel and Gretel, abandoned by their parents, depend on the hospitality of the witch in her house made of gingerbread, cakes, and sugar. The governess, like a witch, is "a persistent, badgering, prying creature" who contributes to the destruction of the children.

Yet another interpretation was offered by Oscar A. Cargill in 1956. According to Cargill, while James cited the "public source" of the story as his conversation with Archbishop Benson at Addington on January 10, 1895, the "private source" was the case history of his mentally ill sister, Alice James. James's way of "shielding Alice's memory" was the employment of "seemingly artless phrases as 'my bogey-tale,' 'irresponsible little fiction,' and 'fairy tale pure and simple,' behind which he could hide".

GUARDIAN ANGEL OR "FALSE FRIEND"

Concerning the governess herself, James made several statements which are susceptible to more than one interpretation. For example, in a letter to H.G. Wells dated December 9, 1898, James appears to give the governess a rather flattering character reference and to vouch for the authenticity of her account:

...I had, about my young woman, to take a very sharp line. The grotesque business I had to make her picture and the childish psychology I had to make her trace and present, were, for me at least, a very difficult job, in which absolute lucidity and logic, a singleness of effort, were imperative. Therefore I had to rule out subjective complications of her own—play of tone, etc., and keep her impersonal save for the most obvious and indispensable little note of neatness, firmness, and courage—without which she wouldn't have had her data.

Glenn A. Reed and Oliver Evans both cite this passage as evidence that James considered the central point of interest in the story to be not the governess and her "subjective complications," but rather the supernatural entities whose activities she accurately reports. On the other hand, however, Goddard reminds us that the "neatness, firmness, and courage" which James ascribes to his heroine do not necessarily require us to accept her account of events because "mental aberration may go hand in hand with strength and beauty of character". Goddard also reads this passage in the light of "a very charming and good-humored, but a nonetheless very unmistakable, side-stepping of questions or comments which had evidently been flung at him" by those correspondents with whom James exchanged letters about The Turn of the Screw.

As evidence he cites James's repeated depreciation of the story in these letters. Goddard perhaps also should have mentioned James's reply to a question of F.W.H. Myers: ...I scarce know what to say to you on the subject on which you wrote, especially as I'm afraid I don't quite understand the principal question you put to me about 'The Turn of the Screw.' However, that scantily matters; for in truth I am afraid I have on some former occasions rather awkwardly signified to you that I somehow can't pretend to give any coherent account of my small inventions 'after the fact'.

Edna Kenton and Oscar Cargill see such positive references to the governess as attempts by James to mislead readers concerning her real nature. In this connection, Edna Kenton reminds us of James's criticism of Thackeray for not sufficiently "loving" his character Becky in Vanity Fair and his praise of Balzac because, in Kenton's words, "Balzac loved his Valerie; he did not expose her; his instinct was to cover her, to protect her..." She suggests that James is never so guileful, so suave and so honied as when he is busily engaged in `protecting.' ...if one is making a collection of his agents of evil, they are not to be found among those endowed with the usual stripes and markings; he loves them even more than Balzac loved his Valerie, and protects them with far finer dexterity.

Cargill, of course, maintains that James attempted to deceive his readers in order to "protect" the mentally ill Alice James, whose case history is one of the story's principal sources. James's letter to Paul Bourget dated August 19, 1898 seems to be a negative evaluation of the work itself (James calls the story "a poor little pot-boiling story of nothing at all"), but it can also be read as an unflattering appraisal of the governess and a denial of the veracity of her account of events. In this story, he says, "Something I have supposed to be a subject turns out on trial really to be none." Does James mean that he began to write a ghost story, but, as the creative process proceeded, the ghosts ceased to be real ghosts, and the governess's account ceased to be a true one? He then says, "The small book in question is really but an exercise in the art of not appearing to oneself to fail".

James could, of course, be referring to his own failure as an artist; he could also, however, be referring to the failure of the mission of a self-deluded governess bent on saving the children from what are, in the last analysis, only her own hallucinations and delusions. James is similarly ambiguous in his letter to Dr. Waldstein dated October 21, 1898: he refers to "the exposure, indeed, the helpless plasticity of childhood that isn't dear or sacred to somebody" and adds, "That was my little tragedy...". Robert Carlton Cole observes that this statement "can be used against the governess" but adds that the word was suggests a possible change—that the author's original intention and his interpretation of the finished work were not the same. Oliver Evans, on the other hand, after citing this passage form the letter to Dr. Waldstein, concludes, That was, indeed, the tragedy: the corruption of the two children by the living servants, and the possession (in the supernatural sense) of them afterwards by the ghosts of those same servants.

This passage, of course, could also easily "be used against" Mrs. Grose in support of the interpretation of C. Knight Aldrich, M.D., who sees the housekeeper as a villain who deliberately takes advantage of the governess's initial instability and drives her into insanity out of possessive jealously toward the children. We might add, also, that this passage can be construed as an indictment of the absent and indifferent uncle—as in the interpretation of John Lydenberg, among others.

The same ambiguity appears in the Preface to Volume 12 of the New York Edition of The Novels and Tales in the course of James's discussion of the reader's response to The Turn of the Screw. He refers there to the reader's "own sympathy (with the children) and horror (of their false friends)". Cole interprets "false friends" as "the governess and Mrs. Grose". On the other hand, Glenn A. Reed, Oliver Evans, and Charles G. Hoffmann also cite this passage but assume that the children's "false friends" are Quint and Jessel.

And, finally, in the Preface to Volume 12 of the New York Edition, James seems simultaneously to give with one hand and take back with the other:

It was 'deja tres-joli,' in 'The Turn of the Screw,' please believe, the general proposition of our young woman's keeping crystalline her record of so many intense anomalies and obscurities—by which I don't, of course, mean her explanation of them; a different matter; and I saw no way, I feebly grant (fighting, at the best, too, periodically, for every grudged inch of my space) to exhibit her in relations other than those; one of which, precisely, would have been her relation to her own nature. We have surely as much of her own nature as we can swallow in watching it reflected in her anxieties and inductions. It constitutes no little of a character indeed, in such conditions, for a young person, as she says, 'privately bred,' that she is able to make her particular credible statement of such strange matters. She has 'authority,' which is a good deal to have given her, and I couldn't have achieved so much had I clumsily tried for more.

James terms the governess's account of the events at Bly "crystalline," but then seems to suggest that her interpretation may be faulty. This could mean that she accurately describes her own thoughts and visions (which may be hallucinations) and the words and actions of herself and others but is deceived about the realty of the apparitions and the corruption of the children. This is the view of Edmund Wilson. "..... these words seem impossible to explain," he says, in his 1934 essay, "except on the hypothesis of hallucination".

Glenn A. Reed, on the other hand, cites the same passage in the course of arguing for a straightforward supernatural interpretation in which the governess is the hero. "...her job is to keep a clear record of these strange happenings at Bly, but she is not to explain them away..." Rather, says Reed, she "records, yet is mystified," in order to "keep the reader held to the very end in the vise of expectant disclosure" as the reader of fairy-tales is led "on step by step to accept impossible happenings without ever attempting a rational explanation of them." We find here, says Reed, "as in fairy stories, many questions left unanswered".

Expanding on the latter point, Roellinger reminds us that members of the Society for Psychical Research frequently considered many different theoretical explanations for what were considered bona fide apparitions. Anent that, of course, Muriel West ("Death" 288) maintains that the governess, not the children, is possessed by the evil spirits. Similarly, John Lydenberg contends that the ghosts—some of whose activities the governess accurately records—are evoked by her own mediumistic powers because of her subconscious need for them, a need rooted in her pride and sense of mission, as well as in her attraction to the uncle. Consequently, in Lydenberg's words, "Just as her words suggest that somehow she calls up the ghosts, and with them the evil, so they suggest that she imposes the meaning upon the events". This is also the position of Katherine Anne Porter.

James's assertion that he did not intend to "exhibit" the governess "in relation to her own nature" has been cited by some critics—for example, Oliver Evans — as evidence that James did not see the psychological problems of the governess as the central focus of the story but rather saw the governess as an objective narrator of supernatural events. Their position seems to be undercut, however, by James's next statement: "We surely have as much of her own nature as we can swallow in watching it reflected in her anxieties and inductions." We have already noted Edmund Wilson's interpretation of the passage's last sentence as an indictment of unreasonable "English authority" as exercised by the governess. This interpretation, however, is vigorously disputed by other critics—for example, Oliver Evans, who insists that James "does not mean that the governess has authority where the children are concerned but where the reader is".

"TO CATCH THOSE NOT EASILY CAUGHT"

There has also been considerable controversy about

James's categorization of the story as a piece of ingenuity pure and simple, of cold artistic calculation, an amusette to catch those not easily caught (the fund of the capture of the merely witless being ever but small), the faded, the disillusioned, the fastidious. In 1924 Edna Kenton quoted this passage to suggest that James saw the story as she did and delighted in catching even otherwise very discerning readers in the vise of an apparitionist interpretation, while rewarding the most astute, such as Edna Kenton, with the pleasure of divining the real secret—"not the children but the little governess was haunted by the ghosts".

Nathan Bryllion Fagin agrees with Kenton that the surface structure of The Turn of the Screw hides a meaning accessible only to the most perspicacious. He, however, considers this deeper level to be not a psychological study but a moral allegory in the Hawthorne tradition. The story is dubbed an amusette, says Fagin, because "James considered allegory to be `one of the lighter exercises of the imagination'".

Louis D. Rubin, Jr., on the other hand, quotes this same passage from the Preface to support his contention that Douglas and Miles are the same person; all readers who fail to perceive this identity, says Rubin, have been "caught," even if they, for the most part, fall within the category of "those not easily caught". An entirely different suggestion is advanced by E.A. Sheppard. Sheppard considers the word amusette to be "merely a rather affectedly depreciatory term" consistent with James's characterization of the story as a "potboiler" and a "jeu d' esprit." She finds in this passage no "implication that James intends to hoax the reader." On the contrary, says Sheppard, James merely "wants to `catch' their attention and interest".

"QUESTIONABLE AND AMBIGUOUS" CORRESPONDENCE

James frequently referred to The Turn of the Screw in correspondence. However, the meanings of many of these references are unclear because James burned the original letters of inquiry to which his letters were replies. Consider, for example, James's apology to the psychiatrist Dr. Louis Waldstein in a letter dated October 21, 1898:

I am only afraid, perhaps, that my conscious intention strikes you as having been larger than I deserve it should be thought. ...as regards a presentation of things so fantastic as in that wanton little Tale, I can only rather blush to see real substance read into them—I mean for the generosity of the reader.

It is impossible to know what interpretation James is denying—i.e., what "conscious intention" and "real substance" Dr. Waldstein saw in the story because Dr. Waldstein's letter is not extant. Similarly, we have, in a letter to F.W.H. Myers dated December 19, 1898, this evasive answer to we know not what question:

...I'm afraid I don't quite understand the principal question you put to me about 'The Turn of the Screw.' However, that scantily matters; for in truth I am afraid I have on some former occasions rather awkwardly signified to you that I somehow can't pretend to give any coherent account of my small inventions 'after the fact.' ...The one thing and another that are questionable and ambiguous in them I mostly take to be conditions for their having got themselves pushed through at all.

We do not know, of course, in the absence of Myers's letters what "questionable and ambiguous" elements are being discussed and what James means by "conditions of their having got themselves pushed through at all." James could be referring to creative processes within his own psyche—he could be saying that production of a very imperfect work—"a very mechanical matter"—was the best he could do. On the other hand, he could be saying that he had to treat circumspectly some emotionally charged topics—having to do, for example, with sexuality or religion—in order for his novella to be publishable.

"SHAMELESS POTBOILER" OR "HIGH DEGREE OF ART"

We cannot be sure of James's assessment of the literary

value of The Turn of the Screw. Certainly James expressed negative assessments. In a letter to H.G. Wells dated December 9, 1898, we find a very sharp depreciation of the story:

Bless your heart, I think I could easily say worse of the T. of S., of the young woman, the spooks, the style, the everything, than the worst any one else could manage. One knows the most damning things about one's self... But the thing is essentially a potboiler and a jeu d' esprit.

In the letter to F.W.H. Myers which we have already quoted, James denigrates the novella as "a very mechanical matter...an inferior, a merely pictorial, subject and rather a shameless potboiler". In the Preface to Volume 12 of the New York Edition of The Novels and Tales, James refers to the work as "this perfectly independent and irresponsible little fiction" and opines that, among literary works, it is "the very kind, as happens, least apt to be baited by earnest criticism, the only sort of criticism of which account need be taken".

On the other hand, a very good case could be made for the contention that James highly esteemed the work. James thought highly enough of the work to insist in a letter to J.B. Pinker dated September 11, 1914 that Martin Secker be allowed to republish the tale in The Uniform Tales of Henry James only with the distinct understanding, please, that he conform literatim ...to [the New York Edition] text. It is vital that he adhere to that authentic punctuation—to the last comma or rather, more essentially, no comma.

In the Preface to Volume 17 of the New York Edition, James congratulates himself for constructing several tales, among them The Turn of the Screw, "in earnest aversion to waste and from the sense that in art economy is always beauty". He sets high standards for a story of the supernatural, standards which he considers Poe's novel The Narrative of Arthur Gordon Pym not to have met. The supernatural story must captivate the reader by realistically "looming through some other history—the indispensable history of somebody's normal relation to something". The Turn of the Screw, he suggests, is successful in this regard. Similarly, in the Preface to Volume 12 of the New York Edition, James emphasizes the difficult task he had set for himself in attempting to construct this story of the supernatural and concludes, "The merit of the tale, as it stands, is accordingly, I judge, that it has struggled successfully with its dangers".

The difficulties were formidable: he wanted to construct a story which would compare favorably with traditional ghost stories and scientifically correct apparitions ("I had to decide in fine between having may apparitions correct and having my story `good.'"); he wanted to "make the reader's general vision of evil intense enough" that the reader's "own experience, his own imagination...will supply him quite sufficiently with all the particulars...released form weak specifications"; he wanted to create "the tone of tragic, yet of exquisite mystification...yet strain the expression of it so clear and fine that beauty would result"; he wanted to construct a fairy tale which would "short and sharp and single, charged more or less with the compactness of anecdote" (such as "Cinderella," "Blue Beard," "or "Little Red Riding Hood") rather than "the long and loose, the copious" type such as we find in the Arabian Nights.

James expresses satisfaction that the novella has met all of these high standards. He assures us that Quint and Jessel are indeed, in the novel's final form, the type of non-traditional, non-psychical ghosts he aimed for: "Here it was...that I felt a high degree of art really required; and here it is that, on reading the tale over, I find my precautions justified". James rejoices that he has constructed a tale of non-specific evil which forces each reader to fill in the blanks from his own experience "with a success apparently beyond my liveliest hope". So successful was he, he maintains, that readers, finding in the story the sexual and other indecencies which their own psyches put there, proceeded to attack the author "with the charge of a monstrous emphasis, the charge of all indecently expatiating." This reaction must come from their "own experience...own imagination" because in the text itself, he maintains, "there is ...from beginning to end of the matter not an inch of expatiation". He was so successful, he says, in constructing a narrator who could "make her particular credible statement of such strange matters" that "I couldn't have arrived at so much had I clumsily tried for more".

He praises the tale for exhibiting the compactness and tight structure of those fairy tales to which he has approvingly alluded: "It is an excursion into chaos while remaining, like Blue-Beard and Cinderella, but an anecdote—though an anecdote amplified and highly emphasized and returning upon itself: as, for that matter, Cinderella and Blue-Beard return". Furthermore, the sincerity and seriousness of James's depreciatory assessment of the story are questionable. Goddard finds in James's letters "a very charming and good-humored, but a nonetheless very unmistakable, side-stepping of questions or comments which had evidently been flung at him" and suggests that, by the time he wrote the Prefaces, his estimation of the tale had risen. Anent that, Cole makes an interesting point: "The New York Edition in itself makes James's comments before 1908 almost irrelevant because he finally revised Turn of the Screw extensively, and it is that revised version we study, not the original".

Robert Ginsberg suggests that the disparaging references in the letters should not be considered literary criticism at all. Ginsberg chides James scholars for having manifested an obstinate disregard of the differences between what an artist does...as a critic (in this case composing his Preface), and what he does in other domains of his private and professional life, such as writing letters to friends or admirers, such as coping with readers who have come up to him with comments about his story...

We see, then, that James took no unequivocal stand on many of the central problems of interpretation, those questions which critics have debated ever since the story's publication—for example, the reality and nature of the apparitions, the sanity and moral stature of the governess, the innocence or corruption of the children, the moral or religious message if there is one. Rather, we have seen that critics of opposing views frequently cite the same passage from James to prove that, were he alive, he would be on their side in a critical debate. Even his estimation of the artistic worth of the novella is open to serious question, although the preponderance of the evidence seems to suggest that his ultimate opinion of the work was very high.

Graham Greene has very succinctly summed up the problems we encounter when we read James's statements about The Turn of the Screw: "We must always remain on our guard while reading..., for at a certain level no writer has really disclosed less". In a similar vein, Mark Spilka has referred to "James' evasive labels", and J.A. Ward has declared, "James' remarks on The Turn of the Screw are typically paradoxical". Commenting on James's statements about the story, Peter Coveney remarked, "One feels the evasion of all this". In this James is perhaps representative of his age. John Enck has remarked, "James, like most important twentieth-century authors, described his books not at all or inscrutably". We have not searched James's comments in some misguided attempt to discover the "true" meaning of the story by ascertaining the author's intentions in writing it.

To do that would be to fall into the intentional fallacy as so many critics have done—for instance, Nathan Bryllion Fagin, who dismisses the psychoanalytic approach of Kenton and Wilson because "it clearly has no relation to James's intention". We agree with Robert Carlton Cole in deploring the approach of those critics who "write almost as if they were influenced more by a concept of property rights than by literary critical judgment". Our purpose, rather, has been to begin our history of the criticism of The Turn of the Screw with a discussion of the critical statements of Henry James himself and to indicate how susceptible they have been to varying interpretations by critics who have taken opposing positions. For this reason we have not discussed here the often-cited notebook entry of January 12, 1895. While this entry may be of value to a student of the creative process, it cannot be considered literary criticism because, at the time the entry was made, the work had not yet been written.

We can, however, make one very definite and very important statement about Henry James as a critic of The Turn of the Screw: James can be said to anticipate the reader-response criticism of Norman Holland, David Bleich, Wolfgang Iser, Jonathan Culler, Stanley Fish, and others. James would almost certainly not have agreed with Alexander E. Jones's criticism of Goddard for including in his critical reading his own "irrelevant" experience as a child in the care of an insane servant. Instead, James might well have agreed with Willen, who suggests that James "appears to be probing a crucial and enormously complicated facet of his central narrator's elemental being" and that the similarities of the governess to the reader's mother as remembered from childhood (because the governess is a mother figure) "sets up a certain receptiveness in the reader" and that, therefore, "each objective analysis...is conditioned by the reader's childhood experiences and emotional responses to them."

The seemingly studied ambiguity of James's comments is consistent with Willen's tolerance of a multitude of interpretations: "I would say then, that the variety of interpretations accorded `The Turn of the Screw' originates in the variety of these experiences and responses." Willen suggests that the "frame" of the story, which critics have discussed so extensively, the multiplicity of narrators, is necessary for a certain distancing which is "absolutely essential if we are to hold on to our illusions and consequently our sanity". The last two paragraphs of James's discussion of The Turn of the Screw in the Preface to Volume 12 of the New York Edition of The Novels and Tales indicate that James would have been very much at home with reader-response criticism. In constructing the tale, James said, he aimed to produce in the reader "that sense of the depths of the sinister," that "portentous evil" which seems "promised and announced as by the hot breath of the Pit".

He then suggests that such a sense of evil cannot be adequately effected by "the offered example, the imputed vice, the cited act, the limited deplorable presentable instance" because no particular evil would be bad enough but, rather, would constitute a "waiting anti-climax". He continues, One had seen, in fiction, some grand form of wrong-doing, or better still of wrong-being, imputed, seen it promised and announced as by the hot breath of the Pit—and then, all lamentably, shrink to the compass of some particular brutality, some particular immorality, some particular infamy portrayed: with the result, alas, of the demonstration's falling sadly short.

After speculating as to what might be "the very worst action small victims so conditioned might be conceived as subject to," James concludes, There is for such a case no eligible absolute of the wrong; it remains relative to fifty other elements, a matter of appreciation, speculation, imagination—these things moreover quite exactly in the light of the spectator's, the critic's, the reader's experience.

He then suggests, as does Frank Kermode in The Genesis of Secrecy, that the literary work—at least this type of literary work—contains a lacuna which each reader must fill in for himself, drawing on his own experience. Only make the reader's general vision of evil intense enough, I said to myself—and that already is a charming job—and his own experience, his own imagination, his own sympathy (with the children) and horror (of their false friends) will supply him quite sufficiently with all the particulars. Make him think the evil, make him think it for himself, and you are released from weak specifications.

James obviously considered the finished product to be suggestive of various readings to people with different experiences, for he claims to have applied this formula "with a success beyond my liveliest hope". He offers as evidence, as we pointed out previously, the indignation of some readers over what they perceived to be material of an objectionable nature—i.e., sexual material. How can I feel my calculation to have failed, my wrought suggestion not to have worked, that is, on my being assailed, as has befallen me, with the charge of a monstrous emphasis, the charge or all indecently expatiating? There is not only from beginning to end of the matter not an inch of expatiation, but my values are positively all blanks save so far as an excited horror, a promoted pity, a created expertness—on which punctual effects of strong causes no writer can ever fail to plume himself—proceed to read into them more or less fantastic figures.

This passage makes more understandable the evasive answers to letters of inquiry and the ambiguous statements which are cited by critics arguing diametrically opposed cases. Perhaps James was deliberately ambiguous to encourage a variety of responses, thinking that specific interpretations, while they might constitute valid readings, would not be correct to the exclusion of alternative interpretations. This is why, perhaps, so many scholars have felt frustrated reading James's criticism of The Turn of the Screw.

This interpretation is also consistent with James's statement to his physician, Sir James MacKenzie, that ambiguity was essential in The Turn of the Screw because "so long as the events are veiled the imagination will run riot and depict all sorts of horrors, but as soon as the veil is lifted, all mystery disappears, and with it the sense of terror". To sum up, then, we find in James's statements about The Turn of the Screw no definitive position on the major questions of interpretation which have continuously exercised the critics but rather pervasive ambiguity in his statements so that the same statements can be quoted as evidence for conflicting claims and evasive replies to letters of inquiry the originals of which he destroyed. A very good case can be made, however, for placing him in the reader-response camp, and such a placement can easily explain at least some of the ambiguity and evasiveness I have discussed.

Chapter 15

Early Criticism: 1898-1933

REVIEWS OF THE TWO MAGICS

The Turn of the Screw first appeared in serial form in Collier's Weekly between January and April of 1898. Then, in October of 1898, it was published in both Great Britain and the United States, together with the undistinguished story "Covering End," in a volume entitled The Two Magics. Accordingly, the first critical reactions to The Turn of the Screw were reviews of The Two Magics. The first point to be made about these initial reactions is that they were, with very few exceptions, favorable. Thus, the critical consensus that The Turn of the Screw is a great work of literary artistry—a consensus that has persisted throughout endless debates concerning questions of interpretation—was present from the very beginning of the long critical discussion.

On October 15, 1898, The New York Times Saturday Review of Books and Art (111, 681-82) began the discussion by terming the novella "a deliberate, powerful, and horribly successful study of the magic of evil, of the subtle influence over human hearts and minds of the sin with which this world is accursed" and by declaring the work worthy of being compared to Robert Louis Stevenson's Dr. Jekyll and Mr. Hyde. Terming the story "the strongest and most affecting argument against sin we have lately encountered in literature," this anonymous reviewer confessed himself unable adequately to "express the awful, almost overpowering sense of the evil that human nature is subject to derive from it [the story] by the sensitive reader." He judged the story "one of the most moving and...most remarkable works of fiction published in many years." On the same day a favorable review appeared in Literature. This reviewer called the work "so astonishing a piece of art that it cannot be described" and one which "exhibits his [James's] subtlest powers".

Other favorable reviews soon followed. The New York Tribune on October 23, 1898, (supp., p. 14) claimed that the story "crystallizes an original and fascinating idea in absolutely appropriate form." On the following day the Detroit Free Press termed the work a "horribly successful study" of depravity, equal in stature to Dr. Jekyll and Mr. Hyde. The Springfield (Mass.) Republican praised the story (October 30, 1898, 8), as did the Overland Monthly (32, November, 1898, 493), the latter publication lauding the author as "unique among storytellers" for his knack of "riveting...the reader's attention on every sentence." Laudatory reviews also appeared in the St. Paul Daily Pioneer Press (November 6, 1898, 26), Life (32, November 10, 1898, 368), the Portland Morning Oregonian (November 13, 1898, p. 22), the Critic (XXXIII, December, 1898, 524), and Ainslee's Magazine (11, December, 1898, 518). The American Monthly Review of Reviews (XVIII, December, 1898, 732-733) termed the story the finest work ... [James] has ever done—for the foul breath of the bottomless pit itself, which strikes the reader full in the face as he follows the plot, puts to shame by its penetrating force and quiet ghastliness the commonplace, unreal 'horrors' of the ordinary ghost-story; it does indeed give an extra 'turn of the screw' beyond anything of the sort that fiction has yet provided.

Book Buyer (XV11, December, 1898, 437) termed the story "one of the most appalling ghost stories ever told." The Nation (67, December 8, 1898, 432) also reviewed the novella favorably. Laudatory reviews continued to appear in 1899. Favorable articles were published in Book Notes (2, January, 48-49), Dixie (1, January, 59-60), and Chautauguan (28, March, 630). The latter publication's praise was effusive:

The intangible is here painted with a skill little short of the supernatural, and in dealing with these subtleties of the mind the author has produced a tale whose suggestiveness makes the blood bund through the veins with unusual rapidity.

There were, of course, a few unfavorable reviews of the novella and scattered unfavorable statements within generally favorable reviews. Some of the unfavorable comments can easily be attributed to a dated Victorian puritanism upon perceiving suggested sexual material in the plot of the novella. Such often obscured moralization, for example, explains "Mr. Chesterton's doubt as to whether the thing ought ever to have been published". It is sometimes difficult— perhaps because turn of the century critics often wrote with less precision than we have since come to expect—to be sure whether the reviewer is devaluing the story as a work of art by objecting to the author's inclusion of unsuitable material or only pointing out that certain happenings within the plot structure would be deplorable if they occurred in real life.

For example, a review in The Outlook (LX, October 29, 1898) declared, "The story itself is distinctly repulsive." The same review, however, characterized the tale as "a ghost story, psychologically conceived, and illustrating a profound moral law." Contrasting the tale with "the ordinary clumsy, materialistic ghost story," this critic stated, "It is hardly necessary to say that Mr. James's tale has nothing in common with the ordinary ghost story; it is altogether on a higher plane both of conception and art." Even more interestingly, a review in The Bookman appears clearly to devalue the story—"We have never read a more sickening, a more gratuitously melancholy tale"—by carelessly assuming an identity between the author's point of view and that of the governess and thereby imputing to the author and his story those defects of character—for example, a tendency to see evil everywhere and easily believe the worst about others—which so many later critics have noted in the governess. These reviewers obviously came close to a positive evaluation of the story. "It has all Mr. James's cleverness, even his grace," they say.

The plotting of the good governess and the faithful Mrs. Grose to combat the evil, very gradually discovered, are marvelously real. You cannot help but assist at their interviews and throb with their anxiety. Their conclusion, however, is that "the clever result is very cruel and untrue," and for that they upbraid the author for the deep mistake of writing the story at all.

A theory has run away with him. It is flimsily built on a few dark facts, so scattered and uncertain that they cannot support a theory at all. The Independent called the work "the most hopelessly evil story that we have ever read in any literature, ancient or modern. "Terming "unaccountable" the author's decision to "make such a study of infernal human debauchery," these reviewers seem to perceive some sort of technical artistic mastery the effect of which is vitiated by the story's reprehensible moral stature. "The study, while it exhibits Mr. James's genius in a powerful light, affects the reader with a disgust that is not to be expressed." The authors do not discuss the theme of the story, but rather seem content to point in horror at the subject matter:

The feeling after perusal of the horrible story is that one has been assisting in an outrage upon the holiest and sweetest fountain of human innocence, and helping to debauch—at least by helplessly standing by—the pure and trusting nature of children.

They conclude, "Human imagination can go no further into infamy, literary art could not be used with more refined subtlety of spiritual defilement." The second major point to be made about these early reviews is that the criticism is predominantly subjective and impressionistic—the reviewers tend mainly to record the effects of the work on themselves and to assume that other readers should and/or would be similarly affected. A brief skimming of the above-cited reviews should make this pattern clear. The New York Times review is predominantly a listing of emotional experiences in store for "the sensitive reader." The Outlook described the novella as "distinctly repulsive." The Bookman called the work "sickening" and "gratuitously melancholy." The Overland Monthly praised James for "riveting the reader's attention on every sentence." The American Monthly Review of Reviews referred to the experience of evil "which strikes the reader full in the face." The Independent claimed the tale "affects the reader with a disgust that is not to be expressed" and then proceeded to comment on said reader's "feeling after perusal of the horrible story." Chautauguan assured its readers that James's story "makes the blood bound through the veins with unusual rapidity."

Reviews, of course, are not scholarly monographs. Even today reviews tend to be much less analytical and more impressionistic than scholarly discussions of a literary work which has been available for a longer period of time. Nevertheless, there are some rather striking omissions: The Outlook, for example, assures us that The Turn of the Screw "has nothing in common with the ordinary ghost story" but does not tell us in what way it differs from such a story—we are told only that this story is "altogether on a higher plane both of conception and art"; the same review terms the tale "a ghost story, psychologically conceived, and illustrating a profound moral law" but offers no hint as to what the reviewers mean by "psychologically conceived" and what "profound moral law" they find in the story.

The review in The Independent is unrelieved invective which sheds no additional light on the meaning, structure, or value of the literary work. The review in The American Monthly Review of Reviews is almost wholly evaluative — we are not told what specific techniques James has employed to make this story "horribly absorbing" and full of "penetrating force" and "capable of producing such a living, vivid, indelible impression upon the mind"—instead, the reviewers bombard us with generalities: "...there is a completeness, a finish, a sense of easy mastery and boundless reserve force about this story which are entirely fascinating."

The review in Literature contains unexplained statements—e.g., "We cannot enter into the morbid psychology of such a work as this" and "It is fiction, but it is not a novel; it is full of apparitions, generally in broad daylight, but it is not a ghost story." We wonder, in particular, why the work is "not a ghost story," since the reviewers obviously adhere to a supernatural interpretation, terming the "subject" of the story "nothing less than the demoniac possession of two young and otherwise delightful children." The Sewanee Review complimented James without offering any explanations for the compliments: "His character analysis...deserves not a little praise, and his manner of dealing with the supernatural is quite unique."

There were, however, some very perceptive comments in these early reviews which anticipated the concerns of later critics. For example, at least one reviewer immediately perceived the governess as possibly an unreliable narrator. The governess, according to The Critic, has nothing in the least substantial upon which to base her deep and startling cognitions. She perceives what is beyond all perception and the reader who begins by questioning whether she is supposed to be sane ends by accepting her conclusions and thrilling over the horrors they involve.

However, this reviewer seems to suggest, not all readers "end by accepting her conclusions":

...if, when the lids of the books are closed, he is not convinced as to the possibility of such horrors, he is at least sure that Mr. James has produced an imaginative masterpiece.

And, of course, as we have seen, the reviewer in The Bookman came close to seeing the governess as unreliable by questioning the corruption of the children—"we must deny the continuity and the extent of the corruption as suggested here"—but then hastily and carelessly imputed the presumed fault not to the fictional narrator, but rather to the author of the story.

A few reviewers appeared to recognize the pervasive ambiguity of The Turn of the Screw, which James boasted of in his correspondence about his story and in the Prefaces to Volumes 12 and 17 of the New York Edition and which has spawned so many different interpretations of the tale.

The review in The New York Times stated,

The work is not horrible in any grotesque or 'realistic' sense...it is ...free from the slightest hint of grossness. Of any precise form of evil Mr. James says very little, and on this head he is never explicit.... The most depraved 'realist' could surely not be more powerful, though he might, in his explicitness, defeat his supposed purpose.

This reviewer considered James eminently successful in employing ambiguity. "No eloquent outpouring of a Jeremy Collier or other avowed enemy of specified evils could produce a feeling of grater abhorrence for the object attacked."

The review in Literature began, "It is not our fault if we fail to understand Mr. James's new book. He leaves everything unexplained." Presumably the author simply "explains" a story to readers. This reviewer attributed the ambiguity of the story to the nature of its subject matter, "the action and reaction of good and evil in childhood," concluding that "the subject does not admit of any plausible statement." The discussion concluded with the words, "Mr. James, though one of the most interesting of writers, is not also the most lucid."

The Overland Monthly, in a similar vein, called the story "as interesting as a Chinese puzzle," and The Critic termed it "so super-subtle as to be almost impalpable." Some reviewers viewed the story as a moral allegory, and thus began a long series of religious and moral readings which still continue. Interestingly, however, some seemed a bit uncomfortable with such an interpretation—anticipating Heilman, the moral interpreter par excellence of The Turn of the Screw, who, nevertheless in 1948, warned us not to "fall into much more blunt statements than we ought make. We say, too forthrightly, that Bly `becomes' a Garden of Eden".

The New York Times review, for example, compared the story to Dr. Jekyll and Mr. Hyde in that, like Stevenson's work, James's is a "horribly successful study of the magic of evil, of the subtle influence over human hearts and minds of the sin with which this world is accursed." However, the reviewer then added, "This is not akin in any other sense than the one here specified... Mr. James's story is perhaps as allegorical as Stevenson's, but the allegory is not so clear." Later, after insisting that James "is the seer and the moralist, whether designedly so or not," this reviewer says, "The allegory is plain or not, according to the reader's aptitude for discovering allegories. We do not insist upon that."

Literature, as we have previously mentioned, considered the novella to be about "the action and reaction of good and evil in childhood." The review in The Bookman saw the story as a depiction of "a sink of corruption, never uncovered, but darkly, potently hinted" underlying "purity, beauty, and joy," which "on the surface" are "resplendent." Thus, according to this reviewer, "the situation of Maisie is reversed," for What Maisie Knew was a triumph of beauty in the end. Its theme was that purity and candor and joy could be strong enough in the heart of a young creature to counteract the miasma of the evil amid which she lived.

This reviewer—who, in my opinion imperceptively, attributed the unreliability of the governess's conclusions to the author of the novella and considered the work thereby to be defective—considered the two dead servants to be symbols:

Mr. James has used symbolism to help him out with theme; so, at least, we may speak of the two ghosts—one of a rascally valet, the other of an iniquitous governess—the origins of the evil in their lifetime, who haunt the children after their death— but thought the symbolism "clumsy," opining, "...only there in the story has Mr. James actually failed."

The American Monthly Review of Reviews, meanwhile, saw the theme of the story as "the mysterious legacy of evil that may continue in force after death." Notably absent from these early reviews were any perceptive comments about the narrative structure of the story—the frame of story within story as told by three fictional narrators—which later critics as diverse as Alexander E. Jones, Louis D. Rubin, Jr., and Shoshana Felman have found so significant. Instead, almost all reviewers ignored the prologue, while The American Review of Reviews dismissed it as "a needlessly awkward method of starting the story," and The New York Times nonchalantly said, "The introduction to this tale is sufficiently conventional, but one decides, in looking back, that it serves better than another would."

This early criticism is almost entirely impressionistic and subjective. The critics—in marked contrast to so many later literary scholars—assume that it is the task of the author to leave nothing ambiguous or unexplained; these critics are thus unable to articulate some of the most important elements of the work, those connected with its ambiguities.

In 1908 The Turn of the Screw was published in revised and definitive form as part of Volume 12 of the New York Edition of The Novels and Tales of Henry James, along with the famous Preface discussed extensively in the preceding chapter of this book. The differences between the later version and the one published in The Two Magics and the importance of these differences for the interpretation of the narrative have been greatly exaggerated by some critics—most notably, Edel in The Ghostly Tales of Henry James and in The Psychological Novel: 1900-1950, Cranfill and Clark in An Anatomy of The Turn of the Screw, and Kimbrough in his Norton Critical Edition to The Turn of the Screw.

In the latter volume Kimbrough succinctly summarizes the differences he and other critics have perceived:

...major revisions appear in the 1908 New York version. Here James seemed intent on shifting the centre of attention away from the details of action observed by the governess to the reactions felt by the governess. By removing commas...he came closer to approximating the streams of her consciousness.... By increasing the use of the possessive pronoun 'my' and by replacing verbs of perception and thought with those of feeling and intuition...James draws us intimately into the course of her narrative. The effect is more vital and vivid...

This view has, I think, been convincingly refuted by E.A. Sheppard in Appendix 1 of Henry James and The Turn of the Screw. A detailed collation of the two editions, according to Sheppard, fails consistently to support the patterns Edel and the other critics have suggested—indeed, it provides numerous counter examples. Sheppard has convincingly argued, citing quite a few examples, that James's revisions in The Turn of the Screw not only were stylistic, and merely stylistic, in intention but also, as regards character and incident, effect no change whatever in the impression conveyed to the reader.

Sheppard also cites differences between the two texts

which can scarcely be considered improvements and, in so doing, calls into question the prevalent assumption that the 1908 revision is superior to the version published in The Two Magics. "But indeed there is no question," says Sheppard, "that many of James's alterations are unnecessary, or inept, or both, and that they may justly be described as the perfectionist's obsessional tinkering with his work".

In any case, the 1908 version should not be considered a new or different literary work. As I pointed out in my discussion of the reviews of The Two Magics, many of the important insights of later critics were present in seminal form in the critical reactions of 1898 and 1899. Also, as we saw in the preceding chapter, James's ambiguous and seemingly contradictory remarks about the story began before the 1908 revision and continued in the Prefaces to Volumes 12 and 17 of the New York Edition.

This is perhaps why, in surveying the reviews of the New York Edition, we find nothing of substance that is new about The Turn of the Screw. Indeed, most of the reviews are perfunctory comments about the New York Edition as a whole or substantial parts of it—several volumes, for example—and contain nothing but platitudes and generalities.

For example, the Nation (August 6, 1908) devoted only one paragraph to Volumes 11 and 12 of the New York Edition, and that paragraph was mainly a perfunctory discussion of the Prefaces. After remarking that "the prefaces are, as usual, devoted to Mr. James's suggestive criticisms of his own writings," the reviewer devoted one sentence to The Turn of the Screw: "'The Turn of the Screw' was written as a 'Christmas-tide toy,' based on 'the vividest little note for sinister romance' that Mr. James had ever jotted down."

Similarly, in a brief article entitled "Writers of Books: The Literary World of Today," the Boston Evening Transcript (August 26, 1908) devoted three brief paragraphs to four volumes of the New York Edition, including the volume containing The Turn of the Screw. Two of these paragraphs were devoted to The Awkward Age. The third paragraph briefly mentioned The Turn of the Screw in a listing containing six other short works, only to point out that "upon these James [in his prefaces] is no less introspective than he is upon his longer novels." After some discussion of The Aspern Papers, the reviewer summarily concluded, "Surely nothing more weird and strange than these introductions has ever been offered to the reading public."

The Bookman (September, 1908) devoted only one paragraph to the New York Edition and did not mention The Turn of the Screw. This reviewer was general and perfunctory:

The prefaces to these volumes, in which he has, so to speak, turned the sharp edge of his critical faculty against himself, promise to constitute in their entirety one of the most interesting of personal documents.

The San Francisco Chronicle (October 11, 1908) reviewed Volume 12 in two sentences:

The twelfth volume comprises 'The Aspern Papers,' a charming study of Italian life; 'The Turn of the Screw,' 'The Liar,' and 'The Two Faces.' Henry James' prefaces furnish good reading, as they throw much light on the conception and development of these tales.

The Chicago Evening Friday Literary Review (August 20, 1909) devoted only one paragraph to the entire New York Edition.

Thus, it is easy to see why James complained in a letter to Edmund Gosse (August 25, 1915) that the New York Edition "never had the least intelligent critical justice done it—or any sort of critical attention at all paid it" (Letters IV 778). Foley summarizes the situation thus:

...when this work met with so little appreciation and so much contempt or neglect, he was sorely disappointed. There was surprisingly little comment about the edition in the magazines. After the excitement occasioned by the announcement of the scheme and the appearance of the first few volumes had subsided, succeeding volumes were either merely announced or ignored.

There were a few exceptions, of course. Edward Marsh, for example, in October of 1909, published a five page review entitled "Henry James: Auto-Critic" in Bookman, concentrating on the prefaces as "a complete, thoroughgoing analysis" of James's creations which, since they came from the artist himself, should be considered "without a parallel in literature." He praised James for "the fullness and richness of his exposition of a whole set of relations commonly ignored by the novelist". This review, however, contained no significant discussion of The Turn of the Screw. Similarly, a five page review in the London Times, which was reprinted in Living Age made quite perceptive comments about a number of the novels and tales but did not mention The Turn of the Screw.

I have suggested as a main reason for the paucity of perceptive reviews of the 1908 version the essential identity between the revision and its predecessor—the former having been characterized by Sheppard as "the perfectionist's obsessional tinkering with his work". This hypothesis is confirmed by Foley's conclusion upon surveying the reviews of the New York Edition in American periodicals: "...the prefaces were welcomed and applauded, but the revisions of the individual stories...were resented and ridiculed". It is hardly surprising, also, to find no plethora of detailed and insightful analyses of the two Prefaces in which The Turn of the Screw was discussed, since the ambiguities and subtleties of these Prefaces, would probably not be immediately apparent to reviewers.

GODDARD

The most important criticism of The Turn of the Screw prior to Edmund Wilson's famous 1934 article, "The Ambiguity of Henry James," is undoubtedly Harold C. Goddard's "A Pre-Freudian Reading of the Turn of the Screw." Although Goddard's essay was not published until 1957, he wrote the essay—according to his daughter, Eleanor Goddard Worthen—"about 1920 or before" and, year after year, read it to students of literature at Swarthmore College, where he was a professor of English. Leon Edel in his "Prefatory Note" to Goddard's article, accepts Ms. Worthen's estimate of the date because Goddard, in the essay, refers to no critic of the story "later than William Lyon Phelps," whose first comments appeared in The Yale Review in 1916, although Phelps did offer further remarks in his Howells, James, Bryant, and Other Essays, which was published in 1924 and in his Autobiography with Letters, which was published in 1939. I am not aware of any evidence which would contradict Goddard's daughter's estimate of the date of composition.

Ms. Worthen, after her father's death, forwarded the essay to Edmund Wilson, who, in turn, gave it to Leon Edel. Edel then provided the title for the previously untitled essay and published it in Nineteenth Century Fiction, XII, No. 1 (June, 1957), 1-36—along with a "Prefatory Note" of his own. In his "Prefatory Note" Edel extends to Goddard "the credit of being the first to expound, if not to publish, a hallucination theory of the story" (Goddard 1). Edel also—probably in order to justify his choice of a title for the essay—contends that Goddard's achievement was effected without the aid of Sigmund Freud. Goddard's essay is a singularly valuable example of textual study. He relied wholly on what James had written, and he gave the tale that attentive reading which the novelist invited when he called his work `a trap for the unwary'.

Here Edel seems to suggest that Goddard's essay is a specimen of the New Criticism. And, indeed, Goddard seems to arrive at and present his interpretation by a thoughtful reading of the story itself. He does not refer to psychoanalytic literature or employ even very common psychoanalytic terminology, such as Oedipus complex, hysteria, conversion, or transference. Instead he, in his own words, attended closely to "the facts of the story" and, in Edel's words, not only sought to understand the psychology of the governess but examined that heroine from the viewpoint of the children entrusted to her, noting such things as `the governess' account of the wild look in her own eyes, the terror in her face'.

Indeed, Goddard's methodology seems to be to "read between the lines" of James's story and decipher another story—what the characters probably thought and feared and wished for—given the evidence presented in the text. In so doing, Goddard relies not on technical and abstruse theory, but rather on the sort of "common sense" understanding of human nature which would be available to any sensitive and intelligent reader. Goddard first of all reminds us of some facts about the background, personality, and situation of the governess before the advent of the apparitions—facts which are related by Douglas in the prologue or by the governess herself in the course of her narrative: for example, "the eccentric nature" of her father; her troubled family "where things were not going well"; her inexperience; her infatuation with her employer; the hopeless nature of this infatuation, given the social and economic realities of Victorian Britain; her tendency to insomnia and mood swings, which she admits in the first chapter of her narrative; the "really great loneliness," as Douglas puts it, of the position which she accepted; her poor judgment, as evidenced by her accepting, because of a hopeless romantic attraction, a position requiring such an unusual and unwise commitment—"that she should never trouble him—but never, never: neither appeal nor complain nor write about anything..." (Prologue).

We have, concluded Goddard, "a girl of no worldly experience and of unstable psychical background" in a situation which is intolerable for her. Goddard then attempts to demonstrate how, naturally, "that inveterate playwright and stage manager, the subconscious" of the governess would piece together the incomplete information available about the children and their former guardians to construct an "internal drama" in which she would execute "imagined deeds of extraordinary heroism or self-sacrifice done in behalf of the beloved object," the children's uncle. According to Goddard, the main elements of the "witch's broth" of incomplete information out of which the governess constructs her bizarre interpretation of reality are the following: first, "the master's strange stipulation" that she never contact him again—"something extraordinary, she was convinced, lurked in the background"; second, her discovery that "the boy, Miles, is dismissed from school for no assigned or assignable reason"; third, Mrs. Grose's "inadvertent hint" in chapter two about some mysterious man who liked "young and pretty" women; fourth, Mrs. Grose's oblique remark in the same conversation about the mysterious end of the former governess, Miss Jessel, who "was not taken ill, so far as appeared in this house," but who began a holiday and "went off to die".

The governess's motivation for selecting the particular pattern which she finally chooses to impose on the above incomplete and hitherto formless picture is her need to execute "some act of unexampled courage" for the man she loves but cannot possess. "When a young person," says Goddard, especially a young woman, falls in love and circumstances forbid the normal growth and confession of the passion, the emotion, dammed up, overflows in a psychical experience, a daydream, or internal drama which the mind creates in lieu of the thwarted realization in the objective world... Her whole being tingles with the craving to perform some act of unexampled courage. To carry out her duties as governess is not enough. They are too humdrum. If only the house would take fire by night, and both children be in peril! Or if one of them would fall into the water! But no such crudely melodramatic opportunities occur. What does occur is something far more indefinite, far more provocative to the imaginative than to the active faculties...—namely, the hints and particles of information we have listed.

"This material and plan on which the dreaming consciousness of the governess sets to work" begin to take definite form when she sees Quint for the first time. The governess has been wandering around Bly on a June evening daydreaming about the employer and imagining how wonderful it would be for him suddenly to appear and smile in approval of how well she is discharging her duties, when she sees a male figure looking down at her from a distant tower. "Instantly, however, she perceives her mistake. It is not he. In her heart she knows it cannot be. But if her love is too good to be true, her fears, unfortunately, are only too true. And forthwith those fears seize and transform this creation of her imagination". The governess has combined this vision with Mrs. Grose's earlier hints about Peter Quint to fashion "the specter who is to dominate the rest of the tale," a being who, "because he is an object of dread... becomes the raw material of heroism." Consequently, at the time of the second vision of Quint, she experiences, in her words, "the shock of a certitude that it was not for me he had come. He had come for someone else."

Goddard sees no reason for this inexplicable certitude that the children are the threatened ones other than "the creative logic of her hallucination," which requires that "she must not merely be brave; she must be brave for someone's sake... She must save the beings whom he has commissioned her to protect". This "creative logic" combines with the ignorance and superstition of Mrs. Grose, who precipitately concludes that the man and woman the governess has seen are Quint and Jessel because of the housekeeper's belief in ghosts and her dislike of Quint and Jessel.

Goddard correctly points out that it is the governess, not Mrs. Grose, who identifies the female apparition as the former governess and that the governess's description of the apparition is not at all detailed—the only specifics are that the woman was pale, beautiful, and dressed in black.

He also argues quite persuasively that Mrs. Grose, during her conversation with the governess immediately following the second appearance of Quint, has not paid much attention to the detailed description the governess has offered but instead has hastily identified the specter on the basis of only two facts, since these are the two facts that Mrs. Grose repeats in her "breathless affirmative groan" that the man was hatless and dressed in some other man's clothes.

With his usually memorable and quotable prose, Goddard suggests that the "intellectual level" of such reasoning is "the level, as anyone who has ever had the curiosity to attend one knows, of a fifth-rate spiritualistic seance," adding, "As if good ghosts always wore hats and bad ones carried their terrestrial pilfering into eternity!"

Goddard suggests that Mrs. Grose is moved to make this hasty identification because of the governess's suggestion that the figure is somehow a menace to the children, of whom the housekeeper is so fond and toward whom she is so possessive: "So do the governess' fears and repressed desires and the housekeeper's memories and anxieties unconsciously collaborate". Then, throughout the remainder of the narrative, the governess continually "seizes the flimsiest pretexts for finding confirmation of her suspicions".

While Goddard has offered an ingenious and convincing explanation of the "identification scene"—the conversation in which Mrs. Grose identifies the male figure as the ghost of Peter Quint—which allows us to believe in the innocence of the children, he has been equally ingenious and thorough in his discussion of the final scene of the story in which Miles dies after "his supreme surrender of the name" of Quint. Goddard points out that Mrs. Grose in chapter 21 does not guarantee that the children have not met after the second vision of Jessel at the lake and the ensuing emotional confrontation between the governess and Mrs. Grose. When the governess asks if they have met, Mrs. Grose is "quite flushed" and answers,

Ah, Miss, I'm not such a fool as that! If I've been obliged to leave her three or four times, it has been each time with one of the maids, and at present, though she's alone, she's locked in safe. And yet—! (qtd. in Goddard 26).

Secondly, Goddard reminds us that, in the final scene, Miles's first question is, "Is she here?" If the governess's interpretation of events were correct, we should expect Miles to use the masculine pronoun and refer to Quint. He would use the feminine pronoun if the idea of spectral visitation came from his sister, whom the governess has terrified with her insane ravings about Miss Jessel, rather than from his own secret consorting with Quint. Then, when the governess screams, "It's not Miss Jessel!" he would naturally think of the other former guardian, Miss Jessel's paramour, who is also deceased.

While Goddard provides a detailed and insightful analysis of the psychological processes of the governess, he does not, as Thomas has justly accused some psychoanalytic critics of doing, "approach 'The Turn of the Screw' as if it were a psychiatric case study rather than a work of fiction". First of all, Goddard combines his analysis of "the creative logic of her hallucination" with an analysis of "the creative logic" James has employed to make the story credible to the reader as he hypnotizes us into forgetting that it is the governess' version of the story to which we are listening, and lures us, as the governess unconsciously lured Mrs. Grose, into accepting her coloring of the facts for the facts themselves.

The story is perceived as more credible than most stories of the supernatural, according to Goddard, because the reader, even if not consciously, perceives the real plot, which is believable: "Two children, under circumstances where there is no one to realize the situation, are put, for bringing up, in the care of an insane governess". This plot is made credible by the introduction of two characters who, together, would be likely to provide the governess with an opportunity to continue her depredations undetected: namely, the totally indifferent employer and the superstitious, ignorant, and easily intimidated housekeeper. The final element, of course, is the isolated location of Bly.

We are led to forget, suggests Goddard, that no facts—only her bare assertions, accepted, for the most part, by Mrs. Grose—are presented to support her contentions that the ghosts are a threat to the children and that the children see them because she matter of factly relates wild hypotheses as facts and includes them in a narrative containing some true information. The governess offers without differentiation facts and interpretations of facts—for example, when she in chapter ten relates the fact that she sees Miles on the lawn and the assertion that Miles is looking above her at some person on the tower or when in chapter seven she relates in the same breath the fact that she saw Miss Jessel and the assertion that Flora also did. We are offered her interpretations of the children's behavicur as if these interpretations were facts when in chapter seventeen Miles's reference to "this queer business of ours" is taken to refer to secret visits with Peter Quint and, in chapter twenty-three, his reference to "the others," the servants at Bly, is interpreted as a reference to the ghosts.

Finally, in duping the reader, the governess is aided by that scintilla of truth which her interpretation contains: the fact that Miles and Flora are not "just happy natural children." This fact is made apparent by, among other things, "the fearful language that Flora uses in her delirium, the boy's lie about the letter, the clear evidence at the end that he has something on his mind that he longs to confess".

A careful reading of the story, however, suggests Goddard, indicates that whatever abnormal behaviour the children exhibit can most plausibly be attributed not to the influence of Quint and Jessel but rather to that of the governess herself. Fear is like faith: it ultimately creates what at first it only imagined. The governess, at the beginning, imagines that the actions and words of the children are strange and unnatural. In the end they become strange and unnatural for the good and sufficient reason that the children gradually become conscious of the strangeness and unnaturalness of her own attitude toward them.... Thus do her mania and their fear feed and augment one another...

Goddard is also to be distinguished from those psychoanalytic critics such as Cargill, Cranfill and Clark, and C. Knight Aldrich, M.D., among others, who seem to treat the work as the case history of a real psychiatric patient rather than as a work of art, by his paramount concern with the effect of the work on the reader. All Goddard's analysis of the narrator's psychology is clearly subordinated to this latter primary concern, explaining the story's effect on its readers. First, as we have seen, Goddard's analysis of the psychology of the governess is subordinate to his attempt to explain the terror the story induces which so many other supernatural tales do not—a terror dependent upon "the quality of being entirely credible, even by daylight", for even skeptical readers can recognize the plausibility of the true plot—"two children...in the care of an insane governess", especially when the author creates two other characters—namely, the employer and Mrs. Grose—whose characteristics complement those of the governess so that the reader is not disturbed by "the unlikelihood of this situation's occurring...the fact that in real life someone would recognize the insanity and interfere to save the children".

Secondly, and perhaps more importantly, Goddard employs his analysis of the psychological processes of the governess to construct an interpretation which can account for the "beauty" of the story and perhaps, in his words, "redeem the narrative from the charge of ugliness and render even its horror subordinate to its beauty". For, if we accept his interpretation, Goddard argues, the story becomes not "a tale of corrupted childhood," but rather "a tale of incorruption childhood" in which the children remain "incarnations of loveliness and charm" who are "withered at last in the flame of the governess' passion. ...And the withering of them in the flame is rendered tragic rather than merely horrible by the heroism that they display." Consequently, the reader of this work sees "justice done to the incredible, the appalling courage of childhood." Furthermore, in Goddard's view, the governess herself can be seen as a tragic figure, a literary demonstration of the truth that "mental aberration may go hand in hand with strength and beauty of character... The governess is deluded, but she rises to the sublime in her delusion". Because of this paramount concern with the effect of the story on the reader, Goddard is undogmatic about the existence of the ghosts:

Whether the insane man creates his hallucinations or whether insanity is precisely the power to perceive objective existences of another order, whether higher or lower, than humanity, no open-minded person can possibly pretend to say, however preponderating in the one direction or the other present evidence may seem to him to be. Goddard, therefore, considers the story "susceptible of various readings". This insight, it seems to me, is one of the most important strengths of Goddard's essay, since no reading's claim to be exclusively correct can be reconciled with the enigmatic and seemingly contradictory statements of the story's foremost critic, Henry James himself. Also, Goddard's interpretation can easily be read in conjunction with other outstanding interpretive essays—most notably those by Lydenberg and Firebaugh—which effect a synthesis between the Freudian and non-

Freudian readings, claiming that the personal problems of the governess interact synergistically with objectively evil presences to bring about the downfall of the children. A few other early critics seemed to perceive dimly the necessity of such a synthesis—for example, Elton and Woolf; the weakness of these critics, however, is that they offer unsupported assertions not grounded in the detailed analysis of the text which Goddard has provided.

From the foregoing discussion the major strengths of Goddard's outstanding essay should be readily apparent. The major weaknesses of the essay in my opinion are Goddard's failure to explain the psychodynamics of the governess's later apparent sexual attraction to Miles (Some psychoanalytic critics have attempted to explain this) and Miles's dismissal from school. Some critics—for example, Alexander E. Jones—have cited as a weakness Goddard's "irrelevant" inclusion of his childhood experiences with an insane servant who used to tell him and his sister of her nocturnal visions of ghosts. It is easy, however, to dispute the "irrelevance" of such personal material by considering the literary work's all-pervasive ambiguity together with the author's explanation, in the Preface to Volume 12 of the New York Edition, of the artistic function of that ambiguity, an explanation which seems to invite the inclusion of a critic's personal experiences:

There is ...no eligible absolute of the wrong; it remains relative to fifty other elements, a matter of appreciation, speculation, imagination—these things moreover quite exactly in the light of the spectator's, the critic's, the reader's experience. Only make the reader's general vision of evil intense enough...and his own experience, his own imagination...will supply him quite sufficiently with all the particulars. Make him think the evil, make him think it for himself, and you are released from weak specifications. Willen suggests that the story is told by a governess rather than a mother and that her narrative is included in the reports of two other narrators in order to shield "the reader from direct and possibly inhibiting contact with his own childhood fantasies, thus freeing him for an apparently objective analysis of the story." But such an apparent freedom is, in Willen's view, spurious, for he states categorically, "Each objective analysis, however, is conditioned by the reader's childhood experiences and emotional responses to them".

Goddard's interpretation, moreover, is not mere assertion supported only by a personal anecdote; he offers abundant evidence from the text to support his particular reading of the story. Furthermore, he offers a reasonable explanation for his inclusion of the anecdote:

It may be that this experience subconsciously accounts for my reading of The Turn of the Screw. If its influence is justified, it is worth recounting. If it is unjustified, it should be narrated that the reader may properly discount its effect on my interpretation of the tale.

The distinction that Goddard makes between those personal considerations which may have influenced his reading and the evidence in the text which validates his reading and which, he holds, should be convincing to any reader and his emphasis on the latter rather than the former distinguish Goddard's criticism from the later reader-response approach of such critics as Norman Holland.

It is interesting by way of contrast to consider Holland's essay on "The Purloined Letter," an exploration of how his concerns with adolescent masturbation coincided with certain elements in the story's structure to produce a particular reading experience in the pubescent Holland. In Holland's essay the critic's personal experience is primary; in Goddard's it is tangential.

A very conservative New Critic might fault Goddard for the inclusion of another kind of "irrelevant" material: James's comments about the story in several letters and in the Preface to Volume 12 of the New York Edition. Goddard, however, can hardly be accused of the intentional fallacy, for he seems to cite James as one critic who may be in agreement with him, as a way of emphasizing the plausibility of his interpretation. His disclaimer at the end of his essay indicates that he does not consider such evidence decisive, or even, perhaps, very important:

I may be guilty of twisting perfectly innocent statements to fit a hypothesis. They do appear to fit with curiously little stretching. But I do not press the point. It is not vital. It in no way affects the main argument. For in these matters it is always the work itself and not the author that is the ultimate authority. It could also, of course, be argued that the "elemental human psychology" which Goddard employs would not seem elemental to one who had not done some reading in psychoanalysis.

This, however, is a problem with almost all New Criticism. Literary critics do a tremendous amount of reading not only in literature but in psychology, history, philosophy, theology, anthropology, and other disciplines. Some of this knowledge always influences their approach to a particular text. Their desire to look exclusively at the literary work in question can only be partially successful.

The New Criticism has also been indicted—quite recently by Terry Eagleton—for ignoring the larger social, political, and economic realities of the society in which the literary work was produced and the work's political implications for the critic's own historical milieu. It is thus interesting to note that Goddard's analysis includes a basis for the development of a sociological, even a Marxist, reading:

The reaction upon a sensitive and romantic nature of the narrowness of English middle class life in the last century: that, from the social angle, is the theme of the story. Goddard's essay—with its detailed and plausible account of the psychology of the governess, its insightful tracing of James's artistry in "[throwing] the reader off the scent" to produce terror of a special kind, its preeminent awareness of literary values, its ingenious readings of the identification scene in chapter 5 and the final scene in chapter 24 to refute arguments against hallucination theories, and its provision of bases for readings which combine psychoanalytic, theological, and sociological considerations—is one of the most outstanding in the history of Jamesian criticism and certainly the most outstanding critical response to The Turn of the Screw in the period prior to Edmund Wilson's famous essay.

EDNA KENTON

Edna Kenton has an important place in the history of the criticism of The Turn of the Screw because she was the first critic to publish a categorical declaration that the ghosts do not exist outside the mind of the governess. Her famous essay "Henry James to the Ruminant Reader: The Turn of the Screw" was published in The Arts, VI (November, 1924), 245-255.In this article, Kenton disputed what she termed "the traditional, we might almost call it lazy version of this tale"—namely, "the children hounded by the prowling ghosts." On the contrary, declared Kenton, "Not the children, but the little governess was hounded by the ghosts". The ghosts, maintained Kenton, "are only exquisite dramatizations of her little personal mystery, figures for the ebb and flow of troubled thought within her mind, acting out her story".

Kenton's claim to be the first to propound a hallucination theory of the story is disputed by Wagenknecht:

Though Edna Kenton is generally given the credit (or blame) for having first suggested that the ghosts in 'The Turn of the Screw' are hallucinations, this is not strictly accurate. The idea had been advanced before 1924 by a number of writers, some of them distinguished... .

Wagenknecht, however, does not give the names of any of these writers, and my research has failed to uncover any. I suspect that Wagenknecht has not carefully read the writers he may have in mind.

Ezra Pound, for example, in 1920, called the work

a Freudian affair which seems to me to have attracted undue interest, i.e., interest out of proportion to the importance as literature and as part of Henry James's own work, because of this subject matter. The obscenity of 'The of the Screw' has given it undue prominence. This is not the same as saying the ghosts are hallucinations.

Similarly, an anonymous reviewer in The Critic (XXXIII, ops., December 1898, 523-524) had stated that the governess "has nothing in the least substantial upon which to base her deep and startling cognitions," but had then added, She perceives what is beyond all perceptions, and the reader who begins by questioning whether she is supposed to be sane ends by accepting her conclusions and thrilling over the horrors they involve.

This is certainly not an unequivocal statement that the ghosts are hallucinations; it could easily be interpreted to mean that the governess is a clairvoyant who "perceives what is beyond all perception" and that the reader "ends by accepting her conclusions" because his horizons have been broadened.

Likewise, Oliver Elton, in 1907, referred to the reader's "doubt, raised and kept hanging, whether, after all, the two ghosts who can choose to which persons they will appear, are facts, or delusions of the young governess who tells the story." Such a reference can hardly be interpreted as a commitment to a non-apparitions reading; indeed, Elton seems committed to the opposing proposition. He refers to "the courage of the young English lady who, desperate and unaided, vainly shelters the children" and to "the distrust with which others regard her story, and the aversion towards her inspired by the ghosts in the children themselves." He also says that the apparitions figure as the survival of the poison which they had sown while living in the breasts of the innocents. And when this influence reawakens, the earthly forms of the sowers gather visible shape, at once as symbols and as actual combatants.

Virginia Woolf in 1918 opined that Quint and Jessel "have neither the substance nor the independent existence of ghosts" but rather should be seen as "an illustration, not in itself specifically alarming, of a state of mind which is profoundly mysterious and terrifying". However, she seems to mean here not that the ghosts are hallucinations per se but that they represent some evil that is within all of us in addition to existing externally:

The governess is not so much frightened of them as of the sudden extension of her own field of perception, which in this case widens to reveal to her the presence all about her of an unmentionable evil. Woolf's remarks in a 1921 essay seem incompatible with any interpretation which would locate the ghosts only in the mind of the governess, and even more incompatible with any attempt to account for them by a psychoanalytic interpretation. Woolf says that, when we read the novella, "it is not a man with red hair and a white face whom we fear. We are afraid of something, perhaps, in ourselves." But this "something" seems also to have a real existence outside our minds:

It is unspeakable. We know that the man who stands on the tower staring down at the governess beneath is evil. Some unutterable obscenity has come to the surface. it tries to get in; it tries to get at something .... Is it possible that the little girl, as she turns back from he window, has seen the woman outside? Has she been with Miss Jessel? Has Quint visited the boy?

Furthermore, this "something" seems not to be explainable through psychoanalytic or any other theory: "It is Quint who must be reasoned away, and for all our reasoning returns".

Wagenknecht is also unfair to Kenton when he characterizes her essay as "primarily a long purr of self-satisfaction at having been clever enough to perceive something that nobody else could see" buttressed by "little or no argument". On the contrary, her article is a closely reasoned argument which relies on evidence of two kinds: James's statements about The Turn of the Screw itself and about other literary works and internal evidence gleaned from the story.

Kenton, first of all, cites passages from the Prefaces which, in her opinion, suggest that James intended to deceive the readers of the story. She reminds us, in this connection, of James's characterization of the story in the Preface to the 1908 New York Edition version:

It is a piece of ingenuity pure and simple, of cold artistic calculation, an amusette to catch those not easily caught (the 'fun' of the capture of the merely witless being ever but small), the jaded, the disillusioned, the fastidious.

She also recalls his statements about supernatural tales in the Preface to Volume 17 of the New York Edition. James had proceeded, she tells us, "with a scruple for nothing but any lapse of application, on the credulous soul of the candid, or, immeasurably better, on the seasoned spirit of the cunning reader." He later concludes, "Attention of perusal, I thus confess by the way, is what I, at every point, absolutely invoke and take for granted".

That James intended to "catch" the readers by making them believe in the account of an unreliable narrator is evident, suggests Kenton, from James's discussion in the same Preface of the objections raised by a reader capable, evidently, for the time, of some attention but not quite capable of enough, who complained that I hadn't sufficiently `characterized' my young woman engaged in her labyrinth; hadn't endowed her with signs and marks, features and humors; hadn't in a word invited her to deal with her own mystery as well as with that of Peter Quint and Miss Jessel.

James's answer to this objection, Kenton reminds us, was to state, "We have surely as much her own nature as we can swallow in watching it reflect her anxieties and inductions". That James intended "her own nature" to have a distorting effect on her perception of reality is evident, according to Kenton, from the distinction James makes in the same paragraph between "her record of so many intense anomalies and obscurities" and "her explanation of them, a different matter." Finally, James, in Kenton's view, implies that asking the reader to believe the governess is asking quite a bit, perhaps too much:

It constitutes no little of a character, indeed, in such conditions, for a young person, as she says, 'privately bred,' that she is able to make her particular credible statement of such strange matters. She had 'authority,' which is a good deal to have given her, and I couldn't have achieved so much had I clumsily tried for more.

Furthermore, says Kenton, if the governess had undesirable traits, we would not expect James to make them obvious, considering his remarks on Thackeray and Balzac in his essay "The Lesson of Balzac." In this essay James criticizes Thackeray for insufficient "protection of character" in his treatment of Blanche and Becky in Vanity Fair, in contrast to Balzac's treatment of Valerie Marneffe. In James's "book of golden rules," says Kenton, "no character is worth doing unless it is worth loving, and no lover is worthy of his love if he lacks the instinct to protect the beloved." Accordingly, maintains Kenton,

...if one is making a collection of his agents of evil, they are not to be found among those endowed with the usual stripes and markings.

He loves them even more than Balzac loved Valerie, and protects them with far finer dexterity. In The Turn of the Screw the protection of character, by all the evidence, reached its apotheosis: not until he came to the writing of The Golden Bowl was James to lean quite so heavily on the strong arm of the novelist's finer technic.

Next, Kenton turns her attention to the story itself. She points out that the prologue—"the submerged and disregarded forward to the tale"—presents a narrator who is young, inexperienced, and possessed by a never-to-be-requited infatuation for her employer. She reminds us that this infatuation continues after the governess arrives at Bly and that the first vision of Quint occurs while the governess is walking around the estate daydreaming about the man she loves. Kenton also emphasizes a point she suspects many readers may tend to forget— that it is she [the governess]—always she herself—who sees the lurking shapes and heralds them to her little world. Not to the charming little Flora, but behind Flora and facing the governess, the apparitional Miss Jessel first appeared.

Those critics who see "the children hounded by the prowling ghosts" need to be reminded, contends Kenton, that "no reader has more to go on that the young governess's word for this rather momentous and sidetracking allegation". Kenton also directs our attention to the governess's discussion of her own "moods" or psychological states which seemed to presage the appearance of the ghosts:

There were states of the air, conditions of sound and stillness, unspeakable impressions of the kind of ministering moment, that brought back to me, long enough to catch it, the medium in which, that June evening out of doors, I had my first sight of Quint... I recognized the signs, the portents—I recognized the moment, the spot (qtd. in Kenton 254).

Kenton concludes,

So she made the shades of her recurring fevers dummy figures for the delirious terrifying of others, pathetically trying to harmonize her own disharmonies by creating discords outside herself .

Kenton's analysis of the story itself is much less detailed than Goddard's. We are told that the apparitions "are only exquisite dramatizations of her little personal mystery, figures for the ebb and flow of troubled thought within her mind, acting out her story", but we are never told precisely what her "story" is — i.e., how her unrequited love for the children's uncle and/or her other problems cause her to need the apparitions of Quint and Jessel; and the only insight we are given into her "little personal mystery" is to be reminded of her unwholesome infatuation toward the employer. One of the main strengths of Goddard's essay, on the other hand, is his detailed analysis of why the governess needs the ghosts.

Furthermore, Kenton does not provide, as do Goddard and some other critics, detailed answers to the arguments of the apparitionists. She does, however, tie her analysis of the story to James's critical statements in a way Goddard does not. She ties "the protection of character" which James praised in Balzac and incorporated in his own "book of golden rules" for fiction to his avowed intention in the Preface to Volume 17 of the New York Edition to "rouse the dear old sacred terror"—i.e., "the tone of suspected and felt trouble of an inordinate and incalculable sort" without presenting "the offered example, the imputed vice, the cited act, the limited deplorable presentable instance" so as to avoid the artistic failure of presenting to the reader

some grand form of wrong-doing, or better still or wrong-being, imputed, . . .promised and announced as by the hot breath of the Pit which would "then, all lamentably, shrink to the compass of some particular brutality, some particular immorality, some particular infamy portrayed: with the result, alas, of the demonstration's falling sadly short.

James has created an air of unspecified evil, Kenton maintains, by creating a narrator who "could not specify" so that "readers of her tender, moving tale have of necessity had to think the evil for themselves." Consequently, contends Kenton, the ironic beauty of his subtle device for best expressing the depths of evil is that it was at the same time the calculated trap of traps for the guarding of his heroine. The eager, thrilled, horrified reader, joined with her in her vivid hunt after hidden sins, has failed to think sufficiently of her; and has, all oddly, contrived to protect her quite as romantically as her creator permitted her to protect herself in her charming recital of the happenings at Bly. Her own story, so naively sympathetic, of the ghosts and children, has been her simple bulwark—even the cunning reader has been credulous.

The reader, in other words, "protects" the governess by "specifying," from his own experience, the exact nature of the threat posed by Quint and Jessel and, in the process, forgetting that her assertion is the only evidence that Quint and Jessel pose any threat at all.

The extremely perceptive reader, however, Kenton maintains, experiences much more. The story produces its fullest effect when the reader, persistently baffled, but persistently wondering, comes face to face at last with the little governess, and realizes, with a conscious thrill greater than that of merely automatic nerve shudders before 'horror, 'that the children have been destroyed not by malevolent ghosts but by a self-deluded narrator who has also deceived the reader "joined with her in her vivid hunt after hidden sins".

In her analysis of the reader's response to the story, Kenton is, of course, very close to Goddard. Goddard also maintains that the reader is hoodwinked by the superficial plausibility of the account of a seemingly straightforward narrator and that the reader's experience is deepened and enriched if he realizes, upon considering the clues in the story—such as the information about the governess in the prologue—that the children are, in fact, the innocent victims of a well-intentioned but deranged woman. The main difference between these two critics lies in the importance assigned to the author's intention when considering the reader's response to the literary work. Goddard considers the critical task to be the examination of the literary work itself, which, as a New Critic, he considers a self-contained entity. Accordingly, he relies only marginally on statements James made in the Prefaces and in correspondence, stating, at the end of his essay, that James's intention, even if ascertainable, "in no way affects the main argument.

For in these matters it is always the work itself and not the author that is the ultimate authority". Kenton, on the other hand, appears to see the literary work as a communication from the author to the reader and to view the critical task as the ascertaining of what it was the author intended to communicate. In other words, she seems to approach The Turn of the Screw as though it were an enigmatic letter or a cryptic diplomatic communication. The critic would then be a decoder, attempting to discover, from his knowledge of the author and the totality of the situation surrounding the composition of the missive, what the author intended to convey. Thus, the reader who "sees through" the spurious account of the governess achieves, by this insight, not only a private artistic experience but an interpersonal experience, a communication with the author. The insightful reader has worked for it all, and by that fruitful labour has verified James's earliest contention that there was a discoverable way to establish a relation of work shared between the writer and the reader sufficiently curious to follow through.

In other words, the hermeneutic enterprise forges a bond between writer and reader—both have labored, and their labors have combined to produce a particular result, the specific reading experience which the author intended to effect. For this reason Kenton is unapologetic in citing statements from the Prefaces as evidence. Indeed, one of her complaints is that "old reactions to the novels and tales have not undergone re-evaluation; old criticism has not been re-written" following the publication of the New York Edition Prefaces. Kenton cannot be classified as a New Critic. She cannot be classified as a reader-response critic a la Norman Holland because she does not attempt to account for a reading experience unique to one reader because of that reader's individual psychology; she is interested, instead, in the type of reading experience the author intended any sufficiently perceptive reader to obtain.

Because of her emphasis on the reader's apprehension of the author's intention— i.e., a meeting of two psyches, we might label Kenton a phenomenological critic. For Iser, the characteristic differentiating phenomenological critics from others is the former's concern with "not only the actual text but also, and in equal measure, the actions involved in responding to that text".

Kenton, like other phenomenological critics, attempts to achieve a "union" with the consciousness of the author by first identifying with the consciousness of a fictional character, the governess.

This is precisely the approach of David Halliburton in Edgar Allan Poe: A Phenomenological View. Halliburton "discovers the authorial intentionality in a story by identifying with the main character". Kenton would probably agree with J. Hillis Miller, who maintains, The comprehension of literature is a process of what Gabriel Marcel calls `intersubjectivity.' ...If literature is a form of consciousness the task of a critic is to identify himself with the subjectivity expressed in the words, to relive that life it anew in his criticism (Guerrin ix).

Kenton must be distinguished, however, from other critics who are interested in apprehending the communication the author intended for the reader. Although Kenton tells us that James's methodology involves enchanting us with the story of an enchanted but seemingly straightforward narrator, she does not provide us with a detailed analysis of how this deception is produced. We thus cannot call her criticism rhetorical because she is not concerned with analyzing rhetoric. And we cannot term her criticism technical or philological as Hall defines these terms—"ascertaining the intention, meaning, and spirit of a work of literature, through its mode of expression". For we find in her essay nothing like the detailed textual analysis which we find in Maynard Mack's "The World of Hamlet" and which is recommended in R. P. Blackmur's "A Critic's Job of Work" Instead, Kenton intuits gestalts from the text and relays them to the reader. Thus, she unapologetically refers to her first experience with the story:

...I read it first 'at night,' in a 'country house' — and in a long ago 'first edition' — into and long past the midnight hours. The conditions were ideal, and all the admiring and admirable reactions to this 'finest ghost story in the world' were mine; of all the thrills and spiral shudders born of the creeping ghosts and 'haunted children' I had the full effect, but it was an effect differing in some inconsequential ways from many of the admiring and admirable reactions to his tale; even enhanced a little, I must now believe, by another kind of wondering that developed steadily along side the prime inevitable wondering over 'story' and 'plot.'

There was the wondering over the portentous Evil that, from the first page to the last, floated through the great room of the story; but there was wondering also over the beauty no less portentous in the working of the evil spell. There were the 'ghosts'; but there was also the way they came. There were the lovely 'corrupted' children; but there was the exquisite little governess too, guarding her charges so explainingly—even she seemed a little infected by the sinister air she breathed in and out so pantingly. ...Strange indeed, today, how this wondering over matters that few fictions generates blurred any serene certainty, at the end, of what the story was about; and so, in this particular instance, enhanced the first effect of The Turn of the Screw. Because here was a little oasis in the wordy desert of fiction; a spot inviting one to linger on a while and search about in all leisure for some possible buried treasure; a find, in short, worth any waste of curiosity in the hunt for the 'fun' that might come out of it.

Kenton accepted the invitation. She lingered to "search about in all leisure for some possible buried treasure" in her experience of this literary work, and the treasure she found is still studied by those who seek to understand what they can of The Turn of the Screw.

OTHER CRITICAL REACTIONS

Although the history of the criticism of The Turn of the Screw during this period is dominated by Goddard and Kenton, it is nonetheless important to recall that a number of distinguished writers published statements about the novella prior to Edmund Wilson's famous essay—most notably, Walter de la Mare in 1915, Rebecca West in 1916, Ezra Pound in 1918 and 1920, Virginia Woolf in 1918 and 1923, and Edith Wharton in 1924. We find, throughout the period, distinguished writers and critics on both sides of the apparitionist/non-apparitionist controversy, although the preponderance of opinion seems to be apparitionist.

Walter de la Mare took an apparitionist stand, seeing in the story's "blind groping of love amid the debauched innocence of childhood" a powerful revelation of "a subliminal world those centuries of psychical research can only supplement". Rebecca West was also an unequivocal apparitionist, viewing the events at Bly as they "are seen by the clear eyes of the honorable and fearless lady who tells the tale". Similarly, Carl Van Doren read the story straightforwardly as a tale of "two children so corrupted by wicked servants that words will not utter the evil in them". And Edith Wharton—one of James's most intimate friends—also stands with the apparitionists, referring without irony to "the poor little governess" and "the two figures of evil with whom she is fighting for the souls of her charges".

Ezra Pound, on the other hand, appeared to read the story non-apparitionally. In 1920 Pound dismissed the story as "a Freudian affair which seems to me to have attracted undue interest". His designation of the story as "Freudian" does not, in itself, however, place him definitely in the non-apparitionist camp; for some critics a story is "Freudian" if it arouses certain responses in the reader. However, two years earlier, Pound had categorized The Turn of the Screw, along with The Tragic Muse, as the artistic product of a "hater of tyranny" and as a literary protest "against all the sordid petty personal crushing oppression, the domination of modern life."

He considered the subject of the story to be "`influence,'

the impinging of family pressure, the impinging of one personality on another; all of them in highest degree damn'd, loathsome, and detestable". Pound could, of course, be referring to the influence on the children exerted by Quint and Jessel, but that would appear to be a rather forced interpretation of his remarks. When a critic uses terms such as "pretty personal crushing opposition," "domination of modern life," and "impinging of family pressure," to describe a writer's preoccupations, we do not ordinarily think the writer is calling for more exorcisms.

These descriptions would, on the other hand, fit in quite easily with an interpretation of the story in which the governess would be driven to oppress the children because of her own unconscious conflicts, conflicts which could be traced—as some critics (for example, Spilka), have suggested—to the social and economic inequities of Victorian Britain. Another interesting non-apparitionist statement was proffered by F. L. Pattee in 1923. Speculating about the author's creative process, Pattee suggested that the story "is the triumph of science over romance."

James began, suggests Pattee, to write a ghost story strongly on the side of the emotional and the romantic... yet so fundamental was his scientific habit, his recording only that which had come within the range of his material experience, that the story may be read not as a ghost story at all, but as the record of a clinic: the study of the growth of a suggested infernal cliche in the brain of the nurse who alone sees the ghosts, of her final dementia which is pressed to a focus that overwhelms in her mind every other idea, and makes of the children her innocent victims.

This, suggests Pattee, was the way James had to metamorphose Bishop Benson's anecdote because of the type of man and artist James was. "Never did he work from his emotions: always he viewed life objectively, coldly, accurately, recording only what he saw within the area he thought worthy of study". We listed as one of the major strengths of Goddard's essay the fact that his interpretation leaves room for syntheses of apparitionist and non-apparitionist approaches—for example, the 1957 essays by Lydenberg and Firebaugh, both of which suggest that the psychological problems and mediumistic powers of the governess facilitate—and perhaps even make possible —the destruction of the children through the agency of objectively existing demonic forces. It is, therefore, interesting to note that several other early critics either attempted some synthesis of the apparitionist and non-apparitionist approaches or offered some other explanation of the ghosts—rejecting both the view that they are objectively existing demonic entities and the contention that they are hallucinations of the governess.

For example, Oliver Elton, in 1907, declared that the question as to whether the apparitions are "facts or delusions of the young governess who tells the story" is "kept hanging". He suggested, however, that the question need not be resolved because the ghosts fulfill a literary function which is distinct from the seemingly mutually exclusive functions assigned them by apparitionist and non-apparitionist critics. The ghosts play their part in the bodily sphere as terrifying dramatis personae—neither substance nor shadow; they are there, as Gorgon faces at the window; while, spiritually, they figure as the survival of the poison which they had sown while living in the breasts of the innocents. And when this influence reawakens, the earthy forms of the sowers gather visible shape, at once as symbols and as actual combatants.

Arthur Waley took a somewhat similar position in a 1918 article. Waley declared that the work is not a ghost story but a literary statement about childhood. "It deals with the fact that children have an interior life, carefully hidden from their elders." Waley considered James's statements about the ambiguity of the story to be "quite untrue"; he considered the wickedness of the servants and the corruption of the children—their bad language, for example—to be unquestionably sexual. Quint and Jessel function as literary devices, according to Waley, "materializations" of "this contamination" in order to convey the story's theme—"beneath this mask of 'absolutely unnatural goodness,' of 'more than earthly beauty,' the old contamination lurks."

Virginia Woolf, in 1918, effected a synthesis of the apparitionist and non-apparitionist approaches which is different, in a subtle way, from the approaches of Firebaugh and Lydenberg. She does not argue that the psychological problems and mediumistic powers of the governess facilitate the materialization of extrinsically existing demonic entities, but rather that the evil which the governess perceives is so deep and so pervasive that it eludes any compartmentalization as exterior or interior, being both at once. Quint and Jessel, she contends, have neither the substance nor the independent existence of ghosts. The odious creatures are much closer to us than ghosts have ever been.

The governess is not so much frightened of them as of the sudden extension of her own field of perception, which in this case widens to reveal to her the presence all about her of an unmentionable evil. The appearance of the figures is an illustrations, not in itself specially alarming, of a state of mind which is profoundly mysterious and terrifying... The horror of the story comes from the force with which it makes us realize the power that our minds possess for such excursions into the darkness; when certain lights sink or certain barriers are lowered, the ghosts of the mind, untraced desires, indistinct intimations, are seen to be a large company.

In 1921 she reiterated these points, declaring that James's ghosts "have their origin within us. They are present whenever the significant overflows our powers of expressing it; whenever the ordinary appears ringed by the strange". Woolf made it clear in this article that she did not consider the ghosts to be hallucinations but instead to be adumbrations of a depth of evil which is terrifyingly real. We know that the man who stands on the tower staring down at the governess beneath is evil. Some unutterable obscenity has come to the surface. It tries to get in; it tries to get at something. The exquisite little beings who lie innocently asleep must at all costs be protected. But the horror grows.

She also suggests, in this article, that no explanation—and thus, I suppose, no psychoanalytic theory—can fully elucidate the realities at Bly. "It is Quint who must be reasoned away, and for all our reasoning returns. After all critical speculation, something remains unaccounted for". A great merit of Woolf's approach is her location of the source of the story's appeal in a certain introspective turn which human consciousness has taken in the twentieth century. Its appeal, she suggested in 1921, is distinctly modern. Mrs. Radcliffe is quaint, according to Woolf, because "we have become fundamentally skeptical" of supernatural horror which assails us from outside ourselves. "Moreover, we are impervious to fear". Increased introspectiveness, in Woolf's view, has gone hand in hand with psychical research in a period "which seeks the supernatural in the soul of man." Consequently, a ghost story like The Turn of the Screw "testifies to the fact that our own ghostliness has much quickened".

At least three critics other than Kenton and Goddard—namely, Virginia Woolf in 1918 and 1921, Edith Wharton in 1924, and Carl H. Grabo in 1928—discussed James's narrative techniques for engineering feelings of fear and horror in his readers, and they came to remarkably similar conclusions. In 1918 Virginia Woolf opined that, in James's ghost stories, "the supernatural is so wrought in with the natural that fear is kept from a dangerous exaggeration into simple disgust or disbelief verging upon ridicule." She contrasted these stories with The Mark of the Beast and The Return of Imray by Rudyard Kipling, which, in her view, "are powerful enough to repel one by their horror, but...too violent to appeal to our sense of wonder". In 1921 she reiterated her conviction that authorial restraint is an important element in the particular sense of horror which The Turn of the Screw engenders.

Perhaps it is the silence that. . .impresses us. Everything at Bly is so profoundly quiet. The twitter of birds at dawn, the far-away cries of children, faint footsteps in the distance stir it but leave it unbroken. It accumulates; it weighs us down; it makes us strangely apprehensive of noise. At last the house and the garden die out beneath it... Edith Wharton made similar points in 1924. She commended James for his authorial restraint in The Turn of the Screw — "the economy of horror is carried to its last degree."

She, like Woolf, opined that ghost stories are easily vitiated by too many and too obvious supernatural effects:

Many a would-be tale of horror becomes innocuous through the very multiplication and variety of its horrors....the fewer the better: once the preliminary horror posited [sic], it is the harping on the string—the same nerve—that does the trick. Quiet iteration is far more racking than diversified assaults; the expected is more frightful than the unforeseen.

This "quiet iteration" was analyzed in more detail by Carl H. Grabo in 1928. Grabo first notes that the novella "directs itself...to a narrow channel; it aims at intensity" by means of its "unity of place" and the small number of characters with which it is concerned. He then analyzes "the successive waves which, with increasing power and frequency,...create the story's rhythm".

The first wave "opens pianissimo with but the faintest single note of the unusual in the excessive pleasure which the housekeeper takes in the coming of the new governess." This wave gathers momentum when the governess, unable to sleep on the first night of her story, seems to hear "'faint and far, the cry of a child'" and later 'a light footstep'". Her uneasiness ceases when she is overcome by the charm of Flora but returns with greater force in chapter two when she receives the letter form the headmaster informing her of Miles's dismissal from school and Mrs. Grose's mysterious "references...to the former governess who went away and shortly after died, and to someone as yet unidentified who liked them young and pretty.'" The wave reaches its climax with the first vision of Quint in chapter three and then subsides.

The tone of naturalness is re-established. The innocence and beauty of the children are again stressed, and an explanation for the appearance of the man on the tower is ostensibly sought. But soon comes "the second wave, more powerful than the first". It begins with the second vision of Quint, which occurs in chapter four. The pace then slackens in the next chapter as Mrs. Grose and the governess discuss what the vision might mean, but it quickens again with the first vision of Miss Jessel, which occurs at the end of chapter six and is hysterically related to Mrs. Grose at the beginning of chapter seven. Then the pace slackens a little as we learn more of Miss Jessel's past, but in vague terms only.... Then it is slowly extorted from Mrs. Grose, with deepening implications of evil, that Miles knew of the relations of Quint and Miss Jessel. The third wave, which begins in chapter nine when the governess confronts Quint on the staircase in pre-dawn darkness, also contains lulls, in the form of contrasting episodes with the children, but the relief which they afford is now only an intensification of horror, for the seeming innocence is more and more stripped from them and we guess them to be little monsters of depravity.

Following the governess's confrontation with Miles on the lawn in the middle of the night at the end of chapter ten, says Grabo, "the purpose of the discarnate demons comes home to the governess with unanswerable conviction". After the conversation between the governess and Mrs. Grose on the following afternoon, events mount with growing rapidity to the close. There is no other appreciable lull. The struggle of the governess for the souls of the obsessed children will permit no intermission.

Grabo is primarily concerned with narrative technique, but his narratology is closely tied to his reading of the story as a moral allegory. For, as the waves succeed one another, according to Grabo, "the horror, it must be noted, has shifted form the merely uncanny, the horror of discarnate devils, to a horror infinitely deeper, the moral horror of the conflict of good and evil".

While Grabo is interesting for his designation of a literary theme through a consideration of narrative technique, Heywood Broun is interesting for his discovery of a literary theme through an analysis of his own psychological reaction to the story. In a January, 1930 preface to a Modern Library edition of the story, Broun recalls reading the novella for the first time in the solitude of the Swiss Alps and being prostrated with anxiety for several days. A sudden insight into the meaning of the story accompanied his recovery from this lamentable psychological state.

Along about the third night that my clammy obsession waked me, and I gaped dry-throated at the face in my starry window, I suddenly remembered that 'The Turn of the Screw' had been written a fair number of years before I had ever read it, and that hundreds, probably thousands, of other unfortunates had stared at that same face in hundreds, probably thousands, of other windows. It was the most healing notion I ever. In fact, I laughed.

The source of Broun's relief was his realization that that wretched monster could hardly have been so multiform as to exist actually in all of those windows. All of us were on the instant preposterous together—preposterous and safe. Any one of us was in mortal danger—all of us together were a comic and protected company.

The conclusion which Broun drew from this experience—and which, he holds, it is "just possible" is the author's intended lesson—appears at first trivial, then sinister when we remember that in 1930 fascism was beginning to sweep over Europe.

All at once I knew why we do cling together, even if sight unseen. I could even understand why we sometimes behave so badly, when we huddle. We can do anything, we must do anything, rather than try to go it alone, with our helpless and terrified loneliness clutching at us in the night.

It is tempting to classify Broun's criticism as reader-response criticism a la Normal Holland. However, while Broun's criticism does bear resemblance to that of Holland and other reader-response critics, there are two important differences. In the first place, we do not find the detailed psychological analysis of a particular reader that we find, for example, in Holland's 1968 essay on "The Purloined Letter." Secondly, Broun's, which is almost entirely narrative, appears to be a hybrid literary form, in between fiction and literary criticism. In this it somewhat resembles Muriel West's novel—if her book can be called a novel—in which a fictional character in a lonely house struggles all night with the meaning of The Turn of the Screw. Broun's account, after all, seems far too overdone to fall outside the realm of fiction. One paragraph bears quoting in its entirety: I did finally bring myself to the scratch. I opened the book, read a little of it, and then a little more, and, of course, finished it in precisely that hideous thralldom that had been its author's wicked purpose.

And there was no clammy sensation I did not sense. There was no sinister horror I did not live through. For nights and nights I would no more than cajole myself to sleep than I would wake staring out of my windows, glazed eyes fixed on the icy peaks, waiting, waiting, for that malign head to appear above the window sill. More than that, a full half the time the head did appear—at least, I could have sworn I saw it.

My muscles were rigid, my nerves were zooming with a horrible intensity, my eyes throbbed with the pain of their protrusion. I cursed Henry James, my 'Beast in the Jungle' friend, my debonair London bookseller. I ached thoroughly for those days of comparative peace when I knew no more of Henry than that he was the brother of William, when Alps were beautiful white Alps and not red-headed evil butlers, and when the fate of little children was a problem academic pure and simple. I was thoroughly badly off. If somebody had come along to tell me of the catharsis value of tragedy, or the ennobling effect of participating in a dignified horror, I would surely have landed him at the foot of my steepest Alp (vii-viii). Granted, the story is deeply affecting—it has been for years one of my favourite stories—but the above paragraph seems a bit excessive.

As we survey the criticism of The Turn of the Screw prior to Edmund Wilson's famous 1934 essay, we find the following broad patterns.

First, we find, from the earliest reviews onward, a broad critical consensus as to the great artistic merits of the story—with only a few scattered dissenting comments, such as those of G.K. Chesterton and Ezra Pound.

Secondly, we find outstanding writers and critics on both sides of the apparitionist/non-apparitionist controversy—with such figures as Walter de la Mare, Rebecca West, Carl van Doren, and Edith Wharton on the apparitionist side and Ezra Pound, Edna Kenton, and Harold C. Goddard in the non-apparitionist camp. We find that most of the critical comments during this period assume the apparitionist position, but that the two greatest critical essays both proceed from a non-apparitionist perspective. We also find early attempts at synthesizing the two perspectives or adopting a third stance which does not require a choice between them. Oliver Elton and Virginia Woolf both effected syntheses of sorts, although neither, in so doing, presented a detailed analysis of the story comparable to the analyses offered by Firebaugh and Lydenberg. Arthur Waley took a position which enabled him to avoid the choice. One of the merits of Goddard's essay, we have seen, is that it can easily be read in conjunction with essays such as those of Firebaugh and Lydenberg which effect a synthesis of apparitionist and non-apparitionist positions.

Thirdly, we have seen that much of the early criticism was subjective and impressionistic—with the critics tending mainly to record the effects of the work on themselves and to assume that other readers should and/or would be similarly affected. This broad stream found issue in two closely related tributaries—the phenomenological criticism of Kenton and the personal narrative criticism of Broun which would reach its zenith in 1964 with the publication of Muriel West's A Stormy Night With the Turn of the Screw.

In contrast to that stream is the New Criticism of Harold C. Goddard, with its emphasis on examining the text as a self-contained unit. Of course, in this case as in other examples of New Criticism, the goal of considering only the text must be seen as an incompletely realized ideal. Goddard himself admitted that certain personal experiences had colored his reading of the story, and, despite the essay's title, it is questionable whether such an interpretation could have been formulated prior to Sigmund Freud.

A number of critics concerned themselves with analyzing the narrative techniques which enabled James, in this story, to affect so many readers so deeply. Three critics—Woolf, Wharton, and Grabo—emphasized the author's restraint in presenting overtly shocking material to the reader, with Grabo offering the most complete such analysis, i.e., his "wave" theory. Goddard and Kenton combined their considerations of the author's narrative techniques with a discussion of the psychological processes of the reader of the story. Goddard suggested that the story seems more credible than most stories of the supernatural because the reader, without realizing it, is reacting to the entirely credible story of two children and an ignorant housekeeper isolated and at the mercy of an insane governess. This analysis, Goddard suggested, might also explain why the story affects so many readers with more than mere fear. The governess, in her insanity, can be seen as a tragic heroine. He also suggested that the reader is seduced by her seemingly matter-of-fact rendition of a narrative which contains obvious elements of truth. Edna Kenton, similarly, suggested that the reader is caught off guard by the charm of the governess and the surface plausibility of her account and is thus unconsciously led to collaborate with James in his "protection" of his character.

Goddard's is the most outstanding work on The Turn of the Screw during this period. Goddard's essay offers a detailed analysis of the psychology of the governess, but does not degenerate into a mere psychiatric case history because Goddard, with the story's reader always uppermost in mind, never loses sight of literary values. Goddard offers insightful comments about the narrative structure of the work—particularly about the techniques whereby James has hoodwinked so many readers—and detailed refutations of apparitionist arguments.

This analysis, as we have seen, can easily be read not only in conjunction with essays such as those of Firebaugh and Lydenberg which offer syntheses of psychoanalytic and theological insights, but also in conjunction with Marxist critiques such as that of Spilka. Edna Kenton's essay is also an outstanding one. It is a closely reasoned argument about authorial intention based on evidence form the text itself and statements of James about this story and other stories. and a demonstration that a non-apparitionist perspective can lead, perhaps, to an even richer literary experience for the reader of this famous "ghost" story.

Bibliography

Baker, Carlos ed. *Ernest Hemingway: Selected Letters,1917-1961.* New York, Charles Scribner's Sons: 1981.

Broccoli, Matthew J., and Margret M. Duggan eds., with the assistance of Susan Walker. *Correspondence of F. Scott Fitzgerald.* New York, Random House: 1980.

Broccoli, Mathew J. *Fitzgerald and Hemingway: A Dangerous Friendship.* New York, Carroll & Graf Publishers, Inc.: 1974.

Brooks, Van Wyck. *The Pilgrimage of Henry James.* New York, Dutton: 1925.

Donaldson, Scott. *Fool For Love.* New York, Congdon & Weed: Distributed by St. Martin's Press: 1983.

Edel, Leon. *Henry James: The Untried Years: 1843-1870.* Philadelphia, New York: J.B. Lippincott Company, 1953.

Edel, Leon ed. *Henry James: Letters, Vol. IV. 1895-1916.* Cambridge, Mass., The Belknap Press of Harvard University Press: 1984.

Edel, Leon and Gordon Ray ed. and intro. *Henry James and H.G. Wells: A Record of Their Friendship, and Their Debate on the Art of Fiction and Their Quarrel.* Urbana, University of Illinois Press: 1958. [I never looked at this, but I suspect that if you are interested in the Wells/James relationship, it would be a good place to start.]

Edel, Leon – 'Oh Henry!What Henry James didn't do with Oliver Wendell Holmes (or anyone else).'

Fitzgerald, F. Scott. *The Great Gatsby.* New York, Charles Scribner's Sons: 1925.

Fitzgerald, F. Scott. *Trimalchio: An Early Version of The Great Gatsby*. Ed. James L. W. West III. Cambridge: Cambridge University Press, 2000.

Habegger, Alfred. *Henry James and the "Woman Business"*. Cambridge, Cambridge University Press: 1989.

James, Henry. *Notes Of A Son and Brother*. New York, Charles Scribner's Sons: 1914.

Novick, Sheldon. *Henry James: The Young Master*. New York, Random House: 1996.

Novick, Sheldon – 'Henry James' Love Life'

MacKenzie, Norman and Jean MacKenzie. *H.G. Wells: A Biography*. New York, Simon & Schuster: 1973.

Milford, Nancy. *Zelda: A Biography*. New York, Harper & Row: 1970.

Ray, Gordon N. *H.G. Wells & Rebecca West*. New Haven, Yale University Press: 1974.

Scott, Bonnie K. ed., an. and intro. *Selected Letters of Rebecca West*. New Haven and London, University Press: 2000.

Spender, Stephen. *The Destructive Element: A Study of Modern Writers and Beliefs*. 1935. Folcroft Library Editions: 1977.

Turnbull, Andrew ed. and into. *The Letters of F. Scott Fitzgerald*. New York, Charles Scribner's Sons: 1963.

Wasserstrom, William. *The Legacy of Van Wyck Brooks; A Study of Maladies and Motives*. Carbondal and Edwardsville, Southern Illionois University Press: 1971.

Wells, H.G. *Boon, The Mind of the Race, The Wild Asses of the Devil, and The Last Trump*. New York, George H. Doran Company: Copyright 1915, Reginald Bliss.

West, Rebecca. *Henry James*. London, Nisbet & Co. LTD.: 1916.